Developmental Assets and Asset-Building Communities

The Search Institute Series on Developmentally Attentive Community and Society

Series Editor
Peter L. Benson, *Search Institute, Minneapolis, Minnesota*

Series Mission
To advance interdisciplinary inquiry into the individual, system, community, and societal dynamics that promote developmental strengths; and the processes for mobilizing these dynamics on behalf of children and adolescents.

DEVELOPMENTAL ASSETS AND ASSET-BUILDING COMMUNITIES:
Implications for Research, Policy, and Practice
Edited by Richard M. Lerner and Peter L. Benson

A Continuation Order Plan is available for this series. A continuation order will bring delivery of each new volume immediately upon publication. Volumes are billed only upon actual shipment. For further information please contact the publisher.

Developmental Assets and Asset-Building Communities

Implications for Research, Policy, and Practice

Edited by

Richard M. Lerner

Tufts University
Medford, Massachusetts

and

Peter L. Benson

Search Institute
Minneapolis, Minnesota

Kluwer Academic / Plenum Publishers

New York, Boston, Dordrecht, London, Moscow

ISBN 0-306-47482-4

©2003 Kluwer Academic / Plenum Publishers, New York
233 Spring Street, New York, New York 10013

http://www.wkap.nl/

10 9 8 7 6 5 4 3 2 1

A C.I.P. record for this book is available from the Library of Congress

Printed in Great Britain by IBT Global, London

Contents

Foreword:
Family-Centered Community Building and Developmental Assets for Youth

Al Gore

Our great nation has been built by the ingenuity and character of Americans working together for centuries to ensure democracy and opportunity for all. The country's future, of course, in great part, relies on the character of today's youth and the extent to which they are prepared to handle the challenges of the future. We as a nation must work to ensure that our communities are strong and provide environments where children and families thrive. I believe we need to take a fresh look at the interaction between family and community and how this interaction can foster strong, healthy environments—an approach I call *family-centered community building.*

Families and communities face an accelerated pace of change and new pressures, often including more work and less family time; more TV and less communication; longer commutes and less sense of community; and shorter childhood and longer old age. Experts are telling us that too many young people are isolated and feel disconnected from each other, their families, and society. Upon closer study we learn that families are often disengaged from the civic life of their neighborhoods and communities. Therefore, families do not have access to the kinds of formal and informal supports they need, not only in times of crisis, but also as a source of strength and nurturance in daily life.

Many traditional community development approaches placed a greater, if not sole, emphasis on physical infrastructure and development. And other community needs, including housing, education, and a healthy environment, were often addressed as singular issues. What national experts, practitioners, educators, and others have realized is that the old way was not working. Some within communities began working together to transcend these barriers and are *working together to build their communities.* This new way of doing things applies strategies that invest in the human *and* social capital of a community as well as its productive and economic capacity. It addresses housing, education, infrastructure, and other needs in a holistic way.

In its essence, family-centered community building focuses on how communities create environmental, social, and educational conditions to enhance individual relationships within families and family relationships within the community. So basically, we move away from isolation to community. The individual exists within the family, the family exists within the community, and the community exists within the nation and the world. The ultimate goal is for young people to grow up with the opportunities, relationships, and guidance they need to become engaged and productive members of our society.

It's neither sufficient nor fair to tell overwhelmed parents that they are solely responsible for building community and doing more for their children. Instead, it is our *shared* task to address more fundamental, systemic questions: Are communities organized in ways that support—rather than thwart—family and human development? Are community policies and institutions accessible to and trusted by families? What kinds of fundamental changes in community life must occur in order to surround families and their children with the relationships, opportunities, and supports they need to thrive?

Answering these questions, both conceptually and practically, requires active dialogue among all parts of the community—young people, parents, neighbors, institutions—in imagining and creating together the ways in which the community can be a place where all children, adolescents, and families can thrive.

I am particularly impressed and heartened by the ideas presented in this important book. The concepts of developmental assets and asset building are giant leaps forward, both in understanding the power of engaged communities to impact family development in positive ways and in creating strategies for improving the well-being of children and families.

The implications of this approach—which draws on all the strength-building capacity of communities—are clearly articulated here. Community building is dynamic. There is no one way to bring about change. The authors model the kinds of dialogue we need to inform comprehensive, effective, and lasting approaches for shaping vibrant communities. This process of exchange and discernment is critical as we as a nation seek to create the models, strategies, and innovations that will, in the end, help residents strengthen their own communities for young people and their families.

In particular, for family-centered community building to be sustainable, the key community members among whom leadership must be encouraged are our young people. These scholars put forth a vision and action agenda that can be extremely effective in building the assets for positive youth development.

Empowering youth helps ensure that family-centered community building is done *with* the community and not *for* the community. It also increases the extent to which sustainable change improves the capacities and life chances for all youth and families, helping to create a legacy of contributions to civil society that will enrich American life for generations to come.

Preface

Young people are resources to be developed, not problems to be managed (Benson, 1997; Benson & Pittman, 2001; Pittman, 1996; Roth, Brooks-Gunn, Murray, & Foster, 1998). Using current conceptual and empirical advances in the study of human development that are predicated on a developmental systems perspective (Lerner, 2002), this book frames current theoretical and research advances regarding the individual and ecological bases of positive youth development through a discussion of the concept of developmental assets, that is, the social and psychological strengths identified by Search Institute that function to enhance health outcomes for children and adolescents.

Introduced in the developmental literature little more than a decade ago at this writing (Benson, 1990), research and application associated with the concept of developmental assets have been integrated with the fields of community change and community building in order, on the one hand, to further understanding of the developmental experiences, resources, and opportunities that contribute to important health outcomes among young people and, on the other hand, to energize and guide community-based approaches to strengthening the natural and inherent socialization capacity of communities in support of youth.

For more than a decade, one of the editors of this volume, Peter L. Benson, and his colleagues at Search Institute in Minneapolis, Minnesota, have developed a conceptual framework to assess the internal and external developmental assets that comprise the resources needed by youth for positive development. Search Institute researchers have found that the more developmental assets an adolescent possesses, the greater is his or her likelihood of positive, healthy development. Benson and his colleagues' conceptualization of developmental assets and their strategic use in communities oriented to build assets in the service of fostering positive youth development finds rich empirical support in the research emanating from Search Institute and other settings.

The purpose of the present book—which is the inaugural volume in the Search Institute Series on Developmentally Attentive Community and Society, sponsored jointly by Search Institute and Kluwer Academic/Plenum Publishers—is to extend this scholarly base for the understanding of the character and scope of the systemic relation between healthy youth development and asset-building communities. The authors present evidence that asset-building communities both promote and are promoted by positive youth development, a bidirectional, systemic linkage that, in accordance with developmental systems theory, furthers civil society by building relational and intergenerational places within a community that are united in attending to the developmental needs of all children and adolescents (Lerner, Fisher, & Weinberg, 2000). In addition, the authors discuss not only the scientific and applied value of the concept of developmental assets but also the challenges for the enhancement of this concept and for the strategic, action agenda for community building associated with the framework of assets by Benson and his colleagues.

Accordingly, this book provides both a guide for further scholarship and a prospectus for future community development and community building. Its aim is to enhance the contribution to science and to society of the concept of developmental assets. All authors in this volume aspire to expand the capacity of communities to promote the positive development of young people and, by so doing, to expand the individual and institutional bases of civil society in America and the world.

There are numerous people to thank in regard to the preparation of this book. First and foremost we are indebted to the contributors. Their scholarship and dedication to the integration of science and application in the service of youth people, their families, and their communities have enabled this volume to come into being and serve as a model of how scholarship can be a dynamic asset in a national effort for community building for youth. We are especially indebted to the Honorable Albert Gore for his generous and visionary foreword to this volume, and to Neal Halfon for his insightful and stimulating afterword.

This book is derived from an invited symposium presented at the August 2000 meeting of the American Psychological Association (APA), held in Washington, D.C. The symposium was sponsored by Division 1 of the APA, General Psychology. We are grateful to Professor Lewis P. Lipsitt of Brown University, then president of Division 1, for extending this invitation and for his interest in informing the members of the APA about the importance of Search Institute's approach to developmental assets for promoting positive youth development.

Our colleagues and students were great resources in the development of this volume. At Tufts we especially want to thank Karyn Lu for her expert editorial assistance, and, at Search Institute, we are grateful for all the support and expertise provided by Eugene Roehlkepartain and Mary Byers. Siiri Lelumees and Michael Williams, our editors at Kluwer Academic/Plenum Publishing, were a constant source of encouragement and collegial support, and we are pleased to acknowledge our gratitude to them.

We gratefully acknowledge financial assistance provided by the Thrive Foundation for Youth toward the preparation of this volume.

Finally, we are, as always, deeply grateful to our families for their love and support during our work. They remain our most cherished sources of strength.

R. M. L.

Medford, Massachusetts

P. L. B.

Minneapolis, Minnesota

References

Benson, P. L. (1990). *The troubled journey: A portrait of 6th–12th grade youth*. Minneapolis, MN: Search Institute.

Benson, P. L. (1997). *All kids are our kids: What communities must do to raise caring and responsible children and adolescents*. San Francisco: Jossey-Bass.

Benson, P. L., & Pittman, K. J. (Eds.). (2001). *Trends in youth development: Visions, realities, and challenges*. Norwell, MA: Kluwer Academic Publishers.

Lerner, R. M. (2002). *Concepts and theories of human development* (3rd ed.). Mahwah, NJ: Erlbaum.

Lerner, R. M., Fisher, C. B., & Weinberg, R. A. (2000). Toward a science for and of the people: Promoting civil society through the application of developmental science. *Child Development, 71*, 11–20.

Pittman, K. (1996). Community, youth, development: Three goals in search of connection. *New Designs for Youth Development, Winter*, 4–8.

Roth, J., Brooks-Gunn, J., Murray, L., & Foster, W. (1998). Promoting healthy adolescents: Synthesis of youth development program evaluations. *Journal of Research on Adolescence, 8*, 423–459.

Part I

Conceptual Foundations

1 Development Assets and Asset-Building Communities: A View of the Issues

Richard M. Lerner
Tufts University

Young people are the resources on which the future must be built. How can segments of society coalesce to ensure that youth develop in ways that enable them to actualize their potential to contribute positively to the healthy development of self, family, and community?

As recently as 10 years ago, the predominant answer to this question was predicated on the assumption that young people constitute—at best—problems waiting to happen. That is, youth were characterized—either explicitly or implicitly, and through deficit models put forward about their attributes—as problems to be managed (Benson, 1997; Roth, Brooks-Gunn, Murray, & Foster, 1998). As a consequence, strategies for promoting healthy development emphasized, if not ameliorative strategies enacted after problems emerged, then preventive strategies undertaken to avoid the otherwise inevitable weaknesses or deficits of young people (Jensen, Hoagwood, & Trickett, 1999).

Theoretical Bases of a Revised Conception of Youth

Today, a new vision of the nature of youth exists: Youth are resources to be developed (Benson, 1990, 1997; Roth et al., 1998). The evolution of this conception of youth has had a scientifically arduous path (Lerner, 2002a). That is, complicating any reconceptualization of the character of youth as resources for positive development of individual, families, and communities was the theoretical approach to development within which the deficit view of young people was often embedded (Lerner, 2002a).

For much of the past century many scholars followed a model that treated the problems of youth development as issues of "only" applied concern—and thus of secondary scientific interest. Not only did this model separate basic science from application, it also disembedded the adolescent from his or her context and treated the variables that were presumed to influence the behavior and development of youth as if they could be studied and understood in a decontextualized, reductionistic manner (Lerner, 2002b; Overton, 1998).

Thus, the conception of developmental process in this model often involved causal splits between individual and context, between organism and environment, or—most generally—between nature and nurture (Gottlieb, 1997; Lerner, 2002a; Overton, 1998). Theories based on this model emphasized either predetermined organismic bases of development, for instance, as in attachment theory (e.g., Bowlby, 1969), ethological theory (e.g., Lorenz, 1965), behavioral genetics (e.g., Plomin, 1986, 2000), psychoanalytic theory (e.g., Freud, 1954), and neopsychoanalytic theory (e.g., Erikson, 1968; A. Freud, 1969), or environmental, reductionistic, and mechanistic bases of behavior and behavior change (e.g., Bijou & Baer, 1961, 1965; Gewirtz & Stingle, 1968).

Other theories stressed more of an interaction between organismic and environmental sources of development (e.g., Piaget, 1950, 1970). Nevertheless, there remained a presupposition that there were two distinct sources of development, that is, that there was a split between organism and environment. As such, it was the role of theory to explain the contributions of these two separate domains of reality to human development (Overton, 1998).

In short, then, scholars studying human development applied a theoretical model that was not useful in understanding the relational nature of development (Overton, 1998) and of the synthesis between basic and applied concerns legitimated by relational models of development (Lerner, 1995, 1996, 1998a, b, 2002a, b). However, these nonrelational, "split" theories of human development are today no longer the predominant ones in the disciplines involved in the study of adolescence (Cairns, 1998; Dixon & Lerner, 1999; Lerner, 1998a). Today, cutting-edge theoretical and empirical scholarship about human development relies on dynamic systems models to understand and enhance the trajectory of change across the life span (Lerner, 1998a, 2002a).

Developmental Systems Models of Human Development

The stress in contemporary developmental theories is on a "healing" of the nature-nurture split (Gottlieb, 1997) and on accounting for how the integrated developmental system functions, that is, for understanding probabilistic epigenesis. Gottlieb (1997, p. 90) defined this process as being "characterized by an increase of complexity or organization—that is, the emergence of new structural and functional properties and competencies—at all levels of analysis (molecular, subcellular, cellular, organismic) as a consequence of horizontal and vertical coactions among its parts, including organism-environment coactions."

As such, the forefront of contemporary developmental theory and research is associated with theoretical ideas stressing that the systemic dynamics of individual-context relations provide the bases of behavior and developmental change (e.g., Ford & Lerner, 1992; Gottlieb, 1992; Lerner, 2002a; Thelen & Smith, 1994, 1998; Wapner & Demick, 1998). In emphasizing that systematic and successive change (i.e., development) is associated with alterations in the dynamic relations among structures from multiple levels of organization, the scope of contemporary developmental theory is not limited by (or, perhaps better, is not confounded by an inextricable association with) a unidimensional portrayal of the developing person (e.g., the person seen from the vantage point of only cognitions, emotions, stimulus-response connections, or genetic imperatives; for example, see Piaget, 1970; Freud, 1949; Bijou & Baer, 1961; and Rowe, 1994, respectively). Rather, the power of the contemporary theoretical stress on processes of dynamic person-context relations is the "design criterion" imposed on research, method, and application pertinent to the study of any content area or dimension of the developing person.

Together, these criteria afford a focus on the understanding, and use for enhancing human development, of systematic *change* (Ford & Lerner, 1992). This focus is required because of the belief that the potential for change exists across the life span (e.g., Baltes, 1987); specific ideas about the person-context relations that are thought to provide the basis of developmental change can be tested by appraising whether induced differences in such relations are associated with theoretically expected changes in behavior and development. In the actual ecology of human development, such induced changes are (depending on their level of organization) community-based actions, for example, programs or public policies (Lerner, 2002a; Lerner & Castellino, in press). Although it is also assumed that systemic change is not limitless (e.g., it is constrained both by past developments and by contemporary contextual conditions), contemporary theories stress that *relative plasticity* exists across life—although the magnitude of this plasticity may vary across ontogeny (Lerner, 1984, 2002a).

There are important implications of relative plasticity for the application of developmental science in regard to young people and their family and community contexts. For instance, the presence of relative plasticity legitimates a proactive search in adolescence for characteristics of individuals and of these facets of their ecologies that, together, can be arrayed to promote positive development (Birkel, Lerner, & Smyer, 1989; Fisher & Lerner, 1994; Lerner, 2002a, b; Lerner & Hood, 1986). Given that the bases for change, and for both plasticity and constraints in development, lie in the relations among the multiple levels of organization that constitute the substance of human life (Ford & Lerner, 1992;

Schneirla, 1957; Tobach, 1981), this search may involve levels that range from the inner biological level, through the individual or psychological level and the proximal social relational level (e.g., involving dyads, peer groups, and nuclear families), to the sociocultural level (including key macroinstitutions such as educational, public policy, governmental, and economic systems) and the natural and designed physical ecologies of human development (Bronfenbrenner, 1979; Riegel, 1975).

These levels are structurally and functionally integrated, thus requiring a systems view of the levels involved in human development (Ford & Lerner, 1992; Lerner, 2002a; Sameroff, 1983; Thelen & Smith, 1994, 1998). The relative plasticity that is a functional feature of this developmental system enables applications that focus not only on preventing undesired developmental trajectories but, as well, on envisioning and promoting systems changes that are associated with health, positive functioning, and the optimization of a young person's life chances.

Implications of Developmental Systems Theory for Policy and Program Design

Simply, then, the vision involved in contemporary developmental systems models of human development is that attributes of individuals and contexts may be integrated in ways that constitute sources of strength and of positive systematic change in young people. We need not, as scientists generating knowledge, or as consumers of that knowledge—community members, practitioners, parents, or young people themselves—take an approach that involves either (a) waiting for problems to occur and then acting to ameliorate or reduce them or (b) avoiding problems through preventive interventions that seek to avoid the actualization of the deficits believed to adhere to individuals in the "youth as problems to be managed" viewpoint. Rather, we can discard entirely an emphasis on problems, deficits, and even prevention. We can, instead, focus on the plasticity and strengths of individuals and their family and community contexts and build an agenda for action that is predicated on integrating these strengths of the developmental system—these assets for positive development—in ways that capitalize on the potential for healthy functioning present in all individuals and settings.

This theoretical perspective affords a vision for policies and programs that is quite distinct from the one associated with deficit conceptions of the human condition. From the developmental systems perspective, prevention is not the same as provision (e.g., Benson, 1997; Lerner, Sparks, & McCubbin, 1999; Pittman, 1996). *Preventing a problem from occurring does not guarantee that youth are being provided with the assets they need for developing in a positive manner.* Even if prevention efforts were completely successful, it is not the case that "problem free means prepared"; that is, preventing problems among young people does not mean that they are capable of making positive, healthy contributions to self, family, community, and civil society (Lerner, Fisher, & Weinberg, 2000; Pittman, 1996). Developmental systems theory advances, then, a new view of young people, one that envisions the possibility of capitalizing on their potential for positive development by promoting their integration with the assets for healthy functioning present in their contexts (e.g., their families and communities).

Building Communities That Promote the Development of Prepared Youth

What community actions may engage the developmental system in a manner that serves well-being and promotes the positive development of young people? One answer is provided by Damon (1997), who has envisioned the creation of a "youth charter" in each community in our nation and the world. The charter consists of a set of rules, guidelines, and plans of action that each community can adopt to provide its youth with a framework for development in a healthy manner. Damon (1997) describes how youth and significant adults in their com- munity (for example, parents, teachers, clergy, coaches, police, business leaders, and government representatives) can create partnerships to pursue a common ideal of positive moral development and intellectual achievement.

Embedding youth in a caring and developmentally facilitative community can promote their ability to develop morally and to contribute to civil society. In a study of about 130 African American parochial high school juniors, working at a soup kitchen for the homeless as part of a school-based community service program was associated with identity development and with the ability to re- flect on society's political organization and moral order (Yates & Youniss, 1996).

In a study of more than 3,100 high school seniors (Youniss, Yates, & Su, 1997), the activities engaged in by youth were categorized into either school- based, adult-endorsed norms or engagement in peer fun activities that excluded adults. Youth were then placed into groups that reflected orientations to (1) school-adult norms, but not peer fun (the "school" group); (2) peer fun but not school-adult norms (the "party" group); or (3) both "1" and "2" (the "all- around" group). The school and the all-around seniors were both high in com- munity service, religious orientation, and political awareness. In turn, the party group seniors were more likely to use marijuana than were the school group (but not the all-around group) seniors (Youniss et al., 1997).

Furthermore, African American and Latino adolescents who were nominated by community leaders for having shown unusual commitments to caring for others or for contributions to the community were labeled "care exemplars" and compared to a matched group of youth not perceived to be committed to the community (Hart & Fegley, 1995). The "care exemplars" were more likely than the comparison youth to describe themselves in terms reflective of moral characteristics, to show commitment to both their heritage and to the future of their community, to see themselves as reflecting the ideals of themselves and their parents, and to stress the importance of personal philosophies and beliefs for their self-definitions (Hart & Fegley, 1995).

Damon (1997) envisioned that, by embedding youth in a community in which service and responsible leadership are possible, the creation of community-specific youth charters could enable adolescents and adults to, together, systematically promote the positive development of youth. Youth charters can create opportunities to actualize both individual and community goals to eliminate risk behaviors among adolescents and promote in them the ability to contribute to high-quality individual and community life. Through community youth charters, youth and adults may work together to create a system wherein individual well-being and, simultaneously, civil society are maintained and perpetuated (Damon, 1997).

What, precisely, must be brought together by such charters to ensure the promotion of such positive youth development? What must be done to ensure that all youth have the opportunity to make such contributions to communities? What must be provided in order to create for young people the resources—the individual and ecological assets—that ensure that they attain the "five C's" of positive youth development: competence, confidence, connection (to family, peers, and community), character, and caring/compassion (Benson & Pittman, 2001; Lerner, 2002b; Pittman, 1996; Roth et al., 1998)? Answers to these questions may be found in the following discussion of developmental assets.

Developmental Assets in Childhood and Adolescence: The Contributions of Search Institute

In 1990, Peter L. Benson introduced the concept of developmental assets, that is, the social and psychological strengths that function to enhance health outcomes for children and adolescents. Related intellectually and strategically to the fields of community change and community building (Kretzmann & McKnight, 1993; McKnight, 1995), Benson and Leffert (2001) conceptualize developmental assets as:

A set of developmental experiences, resources, and opportunities, each of which contributes to important health outcomes, conceived of as both the reduction of health-compromising behaviors and the increase of positive or thriving outcomes such as school success. Though the framework is supported by scientific study, it was purposefully designed to fuel and guide community-based approaches to strengthen the natural and inherent socialization capacity of communities. Therefore, assets include the kinds of relationships, social experiences, social environments, and patterns of interactions known to both promote health and over which a community has considerable control.

Developmental assets, then, represent a framework grounded in scientific study, with the applied aim of reweaving the developmental infrastructure of a community by activating multiple sources of asset building. These include informal, nonprogrammatic relationships between adults and youth; traditional socializing systems such as families, neighborhoods, schools, congregations, and youth organizations; and the governmental, economic, and policy infrastructures which inform those socializing systems. The intent is to encourage the mobilizations of asset-building efforts for *all* children and adolescents within a community.

In line with this conception of, and vision for the strategic utility of deploying, developmental assets, Benson and his colleagues at Search Institute in Minneapolis, Minnesota (Benson, 1997; Benson, Leffert, Scales, & Blyth, 1998; Leffert et al., 1998; Scales, Benson, Leffert, & Blyth, 2000), believe that positive youth development is furthered when actions are taken to enhance the strengths of a person (e.g., a commitment to learning, a healthy sense of identity), a family (e.g., caring attitudes toward children, parenting styles that both empower youth and set boundaries and provide expectations for positive growth), and a community (e.g., social support, programs that provide access to the resources for education, safety, and mentoring available in a community) (Benson, 1997). Such resources may be indexed by the 20 internal and 20 external developmental assets measured in the work of Search Institute (Benson, 1997; Benson & Leffert, 2001; Benson et al., 1998; Blyth & Leffert, 1995; Leffert et al., 1998; Scales & Leffert, 1999; Scales et al., 2000). See Table 1 in Chapter 2.

Benson and his colleagues have found that the more developmental assets possessed by an adolescent the greater is his or her likelihood of positive, healthy development. In a study of 99,462 youth in grades 6 through 12 in public and/or alternative schools from 213 U.S. cities and towns who were assessed during the 1996–97 academic year for their possession of the 40 assets, Leffert et al. (1998) found that the more assets present among youth the lower the likelihood of alcohol use, depression/suicide risk, and violence. For instance, the level of alcohol use risk for youth in grades 6–8 combined and for youth in grades 9–12 combined decreases with the possession of more assets. Youth with zero to 10 assets have the highest risk, followed by youth with 11 to 20 assets, youth with 21 to 30 assets, and youth with 31 to 40 assets. Thus, consistent with Benson's (1997) view of the salience of developmental assets for promoting healthy behavior among young people, the fact that the last group has the lowest level of risk shows the importance of the asset approach in work aimed at promoting positive development in our nation's children and adolescents. Moreover, similar trends were found for males and females in regard to depression/suicide risk, and for combinations of males and females in different grade groupings in regard to violence risk. This congruence strengthens the argument for the critical significance of a focus on developmental assets in the promotion of positive youth development and, as such, in the enhancement of the capacity and commitment of young people to contribute to civil society.

Other data from Benson and his colleagues provide direct support for this argument. Scales et al. (2000) measured the concept of thriving among 6,000 youth in grades 6 to 12, evenly divided across six ethnic groups (American Indian, African American, Asian American, Latino, European American, and multiracial). Thriving was defined as involving seven attributes: school success, leadership, valuing diversity, physical health, helping others, delaying gratification, and overcoming adversity. Most, if not all, of these attributes are linked to the presence of prosocial behavior (e.g., helping others, delaying gratification) and to the behaviors requisite for competently contributing to civil society (e.g., valuing diversity, leadership, overcoming adversity). The greater the number of developmental assets possessed by youth, the more likely they were to possess the attributes of thriving, for example, in regard to helping others, valuing diversity, and leadership.

There are other data that support the importance of focusing on developmental assets both in understanding the bases of positive youth development and in using that knowledge to foster the community building that maximizes attentiveness to promoting developmental strengths for all youth (Benson & Leffert, 2001). Luster and McAdoo (1994) sought to identify the factors that contribute to individual differences in the cognitive competence of African American children in early elementary grades. Consistent with an assets-based approach to promoting the positive development of youth (Benson, 1997; Scales & Leffert, 1999), they found that favorable outcomes in cognitive and socioemotional development were associated with high scores on an advantage index. This index was formed by scoring children on the basis of the absence of risk factors (e.g., pertaining to poverty or problems in the quality of the home environment) and the presence of more favorable circumstances in their lives.

Luster and McAdoo (1994) reported that whereas only 4% of the children in their sample who scored low on the advantage index had high scores on a measure of vocabulary, 44% of the children who had high scores on the advantage index had high vocabulary scores. Similar contrasts between low and high scorers on the advantage index were found in regard to measures of math achievement (14% versus 37%), word recognition (0% versus 35%), and word meaning (7% and 46%).

Luster and McAdoo (1996) later extended the findings of their 1994 research. Seeking to identify the factors that contribute to individual differences in the educational attainment of African American young adults from low socioeconomic groups, Luster and McAdoo (1996) found that assets linked with the individual (cognitive competence, academic motivation, and personal adjustment in kindergarten) and the context (parental involvement in schools) were associated longitudinally with academic achievement and educational attainment.

In sum, Benson's (1997; Benson & Leffert, 2001) conceptualization of the nature of developmental assets, and of their strategic use in communities oriented toward building assets in the service of fostering positive youth development, finds rich empirical support in research emanating from Search Institute as well as from other settings. The purpose of the present book is to extend this scholarly base for the understanding of the character and scope of the systemic relation between healthy youth development and asset-building communities.

The Structure of This Book

When communities marshal their inherent strengths for cohesiveness, caring and compassion, and humane, equitable, and democratic interpersonal connections, they create a web of social support enabling young people to progress through their childhood and adolescence in a manner that not only inculcates in them these very community orientations and values but, in so doing, provides a source in development of the personal character, the confidence, and the competence enabling a young person to make positive contributions to self, family, and community (Benson, 1997; Benson & Leffert, 2001). Simply, asset-building communities both promote and are promoted by positive youth development (Lerner, 1982; Lerner & Walls, 1999), a bidirectional, systemic linkage that furthers civil society (Lerner et al., 2000). Accordingly, as emphasized by Benson and Leffert (2001):

> Asset-building communities are distinguished as relational and inter-generational places, with a critical mass of socializing institutions (e.g.,

families, schools, neighborhoods, youth organizations, religious communities) choosing to attend to the developmental needs of all children and adolescents. Developmental assets become a language of the common good, uniting sectors, citizens, and policy in pursuit of shared targets for all children and adolescents. The commitment of a community and its people, institutions, and organizations is both long term and inclusive.

In Chapter 2, which along with the present one comprises Part I, "Conceptual Foundations," Benson expands the articulation of the systemic interconnectedness of developmental assets, community building, and positive youth development. He explains how a collaborative fusion among people, places, and institutions, both within and across time, must be orchestrated if young people and their communities are to travel together, across generations, toward a more civil society.

The chapters following Benson's provide examples of the individual, interpersonal, and institutional collaborations that are part of as asset-building community. In Part II, "Promoting Positive Youth Development through Community Building," Damon and Gregory discuss the features of a community-building concept they have developed, the "youth charter," and explain how it represents a new era in community-based efforts to promote positive youth development. This era is framed by developmental systems thinking and involves the synthesis of a young person's personal characteristics, especially his or her agency (active, goal-directed participation in community building); the community's assets; the mutual expectations of youth and adults for social responsibility and service; and a key feature of the cognitive and emotional bases for the actions, intentions, and aspirations of all stakeholders in the community partnership for youth: the role of moral values and spiritual or religious faith. The role of youth agency, or participation in community building, is the focus of Chan, Carlson, Trickett, and Earls, who make the point that capitalizing on the ability of youth to play an active and positive role in their own development is an essential component of the development of well-being.

Numerous community institutions may moderate the success of community building on behalf of youth. As noted by Benson and Leffert (2001), families, schools, faith communities, and youth organizations, as well as businesses and media, are among such institutional agents. However, another potentially critical institutional collaborator in any community efforts to promote positive youth development is the philanthropic sector. Hein offers an exemplar of this contribution to young people. Under her leadership, the William T. Grant Foundation is concentrating its resources to support research and applications that are aimed at enhancing the individual and ecological assets for positive development among the diverse young people of America's communities.

Part III, "Building Families and Communities Serving Youth," explores the bidirectional link between positive youth development and asset building in the complex ecology of communities. As emphasized in the integrative, developmental systems perspective that frames both research and applications pertinent to developmental assets (Lerner, 2002a, b), this ecology of human development is composed of several levels of individual and social functioning. The macroecological level of this context includes the social policy and political milieus that impact the community (Bronfenbrenner, 1974; Bronfenbrenner & Morris, 1998), and any community's attempt to build assets for positive youth development will in some way be moderated by policy and politics. This point is richly explained and illustrated in the chapter by Lorion and Sokoloff. They point to both the political antecedents and the consequences of Search Institute's approach to community building and underscore the significance of the institutional climate within which communities strive to foster a healthy context for their young people.

Across the first two decades of life, the family is the key institution linking young people with their communities. Simpson and Roehlkepartain discuss the dynamism and significance of the youth-family-community system in building assets for positive youth development. They note the important role played by parenting practices in asset building and describe the features of family life more generally that enable young people to make valuable contributions to communities.

Of course, parents are not the only adults who can promote positive youth development and community building among young people. Rhodes and Roffman discuss the role of mentors in the positive development of young people. They explain how nonparental adults may be developmental assets for youth but, under some developmental contextual circumstances, may also work against the healthy development of young people.

Successful mentoring brings a young person into an active, reciprocal relationship with an older person and may foster in the youth a greater capacity for initiative and leadership in interpersonal and social situations. Enhancing the ability of youth to take an active, participatory role in their own and their social world's development is a key idea found in developmental systems conceptions of human development (Lerner, 2002a) and, as well, reflects a key feature of effective youth programming (Lerner, 2002b; Roth et al., 1998).

If youth are actively participating in the asset building of their communities, then not only will their well-being (positive development) be enhanced but they

will be collaborating with the other generations of their community in together envisioning and enacting an integrated approach to healthy individual-
ecological change. Several action strategies, or ecologically embedded "methodologies," have been suggested for fostering such collaborations. As noted earlier,
the "youth charter" approach developed by Damon (1997) is an exemplar of
such a strategy.

Across the chapters of this book, authors point to both the value, and the
challenges for the enhanced use, of Benson's (1990, 1997; Benson & Leffert,
2001) conceptualization of developmental assets. That is, contributors note the
issues that must be addressed both to advance science and to enact effectively
the strategic, action agenda associated with developmental assets by Benson
and his colleagues. Accordingly, in Part IV, "A Vision for the Future," Benson suggests clues that emerge in the chapters of this volume for how positive change
can occur at multiple levels in communities and society. He proposes a series of
principles to frame an agenda for advancing the science, practice, and civic engagement needed to transform U.S. communities.

Conclusions

As exemplified by Benson's concluding remarks and as well illustrated by the
scholarship of all the contributors here, the concept of developmental assets and
its link to asset-building communities is, on the one hand, an area of investigation that is predicated on an application to community-based and community-
valued actions. On the other hand, the work associated with the study of developmental assets involves a set of community actions that are inextricably based
in developmental systems theory and research. Benson and Leffert (2001) have
noted this fusion between research and application in the service of civil society:

> Ultimately, rebuilding and strengthening the developmental infrastruc-
> ture in a community are conceived less as a program implemented and
> managed by professionals and more as a mobilization of public will and
> capacity. A major target for this level of community engagement is the
> creation of a normative culture in which all residents are expected by
> virtue of their membership in the community to promote the positive de-
> velopment of children and adolescents. . . . Because these initiatives are
> complex, multisector "experiments" in changing local culture, and because
> they occur in a variety of rural, suburban, and urban settings, there is in-
> creasing investment in learning from these communities about innova-
> tions and effective practices in mobilizing residents and systems, with
> "feedback loops" emerging to inform both the theory of community
> change and the development of practical resources.

In essence, then, the study of developmental assets is framed by a developmental systems perspective that links active young people with their complex and multileveled ecology. As well, the application of knowledge about developmental assets is furthered by actions predicated on integrating all individuals and institutions within the developmental system. The success of such applications— the healthy youth outcomes derived from them—clarifies and fosters the further development of developmental assets theory and research. As such, the link between developmental assets and asset-building communities exemplifies the synthesis between research and application envisioned within a developmental systems approach to scholarship.

It is the hope, then, of all the contributors to this volume that both scholarship and application are furthered by the work presented here. In perhaps no area of human development scholarship and application is there any clearer example of the aspiration of the scholarly community to have its efforts become a decided asset in the promotion of healthier youth, stronger communities, and a more socially just and democratic nation and world.

References

Baltes, P. B. (1987). Theoretical propositions of life-span developmental psychology: On the dynamics between growth and decline. *Developmental Psychology, 23,* 611–626.

Benson, P. L. (1990). *The troubled journey: A portrait of 6th-12th grade youth.* Minneapolis, MN: Search Institute.

Benson, P. L. (1997). *All kids are our kids: What communities must do to raise caring and responsible children and adolescents.* San Francisco: Jossey-Bass.

Benson, P. L., & Leffert, N. (2001). Developmental assets in childhood and adolescence. In N. J. Smelser & P. B. Baltes (Eds.), *International encyclopedia of the social and behavioral sciences.* Oxford: Elsevier.

Benson, P. L., Leffert, N., Scales, P. C., & Blyth, D. A. (1998). Beyond the "village" rhetoric: Creating healthy communities for children and adolescents. *Applied Developmental Science, 2,* 138–159.

Benson, P. L., & Pittman, K. J. (Eds.). (2001). *Trends in youth development: Visions, realities, and challenges.* Norwell, MA: Kluwer Academic Publishers.

Bijou, S. W., & Baer, D. M. (Eds.). (1961). *Child development: A systematic and empirical theory.* New York: Appleton-Century-Crofts.

Bijou, S. W., & Baer, D. M. (Eds.). (1965). *Child development: Universal stage of infancy* (Vol. 2). Englewood Cliffs, NJ: Prentice-Hall.

Birkel, R., Lerner, R. M., & Smyer, M. A. (1989). Applied developmental psychology as an implementation of a life-span view of human development. *Journal of Applied Developmental Psychology, 10,* 425–445.

Blyth, D. A., & Leffert, N. (1995). Communities as contexts for adolescent development: An empirical analysis. *Journal of Adolescent Research, 10,* 64–87.

Bowlby, J. (1969). *Attachment and loss: Vol. 1. Attachment.* New York: Basic Books.

Bronfenbrenner, U. (1974). Developmental research, public policy, and the ecology of childhood. *Child Development, 45,* 1–5.

Bronfenbrenner, U. (1979). *The ecology of human development: Experiments by nature and design.* Cambridge, MA: Harvard University Press.

Bronfenbrenner, U., & Morris, P. A. (1998). The ecology of developmental process. In R. M. Lerner (Ed.), *The handbook of child psychology: Vol. 1. Theoretical models of human development* (5th ed., pp. 993–1028). Editor in chief: W. Damon. New York: Wiley.

Cairns, R. B. (1998). The making of developmental psychology. In R. M. Lerner (Ed.), *The handbook of child psychology: Vol. 1. Theoretical models of human development* (5th ed., pp. 25–106). Editor in chief: W. Damon. New York: Wiley.

Damon, W. (1997). *The youth charter: How communities can work together to raise standards for all our children.* New York: Free Press.

Dixon, R. A., & Lerner, R. M. (1999). History and systems in developmental psychology. In M. H. Bornstein & M. E. Lamb (Eds.), *Developmental psychology: An advanced textbook* (4th ed., pp. 3–45). Mahwah, NJ: Lawrence Erlbaum.

Erikson, E. H. (1968). *Identity, youth and crisis.* New York: Norton.

Fisher, C. B., & Lerner, R. M. (1994). Foundations of applied developmental psychology. In C. B. Fisher & R. M. Lerner (Eds.), *Applied developmental psychology* (pp. 3–20). New York: McGraw-Hill.

Ford, D. L., & Lerner, R. M. (1992). *Developmental systems theory: An integrative approach.* Newbury Park, CA: Sage.

Freud, A. (1969). Adolescence as a developmental disturbance. In G. Caplan & S. Lebovier (Eds.), *Adolescence* (pp. 5–10). New York: Basic Books.

Freud, S. (1949). *Outline of psychoanalysis.* New York: Norton.

Freud, S. (1954). *The standard edition of the complete psychological works.* London: Hogarth Press.

Gewirtz, J. L., & Stingle, K. G. (1968). Learning of generalized imitation as the basis for identification. *Psychological Review, 75,* 374–397.

Gottlieb, G. (1992). *Individual development and evolution: The genesis of novel behavior.* New York: Oxford University Press.

Gottlieb, G. (1997). *Synthesizing nature-nurture: Prenatal roots of instinctive behavior.* Mahwah, NJ: Lawrence Erlbaum.

Hart, D., & Fegley, S. (1995). Prosocial behavior and caring in adolescence: Relations to self-understanding and social judgement. *Child Development, 66,* 1346–1359.

Jensen, P., Hoagwood, K., & Trickett, E. (1999). Ivory towers or earthen trenches? Community collaborations to foster "real world" research. *Applied Developmental Science, 3,* 206–212.

Kretzmann, J. P., & McKnight, J. L. (1993). *Building communities from the inside out: A path toward finding and mobilizing a community's assets.* Chicago: ACTA Publications.

Leffert, N., Benson, P. L., Scales, P. C., Sharma, A. R., Drake, D. R., & Blyth, D. A. (1998). Developmental assets: Measurement and prediction of risk behaviors among adolescents. *Applied Developmental Science, 2,* 209–230.

Lerner, R. M. (1982). Children and adolescents as producers of their own development. *Developmental Review, 2,* 342–370.

Lerner, R. M. (1984). *On the nature of human plasticity.* Cambridge: Cambridge University Press.

Lerner, R. M. (1995). *America's youth in crisis: Challenges and options for programs and policies.* Thousand Oaks, CA: Sage.

Lerner, R. M. (1996). Relative plasticity, integration, temporality, and diversity in human development: A developmental contextual perspective about theory, process, and method. *Developmental Psychology, 32,* 781–786.

Lerner, R. M. (1998a). (Ed.). *The handbook of child psychology: Vol. 1. Theoretical models of human development* (5th ed.). Editor in chief: William Damon. New York: Wiley.

Lerner, R. M. (1998b). Theories of human development: Contemporary perspectives. In R. M. Lerner (Ed.), *The handbook of child psychology: Vol. 1. Theoretical models of human development* (5th ed., pp. 1–24). Editor in chief: W. Damon. New York: Wiley.

Lerner, R. M. (2002a). *Concepts and theories of human development* (3rd ed.). Mahwah, NJ: Lawrence Erlbaum.

Lerner, R. M. (2002b). *Adolescence: Development, diversity, context, and application.* Upper Saddle River, NJ: Prentice-Hall.

Lerner, R. M., & Castellino, D. R. (in press). Contemporary developmental theory and adolescence: Developmental systems and applied developmental science. *Journal of Adolescent Health.*

Lerner, R. M., Fisher, C. B., & Weinberg, R. A. (2000). Toward a science for and of the people: Promoting civil society through the application of developmental science. *Child Development, 71,* 11–20.

Lerner, R. M., & Hood, K. E. (1986). Plasticity in development: Concepts and issues for intervention. *Journal of Applied Developmental Psychology, 7,* 139–152.

Lerner, R. M., Sparks, E. S., & McCubbin, L. (1999). *Family diversity and family policy: Strengthening families for America's children.* Norwell, MA: Kluwer Academic Publishers.

Lerner, R. M., & Walls, T. (1999). Revisiting "individuals as producers of their development": From dynamic interactionism to developmental systems. In J. Brandtstädter & R. M. Lerner (Eds.), *Action and self-development: Theory and research through the life-span* (pp. 3–36). Thousand Oaks, CA: Sage.

Lorenz, K. (1965). *Evolution and modification of behavior.* Chicago: University of Chicago Press.

Luster, T., & McAdoo, H. P. (1994). Factors related to the achievement and adjustment of young African American children. *Child Development, 65,* 1080–1094.

Luster, T., & McAdoo, H. (1996). Family and child influences on educational attainment: A secondary analysis of the High/Scope Perry Preschool data. *Developmental Psychology, 32,* 26–39.

McKnight, J. (1995). *The careless society: Community and its counterfeits.* New York: Basic Books.

Overton, W. F. (1998). Developmental psychology: Philosophy, concepts, and methodology. In R. M. Lerner (Ed.), *The handbook of child psychology: Vol. 1. Theoretical models of human development* (5th ed., pp. 107–189). Editor in chief: W. Damon. New York: Wiley.

Piaget, J. (1950). *The psychology of intelligence.* New York: Harcourt Brace.

Piaget, J. (1970). Piaget's theory. In P. H. Mussen (Ed.), *Carmichael's manual of child psychology, 1* (pp. 703–732). New York: Wiley.

Pittman, K. (1996). Community, youth, development: Three goals in search of connection. *New Designs for Youth Development, Winter,* 4–8.

Plomin, R. (1986). *Development, genetics, and psychology.* Hillsdale, NJ: Lawrence Erlbaum.

Plomin, R. (2000). Behavioural genetics in the 21st century. *International Journal of Behavioral Development, 24,* 30–34.

Riegel, K. F. (1975). Toward a dialectical theory of development. *Human Development, 18,* 50–64.

Roth, J., Brooks-Gunn, J., Murray, L., & Foster, W. (1998). Promoting healthy adolescents: Synthesis of youth development program evaluations. *Journal of Research on Adolescence, 8,* 423–459.

Rowe, D. C. (1994). *The limits of family influence: Genes, experience, and behavior.* New York: Guilford Press.

Sameroff, A. J. (1983). Developmental systems: Contexts and evolution. In W. Kessen (Ed.), *The handbook of child psychology: Vol. 1. History, theory, and methods* (pp. 237–294). New York: Wiley.

Scales, P., Benson, P., Leffert, N., & Blyth, D. A. (2000). The contribution of developmental assets to the prediction of thriving among adolescents. *Applied Developmental Science, 4,* 27–46.

Scales, P. C., & Leffert, N. (1999). *Developmental assets: A synthesis of the scientific research on adolescent development.* Minneapolis, MN: Search Institute.

Schneirla, T. C. (1957). The concept of development in comparative psychology. In D. B. Harris (Ed.), *The concept of development* (pp. 78–108). Minneapolis: University of Minnesota Press.

Thelen, E., & Smith, L. B. (1994). *A dynamic systems approach to the development of cognition and action.* Cambridge, MA: MIT Press.

Thelen, E., & Smith, L. B. (1998). Dynamic systems theories. In R. M. Lerner (Ed.), *The handbook of child psychology: Vol. 1. Theoretical models of human development* (5th ed., pp. 563–633). Editor in chief: W. Damon. New York: Wiley.

Tobach, E. (1981). Evolutionary aspects of the activity of the organism and its development. In R. M. Lerner & N. A. Busch-Rossnagel (Eds.), *Individuals as producers of their development: A life-span perspective* (pp. 37–68). New York: Academic Press.

Wapner, S., & Demick, J. (1998). Developmental analysis: A holistic, developmental, systems-oriented perspective. In R. M. Lerner (Ed.), *The handbook of child psychology: Vol. 1. Theoretical models of human development* (5th ed., pp. 761–805). Editor in chief: W. Damon. New York: Wiley.

Yates, M., & Youniss, J. (1996). Community service and political-moral identity in adolescents. *Journal of Research on Adolescence, 6,* 271–284.

Youniss, J., Yates, M., & Su, Y. (1997). Social integration: Community service and marijuana use in high school seniors. *Journal of Adolescent Research, 12,* 245–262.

2 Developmental Assets and Asset-Building Community: Conceptual and Empirical Foundations

Peter L. Benson
Search Institute

The issue that frames this volume is the strengthening of the human development infrastructure in American communities. This infrastructure is concerned with the patterns and rhythms of relationships, resources, opportunities, and experiences—and the programs and policies that undergird them—for raising competent, connected, and successful children and adolescents. Since 1990, my work, and that of my colleagues at Search Institute, has focused on an action research agenda designed both to understand the role of community in human development and to position communities as co-learners with Search Institute in creating sustainable strategies for unleashing their human development capacity. As of fall, 2001, nearly 700 American urban, suburban, and rural communities in more than 30 states have launched initiatives based on this work.

Three core concepts drive this action research. First, *developmental assets* represent a theoretical construct identifying a set of environmental and intrapersonal strengths known to enhance educational and health outcomes for children and adolescents (Benson, 1990, 1997, 1998; Benson, Leffert, Scales, & Blyth, 1998; Benson, Scales, Leffert, & Roehlkepartain, 1999). The 40 elements in this framework represent a synthesis of multiple research literatures and are purposefully positioned as health-enhancing resources over which communities have considerable control. Second, *asset-building community* is an evolving conceptual model describing the nature and dynamics of places and settings that provide a constant and equitable flow of asset-building energy to all children and adolescents (Benson, 1997b; Benson & Leffert, 2001). This vision of developmentally attentive communities names multiple arenas of asset-building capacity, including *individual-level* actions by community residents in informal relationships with children and adolescents, *socializing system* actions (e.g., families, neighborhoods, schools, congregations, youth organizations), and *community-building* actions that can be triggered directly or indirectly by local economic and governmental infrastructures of a community.

Finally, *asset-building society* represents an emerging line of conceptualization and inquiry regarding the roles of social norms, public policy, rituals, and media in advancing the asset-building capacity of individuals, systems, and communities. One initial foray into this work is a poll of a nationally representative sample of adults to identify the social norms that advance or hinder adult engagement in the lives of children and adolescents (Scales, Benson, & Roehlkepartain, 2001).

This chapter provides an overview of these concepts with particular reference to the framework of developmental assets, its utility for triggering community transformation, and the challenge and opportunity of engaging communities as learning partners in understanding the processes and dynamics of mobilizing the natural and inherent capacity of communities to be developmentally attentive, asset-building places. To provide context for this work it is instructive to position developmental assets and asset-building community within a broader conceptual landscape.

The Conceptual Landscape

One primary intent of the stream of work we launched in 1990 is to develop an interdisciplinary, ecological, and applied line of inquiry that both understands and activates the capacity of community to promote developmental strengths. For now, we use two interchangeable names for this work: community-based human development and asset-based community and human development. The latter concept yokes our work directly to several leading approaches to community development: asset-based community development, with its accent on using the real but often hidden strengths of communities to lead and direct the process of change (Kretzmann & McKnight, 1993), and the national healthy community movement, which accents citizen engagement in articulating and addressing local civic, health, economic, and/or ecological issues (Norris, Ayre, & Clough, 2000).

In linking the human development and community development spheres, we draw on a number of intellectual and research traditions. The concept of community within the field of child and adolescent development owes a considerable debt to Bronfenbrenner's (1979) theoretical foundations on the ecology of human development, as well as to the significant work of Jessor and his colleagues on social-cultural influences on adolescent behavior (e.g., Jessor, 1993; Jessor, Graves, Hanson, & Jessor, 1968; Jessor & Jessor, 1977). This line of theory and research helped trigger both a more coherent view of the child's embeddedness within a complex pattern of social institutions (Belsky, 1981; Zigler, 1990) and the design of community-based interventions aimed at a wide range of issues, including school readiness and the prevention of juvenile delinquency (Zigler, Taussig, & Black, 1992).

Lerner's (1986, 1992) work on developmental contextualization has added to the understanding of community context in its articulation of the ecologies that inform development and the ways in which adolescents influence their social contexts. The implications of this work for policy and program are significant (Lerner, 1995).

In conceptualizing the intellectual and practical foundations for integrating the arenas of human development and community development, it is instructive to define the various infrastructures of community life that inform and shape child and adolescent health (Benson, 1997). In brief, these can be construed as the economic, service, program, and human development dimensions of community. The *economic infrastructure* profoundly shapes the overall well-being of families. We know—especially for those families who struggle to meet basic needs for food and shelter—that community success in promoting fair wages, affordable housing, and meaningful work can significantly improve some of the fundamental indicators of child and adolescent health.

The *service infrastructure* distributes a series of resources aimed at ameliorating risks and promoting health, especially among vulnerable populations. The public sector is perhaps the key actor here. A common approach has been service integration in which multiple delivery systems collaborate in serving high-risk youth and families. These kinds of efforts are well documented. However, a number of innovations in service integration designed to promote system reform and cross-system collaboration among service providers face significant obstacles in sustaining the kind of deep systemic reform needed to make collaboration successful (Burt, Resnick, & Norick, 1998). Dryfoos (1998) has recently defined and documented the look and feel of successful service-delivery collaborations within a school context. She provides an important advance in the understanding of how to construct a full menu of effective services for high-risk youth.

Communities also require a *program infrastructure*, providing safe places, adult connections, and competency-building curricula. This infrastructure becomes particularly important for filling the gaps between the school day and the return of the parent and/or guardian from the workplace. Communities across the country are rapidly seeking new energy and new resources to support the growth of these programmatic supports, particularly for vulnerable youth.

America's Promise: The Alliance for Youth is one prominent initiative calling for action regarding safe places, caring adults, and opportunities to serve.

Each of these three infrastructures (economic, service, program) is necessary but not sufficient for promoting the health of children and adolescents. Across these three areas, professionals, bureaucracies, and agencies are the prime actors. Much of the work is targeted at vulnerable populations. And the organizing framework that tends to shape these three infrastructures is a deficit reduction paradigm in which the prevailing goal is to ameliorate social and/or personal pathologies and the conditions that promote them.

The *human development infrastructure* has to do with the patterns, rhythms, and flow of community attentiveness to essential developmental needs and milestones. In essence, we are speaking here of the constancy and equity of core developmental experiences such as support, engagement, empowerment, belonging, affirmation, boundary setting, structure, and connectedness, all of which are grounded less in program and policy and more in how citizens and socializing systems identify and use their inherent, relational capacities (Benson & Saito, 2000).

There is mounting evidence that this human development infrastructure is particularly fragile in American communities. Take, for example, three types of support and connection that are known to be predictive of significant adolescent health outcomes: sustained relationships with nonrelated adults (i.e., embeddedness in intergenerational community), embeddedness in neighborhoods in which adults know and interact with children and adolescents, and engagement in schools that students perceive as caring and supportive. These three forms of support, each of which is essentially about adult attentiveness and connection, are 3 of the 40 developmental assets to be discussed in the next section. In survey-based profiles of hundreds of urban, suburban, and rural communities, we have discovered that these kinds of support mechanisms are relatively uncommon (Benson et al., 1999). To be more precise, an aggregated sample of 99,462 middle school and high school students in 213 cities yields these percentages of youth who possess these developmental assets: intergenerational relationships, 41%; caring neighborhood, 40%; and caring school climate, 25%. In addition, further analyses of these 213 cities as well as the approximately 700 communities profiled since 1997 suggest that the fragility of these support systems, and that of parallel systems of empowerment, structure, and engagement, is generalized across geography and community size. And subgroup analyses of student reports reveal that this "nonnormative" access to these kinds of developmental resources holds across gender, grade, parental education, and race/ethnicity (Benson et al., 1999).

These findings begin to make the case for a profound rupture in the human development infrastructure in American communities. As discussed in a series of publications (e.g., Benson, 1997; Benson, Leffert, et al., 1998), many dynamics within this culture now inhibit the flow of developmental energy. Among these are age segregation and the deep disconnection, particularly during the adolescent years, of young people from long-term, sustained relationships with multiple adults. To these we can add the issue of inconsistent socialization that now describes the journey of human development in most communities. Most communities evidence a kind of dissonance in core messages to children and adolescents about boundaries, expectations, and values (Damon, 1997).

Currently, one of the most discussed phenomena influencing the dynamics of community is "the disappearance of social capital and civic engagement in America" (Putnam, 1996, p. 34). A healthy society, at least in Western terms, requires the mobilization of social networks and social norms to support the pursuit of shared goals (social capital) and the meaningful participation of citizens in building and being community (civic engagement). In the fields of political science and public affairs, the suppression of social capital and civic engagement is widely documented and discussed as a possible explanation for historical downturns in voting behavior and as consequences of rising social mistrust, isolation, and individualism (Benson, 1997).

If we can extrapolate from this literature, the concept of civic engagement also is useful for analyzing processes of child and adolescent development within a community context. We take it as axiomatic that such core developmental processes as the transmission of values and standards, the provision of support, the establishment of checks and balances in behavior, and the promotion of belonging and empowerment depend to a large extent on consistent adult presence and voice. Further, we suggest that these kinds of core developmental processes are best promoted when adult presence and voice are redundant, holding across many of the contexts of child and adolescent development (e.g., family, neighborhood, public gathering places, schools, congregations). This kind of vibrant developmental infrastructure requires considerable civic engagement in the lives of children and adolescents. And that, in turn, requires social norms favoring engagement and a kind of self-selection by most community residents to connect and engage.

It is likely that trends toward civic disengagement from active participation in the lives of children and adolescents are fed, in part, by perceived risks for engagement (e.g., litigation) and a distrust that creates social distance between adults and youth. Recent public opinion poll data on adult views of children and adolescents are also relevant here. When asked to describe American youth, a majority of adults choose negative descriptors (e.g., undisciplined, disrespectful, unfriendly) as their initial response (Farkas & Johnson, 1997). These perceptions may impede engagement.

In a rather pointed critique, McKnight (1995) described the evolution of the American service industry and its unintended consequence of suppressing community social capital and engagement:

> The most significant development transforming America since World War II has been the growth of a powerful service economy and its pervasive serving institutions. Those institutions have [commodified] the care of community and called that substitution a service. As citizens have seen the professionalized service commodity invade their communities, they have grown doubtful of their common capacity to care, and so it is that we have become a careless society, populated by impotent citizens and ineffectual communities dependent on the counterfeit of care called human services. (pp. ix–x)

Intertwined with this social phenomenon is the contemporary dominance of what is often called the deficit reduction paradigm. In this paradigm, research and practice are steered toward naming, counting, and reducing the incidence of environmental risks (e.g., family violence, poverty, family disintegration) and health-compromising behaviors (e.g., substance use, adolescent pregnancy, interpersonal violence, school dropout). This paradigm, it has been argued, dominates the strategies chosen to enhance child and adolescent health and has historically driven resource allocation in favor of federal and foundation initiatives (Benson, 1997). The point here is not that deficit reduction as a way of thinking and mobilizing action is misguided. But as a dominating paradigm, it may unintentionally enhance both the overprofessionalization of care and civic disengagement. These processes may well be symbiotic. That is, civic disengagement and professionalized forms of addressing child and adolescent health may feed each other.

It is not particularly clear from where and what the dominance of the deficit reduction paradigm emanates. Among the candidates is the philosophical tradition of logical positivism with its accents on detached inquiry, the splits between basic research and application and between expert and practitioner. As Boyte (2000) puts it, positivism structures patterns of theory evaluation, assessment, and outcome measures around fixing social problems. "It sustains patterns of one-way service delivery and the conceptualization of poor and powerless groups as needy 'clients.' It shapes the market, the media, health care, and political life. Professionals imagine themselves outside a shared reality with their fellow citizens, who are seen as 'customers' or 'clients,' objects to be manipulated or remediated" (Boyte, 2000, p. 50).

What we have, then, is a culture dominated by deficit and risk thinking, by pathology and its symptoms. This shapes our research, our policy, our practice. It fuels the creation of elaborate and expensive service and program delivery infrastructures, creates a dependence on professional experts, encourages an ethos of fear, and, by consequence, derogates, ignores, and interferes with the natural and inherent capacity of communities to be community.

The theory and research undergirding developmental assets and asset-building community are designed, in part, to assist community residents and their socializing systems to mobilize their capacity to promote developmental strengths. By so doing, we seek to balance paradigms so that communities pursue deficit reduction and asset building with equal vigor.

In defining how communities can focus simultaneously on deficit reduction and asset promotion, it is useful to note briefly how the two approaches draw on different resources and processes. Deficit reduction efforts focused, for example, on reducing adolescent chemical use, school dropout, violence, or pregnancy tend to be shaped and guided by professionals who implement strategies encouraged by federal, state, or foundation mandate. It is often a process of "top-down" change supported by significant funding and aimed largely at vulnerable or marginalized youth. The mobilization of community capacity to build developmental strengths, on the other hand, places citizens and socializing systems (e.g., neighborhood, family, school, congregation) at the center of the action with emphasis more on unleashing natural asset-building capacity guided by a shared vision of "what kids need to thrive" and building more on the energy of personal and collective efficacy, social trust, and pursuit of the common good than on the energy of funding, policy, or mandate. As such, this second paradigm more typically reflects a "bottom-up" change process, with the accent less on implementation and more on unleashing, supporting, and celebrating the inherent power of communities to be community (Benson, 1997; Benson, Leffert, et al., 1998).

The Framework of Developmental Assets

An essential early step, it is argued, for triggering community-wide engagement in reclaiming a developmentally vibrant infrastructure is to introduce and diffuse a set of developmental benchmarks that can be widely embraced by community residents and civic leaders. The taxonomy of developmental assets (Table 1) focuses on a scientifically based set of environmental and psychological strengths that enhance health outcomes for children and adolescents and that at the same time provide citizens and systems with a unifying language.

Table 1. 40 Developmental Assets

External Assets	Support	1. *Family support*—Family life provides high levels of love and support.
		2. *Positive family communication*—Young person and her or his parent(s) communicate positively, and young person is willing to seek advice and counsel from parents.
		3. *Other adult relationships*—Young person receives support from three or more nonparent adults.
		4. *Caring neighborhood*—Young person experiences caring neighbors.
		5. *Caring school climate*—School provides a caring, encouraging environment.
		6. *Parent involvement in schooling*—Parent(s) are actively involved in helping young person succeed in school.
	Empowerment	7. *Community values youth*—Young person perceives that adults in the community value youth.
		8. *Youth as resources*—Young people are given useful roles in the community.
		9. *Service to others*—Young person serves in the community one hour or more per week.
		10. *Safety*—Young person feels safe at home, at school, and in the neighborhood.
	Boundaries and Expectations	11. *Family boundaries*—Family has clear rules and consequences and monitors the young person's whereabouts.
		12. *School boundaries*—School provides clear rules and consequences.
		13. *Neighborhood boundaries*—Neighbors take responsibility for monitoring young people's behavior.
		14. *Adult role models*—Parent(s) and other adults model positive, responsible behavior.
		15. *Positive peer influence*—Young person's best friends model positive, responsible behavior.
		16. *High expectations*—Both parents and teachers encourage the young person to do well.
	Constructive Use of Time	17. *Creative activities*—Young person spends three or more hours per week in lessons or practice in music, theater, or other arts.
		18. *Youth programs*—Young person spends three or more hours per week in sports, clubs, or organizations at school and/or in community organizations.
		19. *Religious community*—Young person spends one or more hours per week in activities in a religious institution.
		20. *Time at home*—Young person is out with friends "with nothing special to do" two or fewer nights per week.

Table 1. 40 Developmental Assets (continued)

Internal Assets	Commitment to Learning	21. *Achievement motivation*—Young person is motivated to do well in school.
		22. *School engagement*—Young person is actively engaged in learning.
		23. *Homework*—Young person reports doing at least one hour of homework every school day.
		24. *Bonding to school*—Young person cares about her or his school.
		25. *Reading for pleasure*—Young person reads for pleasure three or more hours per week.
	Positive Values	26. *Caring*—Young person places high value on helping other people.
		27. *Equality and social justice*—Young person places high value on promoting equality and reducing hunger and poverty.
		28. *Integrity*—Young person acts on convictions and stands up for her or his beliefs.
		29. *Honesty*—Young person "tells the truth even when it is not easy."
		30. *Responsibility*—Young person accepts and takes personal responsibility.
		31. *Restraint*—Young person believes it is important not to be sexually active or to use alcohol or other drugs.
	Social Competencies	32. *Planning and decision making*—Young person knows how to plan ahead and make choices.
		33. *Interpersonal competence*—Young person has empathy, sensitivity, and friendship skills.
		34. *Cultural competence*—Young person has knowledge of and comfort with people of different cultural/racial/ethnic backgrounds.
		35. *Resistance skills*—Young person can resist negative peer pressure and dangerous situations.
		36. *Peaceful conflict resolution*—Young person seeks to resolve conflict nonviolently.
	Positive Identity	37. *Personal power*—Young person feels he or she has control over "things that happen to me."
		38. *Self-esteem*—Young person reports having high self-esteem.
		39. *Sense of purpose*—Young person reports that "my life has a purpose."
		40. *Positive view of personal future*—Young person is optimistic about her or his personal future.

Accordingly, we take particular care in identifying developmental building blocks, or assets, that generalize across gender, race/ethnicity, geography, and community size.

Although the framework is supported by hundreds of scientific studies (Scales & Leffert, 1999), it has been purposefully designed to fuel and guide community-based approaches to strengthening the natural and inherent socialization capacity of communities. Therefore, the framework of 40 assets includes the kinds of relationships, social experiences, social environments, and patterns of interaction known to promote health and over which a community has considerable control.

At the same time, the asset framework is intended to speak to and elicit the engagement of multiple sources of asset-building energy. These include informal, nonprogrammatic relationships between adults and youth; traditional socializing systems such as families, neighborhoods, schools, congregations, and youth organizations; and the governmental, economic, and policy infrastructures that inform those socializing systems. The intent is to encourage the mobilization of asset-building efforts within many settings of a child's life and to increase these efforts for *all* children and adolescents within a community.

The framework is scientifically based on empirical studies of child and adolescent development, as well as applied studies in prevention, health promotion, and resiliency. The development of this conceptual foundation involved a research synthesis that focused on integrating developmental experiences that are widely known to inform three types of health outcomes among adolescents: (a) the prevention of high-risk behaviors (e.g., substance use, violence, sexual intercourse, school dropout), (b) the enhancement of thriving outcomes (e.g., school success, affirmation of diversity, prosocial behavior), and (c) resiliency or the capacity to overcome adversity. The assets are framed initially around adolescent development. We are now in the process of extending the definition and measurement of developmental assets from birth to age 10 (Leffert, Benson, & Roehlkepartain, 1997; Roehlkepartain & Leffert, 2000).

Because the developmental assets framework was designed not only to inform theory and research but also to have practical significance for the mobilization of communities, the 40 assets are placed in categories that have conceptual integrity and can be described easily to the residents of a community. As seen in Table 1, they are grouped into 20 external assets (i.e., environmental, contextual, and relational features of socializing systems) and 20 internal assets (i.e., skills, competencies, and commitments). The external assets include four categories: Support, Empowerment, Boundaries and Expectations, and Constructive Use of

Time. The internal assets are also grouped in four categories: Commitment to Learning, Positive Values, Social Competencies, and Positive Identity. The scientific foundations for the eight categories and each of the 40 assets are described in more detail in Scales and Leffert (1999).

The 40 developmental assets are assessed in a 156–item self-reporting survey instrument, administered anonymously in public school districts in a classroom setting and guided by standardized instructions. The instrument also assesses numerous thriving indicators (e.g., school success, affirmation of diversity) and risk behaviors (e.g., violence, substance use, sexual activity). Students place completed surveys in an envelope that is then sealed and mailed to Search Institute for processing and generation of a school district report. Typically, school districts choose to survey a complete census of all 6th- through 12th-grade students attending school on the day the survey is administered.

Since 1990, approximately 2,000 communities have conducted this survey—many as an early step in launching a community-wide asset-building initiative. There is a significant mix of urban, suburban, and rural districts included in this ongoing survey assessment process. Our recent scientific publications use an aggregate sample of 99,462 6th- through 12th-grade youth from public and alternative schools in 213 cities and towns in the United States who administered the survey during the 1996–97 academic year.

An updated and expanded sample has become the focus of a next wave of analyses, beginning in 2001. This sample of 217,277 6th- through 12th-grade students aggregates across 318 communities. All data were collected in the 1999–2000 school year. Using U. S. census figures, data have been weighted on urbanicity and race/ethnicity. A preliminary comparison of the older and newer samples suggests only minor and largely nonmeaningful charges in asset profiles. Hence, the data presented in this chapter—based on the 1996–97 sample—substantially mirror the newer sample.

The survey is primarily used as a means of communicating aggregate data on a community's youth. A report, developed for each community or school district that uses the survey, often becomes a widely shared document and is used both to frame community-wide discussions and to serve as a focal point to mobilize around raising healthy youth (Benson, Leffert, et al., 1998). A dichotomous form of reporting the assets, whereby each asset is simplified into a single percentage of youth who have, or do not have, each asset, is an effective method for communicating the asset profile to diverse community audiences. This also allows for a simple summation of the average number of assets youth in any given community report having.

Research on Developmental Assets: Primary Themes

A growing body of publications describes the psychometric properties of the survey instrument (Benson, 1997; Benson, Leffert, et al., 1998; Leffert et al., 1998; Scales, Benson, Leffert, & Blyth, 2000), demographic differences in asset profiles (Benson, 1990, 1996a; Benson et al., 1999; Benson & Leffert, 2001; Leffert et al., 1998), and the predictive utility of the asset framework for explaining both risk and thriving behaviors (Benson, 1998; Benson et al., 1999; Leffert et al., 1998; Scales et al., 2000). Two themes dominate across these studies.

The first theme is the consistent finding that most adolescents evidence only a minority of the developmental assets. The mean number of assets is 18.0, based on a scale comprised of 40 binary variables. Nearly two-thirds (62%) of the aggregated sample evidence 20 or fewer developmental assets. When the sample is broken into four asset levels, we find that 20% possess a total number of assets of 10 or less, 42% possess 11–20, 30% have 21–30, and 8% attain 30 or more assets.

By grade, the mean decreases from 21.5 in grade 6 to 17.2 in grade 12. Boys average three assets fewer than girls (16.5 and 19.5, respectively). Means for communities range from 16.5 to 20.0 across all 213 cities. A particularly important finding is that the mean number of assets is relatively similar when comparing students in different community sizes (communities ranging in size from 10,000 to those of 250,000 or more). Although there is variability across communities, it is less than expected and reinforces the idea that all communities have significant proportions of adolescents who lack key developmental building blocks in their lives. It should be noted here that these findings are based on youth who attend American middle schools and high schools. If out-of-school 12- to 18-year-olds were also captured in this assessment, the reported percentages would likely be lower.

Family income is not measured in the survey. However, in a study done in Minneapolis, we looked at how the developmental assets vary as a function of the city's 11 planning districts, which differ substantially in average family income, property values, and resources. Across these 11 geographical areas of the city, the average number of 40 assets ranged from 16.7 to 20.1 (Benson, 1996a). Not surprisingly, as average wealth rises, assets rise. But, putting this in context, note that the difference is only about three developmental assets when we compare the least and most affluent planning districts.

In all demographic categories, there are sets of assets that are particularly fragile. Among these are many of the specific assets in the Support, Engagement, Boundaries and Expectations, and Social Competency categories. Total sample and subgroup percentages for each of 40 assets are reported in a number of publications (e.g., Benson et al., 1999).

The second theme has to do with the cumulative or additive nature of the developmental assets in explaining risk and thriving behaviors. That is, as assets rise in number, profound reductions are seen in each of nine risk behavior patterns (alcohol use, tobacco use, illicit drug use, antisocial behavior, violence, school failure, sexual activity, attempted suicide, and gambling). And the cumulative effect is equally powerful in predicting thriving behaviors, with increases in assets associated with dramatic increases in academic achievement, school grades, leadership, prosocial behavior, the delay of gratification, and the affirmation of diversity. While many of our studies pinpoint subsets of assets that are particularly germane to a particular risk or thriving behavior, addressing a more comprehensive vision of child and adolescent health (i.e., protection from many types of risk behavior and the pursuit of many forms of thriving) requires attention to the full complement of developmental assets.

More sophisticated analyses document the relative power of the asset framework. Regression analyses are used to assess the extent to which the developmental assets are useful in predicting either a reduction in risk behaviors or a promotion of thriving indicators. Those analyses have shown that demographic variables accounted for a range of 5% to 14% of the total variance of each of the models constructed to examine risk behaviors. In each analysis, the developmental assets contributed a significant amount over and above the influence of demographic variables, accounting for 16% to 35% of the variance explained in the reduction of each of the individual risk behavior patterns and for 57% of the variance in a composite index of risk behaviors. The total regression model (assets with demographics) explained 66% of the variance in this composite index (Leffert et al., 1998).

Adolescent health is often understood as the absence of symptoms, pathology, or health-compromising behavior. This incomplete view of well-being mimics, of course, the "medical model" approach to health. The emerging field of youth development places particular emphasis on expanding the concept of health to include the kinds of skills, behaviors, and competencies needed to succeed in employment, education, and civic life. A common mantra in youth development circles is "problem-free is not fully prepared" (Pittman, Irby, & Ferber, 2001).

The concept of thriving indicators has been posited to reflect this domain of positive outcomes (Benson, 1997; Scales et al., 2000). Multiple thriving behavior measures are embedded in the developmental assets survey instrument. Regression analyses show that the developmental assets framework is also a powerful prediction of thriving measures taken one at a time or in combination. Across each of six racial/ethnic groups (African American, Asian American, Hispanic/ Latino, Native American, multiracial, white), developmental assets explained from 47% to 54% of the variance in a composite thriving index (e.g., prosocial behavior, leadership, affirmation of diversity) over and above demographic variables (Scales et al., 2000).

Of particular import is the role of developmental assets in academic achievement. Students who report a high number of assets (31–40) are two times more likely (53% vs. 19%) to report "getting mostly A's" in school compared to students with 11–20 assets and about 8 times more likely than those reporting 10 or fewer assets (7%) (Benson et al., 1999). A recent study in a midwestern city allows us to merge individual asset profiles with school records. We find that developmental assets are strongly linked to grade point average and to actual grades in English, science, and mathematics (Leffert, Scales, Vraa, Libbey, & Benson, 2001). Other research is under way that will link developmental assets with archival data on state benchmark tests.

The observation that assets have a cumulative or "pileup" effect adds to an emerging literature on this phenomenon. Heretofore, most of this research has focused on the pileup effect of risk indicators on problem behaviors. One exception to this, and consonant with the cumulative impact of developmental assets, is Jessor's work on the additive nature of protective factors in reducing several forms of risk taking (Jessor, 1993; Jessor, Van Den Bos, Vanderryn, Costa, & Turbin, 1995).

The Concept of Asset-Building Communities: Reframing Capacity, Accountability, and Power

In summary, studies of many adolescent samples and multiple behavioral domains provide evidence both for the utility and the importance of strategies dedicated to the promotion of developmental strengths. There are several aligned areas of inquiry that are beginning to build what we might call a science of promoting developmental strengths, in contrast to what has become known as the field of prevention science. Some of the conceptual strands that inform a "promotion science" include resiliency (Garmezy, 1985; Luthar, Cicchetti, & Becker, 2000; Masten & Curtis, 2000), protective factors (Hawkins, Catalano, & Miller, 1992), and youth development (Benson & Pittman, 2001). Many of these efforts to study the sources and impact of developmental strengths lead to the formation of strength-building programs and/or policy recommendations (Roth & Brooks-Gunn, 2000).

My colleagues at Search Institute and I have chosen to follow a somewhat different path, with important theoretical, scientific, and practical implications. Although program and policy implications are of strong interest, the developmental assets framework was designed to be an early step in advancing a science and a practice for creating and sustaining developmentally attentive communities.

Accordingly, there are three features embedded in the developmental assets framework that are intended to invite "experiments" by communities to mobilize adults, youth, and socializing systems in a coordinated effort to move the developmental needle. First, the developmental assets model purposefully identifies building blocks of development that have a kind of universal currency. I use the term *universal* here to mean developmental resources that have significance within multiple demographic subgroups and that have face validity for the many and diverse communities of identity and interest within a city. There is considerable empirical data to suggest that the 40 developmental assets, individually and in combination, do have developmental meaning and significance for youth, regardless of family background, race/ethnicity, or geographic location. And there is mounting qualitative evidence to support our intent to position the developmental assets as a "language of the common good," drawing people of a city together into a shared civic work. In the diverse fields of community building and organizational change, this kind of common-good language—sometimes referred to as shared vision—is held up as a necessary but not a sufficient ingredient for producing systemic change. The scientific study of this shared vision dynamic, however, is in its infancy. Little is known about how images of the common good emerge and spread.

Second, the developmental assets framework, when used as a lens to examine the developmental journey of a community's youth, invites deep, community-wide conversation, reflection, and critique of community life. In essence, this is the process of framing how a community knows and understands its role in the development of children and adolescents. The study of developmental assets at a local level is intended to trigger several forms of reframing. One, of course, is the reframing of how a community of people and systems understands the nature of successful development. Here we would argue that our work helps communities expand their shared understanding of healthy development to encompass not only "problem free" but also "asset rich." Another reframing has to do with a community's collective understanding of the population of children and adolescents to be targeted by community interventions. Deficit reduction approaches tend to bifurcate youth into two camps, with the developmental "have-nots" labeled as at risk, vulnerable, high risk, or marginalized. Our approach, supported by hundreds of community asset profiles, is to place development on a continuum that runs from asset depleted on the one end to asset rich on the other. By showing communities that a majority of their 6th- through 12th-grade students are below midpoint, we strategically and purposefully create dissonance in the public's understanding of what the issue is. In more classic community development verbiage, this is the process of expanding citizen ownership of and engagement in the issue. In language that resonates more with community residents, we often speak of shifting the understanding from "some kids need more" to "all kids need more."

This effort to expand the focus from "some kids" to "all kids" also signals a larger social critique, alerting communities, regardless of size or location, to general and widespread ruptures in the American developmental infrastructure. The normative developmental journey, our community studies suggest, includes developmentally inattentive socializing systems (e.g., schools, neighborhoods, families) and a lack of sustained relationships with adults. In this social critique, we join with others concerned about our national capacity to promote healthy development. In a particularly cogent analysis of the ecology of development in the United States, Bronfenbrenner and Morris (1998) conclude:

> The research findings here presented reveal growing chaos in the lives of families, in child care settings, schools, peer groups, youth programs, neighborhoods, workplaces, and other everyday environments in which human beings live their lives. Such chaos, in turn, interrupts and undermines the formation and stability of relationships and activities that are necessary for psychological growth. (p. 1022)

This reframing to "all kids" is an essential strategy for motivating multiple systems within communities to pool their developmental resources in a coherent, long-term, multisystem, and citizen-engaged initiative to promote developmental strengths. It also has other significant advantages. Given the complex and long-term dimensions of community change—as well as the dearth of scientific knowledge about creating developmentally attentive communities—we have chosen to connect hundreds of communities together into a mutually supporting web of action and learning directed toward the comprehensive transformation of community life. The "all kids" reframing, and the underlying societal dimensions it presupposes, puts cities of many sizes and geographies on a common playing field, seeking knowledge and wisdom about similar issues (e.g., the expansion of civic engagement, the creation of developmentally attentive schools, the building of social trust within neighborhoods, the re-creation of intergenerational community). Positioned this way, communities across the country discover a commonality of interest and an eagerness to connect, learn, and teach. And rather than deflecting energy away from marginalized youth, the "all kids" reframing appears to reenergize and strengthen this community engagement.

Finally, embedded within the developmental asset approach is a comprehensive approach to the etiology of developmental strengths. The external assets directly speak to the role of multiple developmental ecologies, including family, neighborhood, school, youth organizations, congregation/synagogue/mosque, and programs. The internal assets invite inquiry and conversation about the multiple sources of competencies, values, identity, commitment and purpose, and the degree to which communities possess the harmony of voice or the deep and sustained relationships necessary for these capacities to develop. As such, the taxonomy of developmental assets provides counterweight to approaches that are overdependent on professionalized services for their implementation.

In summary, the accompanying chart captures some of the salient accents on two different organizing principles for advancing the health and well-being of children and adolescents (Benson, 1997).

	Deficit Reduction	*Asset Promotion*
The Goal	Reduce deficits, risks, and health-compromising behavior	Promote or enhance developmental assets
The Target	Vulnerable children and adolescents	All children and adolescents
The Strategies	Expansion of social services and treatment systems; early interventions; prevention programs targeted at high-risk behaviors	Mobilization of all citizens and socializing systems to act on a shared vision for positive human development
The Actors	Professionals take the lead, citizens support	Citizens take the lead, professionals support

Although there are important strategic and practical differences in the two paradigms, we are not advocating that one should reign supreme. What communities need is a kind of paradigm balance in which deficit reduction efforts are matched in intensity and power with asset-building efforts. An important line of inquiry, heretofore unexamined, is how communities successfully achieve this balance.

The developmental assets framework (and its diffusion) is a first step in triggering community change. The target is the creation of asset-building communities by means of which multiple energy systems are transformed and equipped to serve as strong, vibrant conduits for developmental assets. Developmentally attentive community (a synonym I currently use for asset-building community) provides a potentially useful conceptual framework for exploring and positing optimal configurations of resources, opportunities, experiences, and relationships across many settings (Benson & Leffert, 2001; Benson & Libbey, 2001). The term *community* has rich and varied connotations and a growing number of meanings and uses. In the meaning intended here, we define it more as a geographic area than as a community of association or as one's perceived community. We lean to a geographic definition because much of the strength-building energy that can be mobilized for children and adolescents occurs within geographically overlapping systems of schools, neighborhoods, families, youth organizations, parks, and religious institutions within the boundaries of a particular municipality. When systems of socialization overlap (as when school districts draw students from multiple towns), community must be thought of as several cities, a county, or other area. In large urban centers, the geography that defines a particular child's community might be a neighborhood or section of the city where most socialization is experienced.

The dynamics and processes by which communities mobilize their developmental capacity constitute a relatively unexplored line of inquiry, both theoretically and empirically (Blyth & Leffert, 1995). An initial framework for understanding the asset-building capacity of communities provides a set of core principles and strategies, grounded in the literatures of community development, social marketing, and organizational change (Benson, 1997; Benson et al., 1998). Among these are the principles of *developmental redundancy* (the exposure to asset-building people and environments within multiple contexts), *developmental reach* (a focus on nurturing most or all assets in children and adolescents), and *developmental breadth* (extending, by purpose and design, the reach of asset-building energy to all children and adolescents).

In activating these core principles, five sources of asset-building potential are hypothesized to exist within all communities, each of which can be marshaled by means of a multiplicity of community mobilization strategies. These sources of potential asset-building influence include:

- Sustained relationships with adults, both within and beyond family;
- Peer group influence (when peers choose to activate their asset-building capacity);
- Socializing systems, including families, neighborhoods, schools, playgrounds, congregations, youth organizations, and places of employment;
- Community-level social norms, ceremony, ritual, policy, and resource allocation; and
- Programs, including school-based and community-based efforts to nurture and build skills and competencies.

In brief, we posit that asset-building communities are distinguished as relational and intergenerational ecologies, with a critical mass of citizens and socializing institutions (e.g., families, schools, neighborhoods, youth organizations, religious communities) choosing to attend to the developmental needs of all children and adolescents. Developmental assets become a language of the common good, uniting sectors, citizens, and policy in the pursuit of shared goals for all children and adolescents. The commitment of a community and its people, institutions, and organizations is both long term and inclusive.

Ultimately, rebuilding and strengthening the developmental infrastructure in a community are conceived less as a program implemented and managed by professionals and more as a mobilization of public will and capacity. A major target for this level of community engagement is the creation of a normative culture in which all residents are expected, by virtue of their membership in the community, to promote the positive development of children and adolescents.

While the developmental assets framework—and the reframing principles on which it is based—is designed to create a readiness for new community action, models of asset-rich developmental ecologies are needed to give this energy focus and direction. Drawing on a range of sources, including reviews of system change research, field studies, and interviews with practitioners, a series of recent publications paints conceptual pictures of asset-building contexts. These include, for example, schools (Starkman, Scales, & Roberts, 1999), neighborhoods (Saito, Sullivan, & Hintz, 2000), congregations (Roehlkepartain, 1998), and whole communities (Benson, 1997). As importantly, we also seek to personalize the work as we develop and disseminate portraits of asset-building adults (Benson, Galbraith, & Espeland, 1998a) and adolescents (Benson, Galbraith, & Espeland, 1998b). In the case of adolescents, emphasis is placed on promoting personal ownership and efficacy for development (Lerner, 1982).

Our efforts to describe the nature and dynamics of developmentally attentive people and places are fueled by one of Bronfenbrenner's (1979) insights. He admonishes American social science for its preoccupation with "describing what is" and its inattention to understanding and experimenting "with new social forms as contexts for realizing human potential" (p. 41). He calls for (a) imagining what social ecologies look like when they are developmentally rich and (b) "transforming experiments" designed to move ecologies closer to this ideal.

If "transforming experiments" primarily referred to altering the flow of developmental energy within a single context, as, for example, after-school programs, we might choose to put the experiments in the hands of professional experts. Then, if a series of evaluation studies gave affirming evidence, we would disseminate this new knowledge about effective programs through traditional channels. Because the scope of change needed to enhance the developmental infrastructure is, however, demanding of multiple and coordinated ecological changes, as well as transformation promoting the engagement of adults and adolescents in the relational delivery of developmental assets, the classic formula for change, with its professionally led and expert-driven accents, is inadequate for the kind of comprehensive community change needed to provide depth, reach, and redundancy.

Hence, we have decided to pursue another approach to change. And, it is itself a work in progress. Assuming that all communities have a reservoir of human and social capital that can be realigned (or perhaps reignited) to provide deep and sustained connections to asset-building people and places, our approach at this point tilts in the direction of inviting communities to be co-learners and co-experimenters with us in creating asset-building communities.

Accordingly, I have chosen to pursue a diffusion process grounded in bringing our first wave of ideas on developmental assets and asset-building communities straight to the residents of cities. Methods of diffusion at the local level often include community meetings to premier the local portrait of developmental assets (these forums can draw up to 2,000 or 3,000 people); the strategic use of print, radio, and television media partners; a speakers' bureau that fans out across a community and addresses, potentially, most service clubs, employers, congregations, and neighborhood groups; and the dissemination of print and video resources throughout the community. We also equip local community organizations by building dissemination alliances with their national offices (e.g., youth-serving systems, educational associations, denominations, and Fortune 500 employers with multiple manufacturing and distribution locations).

This grassroots diffusion process is not just about the dissemination and utilization of new knowledge. It might also be understood as the diffusion of capacity and power (i.e., communities and their residents possess resources, efficacy, and capital that can be mobilized to promote developmental strengths).

The rapid spread of the asset-building approach to community building has been significantly advanced by the corporate engagement of Lutheran Brotherhood, a Fortune 500 company with national headquarters in Minneapolis. Although its core business is the sale of financial products such as insurance and annuities, its historical philanthropic mission includes mobilizing hundreds of volunteer branches in all 50 states to promote the social good. Since the mid 1990s, Lutheran Brotherhood has been the corporate sponsor for the national movement, not only providing significant financial resources to undergird our research and product development, but just as importantly providing their national volunteer network with training and resources to assist in community mobilization.

The diffusion process has, by intent and design, created a network of cities seeking to pursue community transformation. Organized along the lines of a social movement, 700 American communities, and several dozen emerging in Canada, are linked to each other and Search Institute through the Healthy Communities · Healthy Youth initiative we launched in 1996. Inclusion in the network requires several community commitments, including a multisector focus, significant youth engagement in leadership and implementation, and a willingness to be in a teaching-learning relationship with other communities in the movement. As of 2001, statewide initiatives have been formed in 22 states to link multiple communities together to provide support, technical assistance, and knowledge diffusion. All of these 22 networks emerged with little or no Search Institute support. And that is precisely how a movement ought to work.

Among the 700 communities are major urban centers, including Seattle, Portland, Orlando, and New York City, as well as hundreds of smaller cities, towns, and suburbs in 44 states. An annual Healthy Communities · Healthy Youth Conference orchestrated by Search Institute draws several thousand participants—both adults and adolescents—into hundreds of learning sessions. A premium is placed on positioning conference participants to exchange their emerging discoveries about citizen and system transformation.

Finally, this national movement provides "laboratories of discovery" for advancing a line of conceptual and empirical inquiry into the processes and dynamics of community and social change. The network of cities offers a rich diversity in size and geography, providing an array of approaches to change as well as insight for advancing both the theory and practice of community change. This arena of study—which we have recently called community-based human development—now propels much of our work (Benson, Scales, & Mannes, in press).

Concluding Thoughts

I would like to offer several ideas in advance of my colleagues' discussions of the meaning of this work and its implications.

I take it as axiomatic that the health and well-being of children and adolescents require as much attention to promoting developmental strengths as to directly combating the risks, environmental threats, and social dysfunction that obstruct human development. These two approaches ought to be complementary and in balance. Currently, it seems they are imbalanced, with the latter approach dominating public dialogue, public policy, and scientific inquiry. It is here that our work joins hands, in a sweeping scientific and cultural critique, with the emerging positive psychology movement (Seligman & Csikszentmihalyi, 2000).

The scientific exploration of a strength-based paradigm requires, however, a deeply interdisciplinary approach, integrating, at a minimum, the fields of anthropology, sociology, and economics with psychology in order to understand and mobilize a full arsenal of ritual, social norms, and system and individual capacities necessary to the complicated but essential task of becoming developmentally attentive communities. If communities are indeed an important context for the "production" of developmental strength, our methods of learning and discovery require approaches that currently are too underused and too undervalued. To a considerable extent, knowledge about crucial asset-building dynamics such as intergenerational community, sustained connections with "elders," and rituals for moving from adolescence to adulthood is vested in "non-experts," in communities organized around race, ethnicity, or worldview. Tapping this wisdom requires a significant shift in how the academy typically works, requiring instead a knowledge generation process that brings community residents and scholars together in the pursuit and production of knowledge (Lerner, Fisher, & Weinberg, 2000).

The production of an interdisciplinary knowledge grounded in the inherent capacity of community also requires a long-term investment in discovering the nature and sequencing of community change. This kind of comprehensive, collaborative, citizen-engaged approach also requires a patient evaluation system. The American way, when it comes to evaluation, is at best an impatient system. The demand by government agencies and foundations to show impact after a relatively short period of time fuels quick programmatic solutions and diminishes inquiry into the complex, long-term, and invigorating exploration of how this culture and its communities can and must reimagine the norms, rituals, ceremonies, relationships, environments, and policies needed to grow healthy, competent, whole, and caring human beings.

References

Belsky, J. (1981). Early human experiences: A family perspective. *Developmental Psychology, 17,* 3–23.

Benson, P. L. (1990). *The troubled journey: A portrait of 6th–12th grade youth.* Minneapolis, MN: Search Institute.

Benson, P. L. (1996a). *Developmental assets among Minneapolis youth: The urgency of promoting healthy communities.* Minneapolis, MN: Search Institute

Benson, P. L. (1996b). *Uniting communities for youth.* Minneapolis, MN: Search Institute.

Benson, P. L. (1997). *All kids are our kids: What communities must do to raise caring and responsible children and adolescents.* San Francisco: Jossey-Bass.

Benson, P. L. (1998). Mobilizing communities to promote developmental assets: A promising strategy for the prevention of high-risk behavior. *Family Science Review, 11,* 220–238.

Benson, P. L., Galbraith, J., & Espeland, P. (1998a). *What kids need to succeed: Proven, practical ways to raise good kids.* Minneapolis, MN: Free Spirit.

Benson, P. L., Galbraith, J., & Espeland, P. (1998b). *What teens need to succeed: Proven, practical ways to shape your own future.* Minneapolis, MN: Free Spirit.

Benson, P. L., & Leffert, N. (2001). Developmental assets in childhood and adolescence. In N. J. Smelser & P. B. Baltes (Eds.), *International Encyclopedia of the Social and Behavioral Sciences.* New York: Elsevier Science.

Benson, P. L., Leffert, N., Scales, P. C., & Blyth, D. A. (1998). Beyond the "village" rhetoric: Creating healthy communities for children and adolescents. *Applied Developmental Science, 2,* 138–159.

Benson, P. L., & Libbey, H. (2001). Minneapolis promise: Reflections on the journey. *The Center,* (Summer), 54–67.

Benson, P. L., & Pittman, K. J. (Eds.). (2001). *Trends in youth development: Visions, realities and challenges.* Norwell, MA: Kluwer Academic Publishers.

Benson, P. L., & Saito, R. N. (2000). The scientific foundations of youth development. *Youth development: Issues, challenges, and directions,* pp. 125–147. Philadelphia: Public/Private Ventures.

Benson, P. L., Scales, P. C., Leffert, N., & Roehlkepartain, E. C. (1999). *A fragile foundation: The state of developmental assets among American youth.* Minneapolis, MN: Search Institute.

Benson, P. L., Scales, P. C., & Mannes, M. (in press). Developmental strengths and their sources: Implications for the study and practice of community building. In R. M. Lerner, F. Jacobs, & D. Wertlieb (Eds.), *Promoting positive child, adolescent, and family development: A handbook of programs and policy innovations.* Newbury Park, CA: Sage.

Blyth, D. A., & Leffert, N. (1995). Communities as contexts for adolescent development: An empirical analysis. *Journal of Adolescent Research, 10,* 64–87.

Boyte, H. C. (2000). The struggle against positivism. *Academe, 86,* 46–51.

Bronfenbrenner, U. (1979). *The ecology of human development: Experiments by nature and design.* Cambridge, MA: Harvard University Press.

Bronfenbrenner, U., & Morris, P. A. (1998). The ecology of developmental processes. In R. M. Lerner (Ed.), *The handbook of child psychology: Vol. 1. Theoretical models of human development* (5th ed., pp. 993–1028). Editor in chief: W. Damon. New York: Wiley.

Burt, M. R., Resnick, G., & Novick, E. R. (1998). *Building supportive communities for at-risk adolescents.* Washington, DC: American Psychological Association.

Damon, W. (1997). *The youth charter: How communities can work together to raise standards for all our children.* New York: Free Press.

Dryfoos, J. G. (1998). Full-service schools: A revolution in health and social services for children, youth, and families. San Francisco: Jossey-Bass.

Farkas, S., & Johnson, J. (1997). *Kids these days: What Americans really think about the next generation.* New York: Public Agenda.

Garmezy, N. (1985). Stress-resistant children: The search for protective factors. In J. E. Stevenson (Ed.), *Recent research in developmental psychopathology. Journal of Child Psychology and Psychiatry Book Supplement, No. 4* (pp. 213–233). Oxford: Pergamon Press.

Hawkins, J. D., Catalano, R. F., & Miller, J. Y. (1992). Risk and protective factors for alcohol and other drug problems in adolescence and early childhood: Implications for substance abuse prevention. *Psychological Bulletin, 112,* 64–105.

Jessor, R. (1993). Successful adolescent development among youth in high-risk settings. *American Psychologist, 48,* 2117–2126.

Jessor, R., Graves, T. D., Hanson, R. C., & Jessor, S. L. (1968). *Society, personality, and deviant behavior: A study of a tri-ethnic community.* New York: Holt, Rinehart and Winston.

Jessor, R., & Jessor, S. L. (1977). *Problem behavior and psychosocial development: A longitudinal study of youth.* New York: Academic Press.

Jessor, R., Van Den Bos, J., Vanderryn, J., Costa, F. M., & Turbin, M. S. (1995). Protective factors in adolescent problem behavior: Moderator effects and developmental change. *Developmental Psychology, 31*, 923–933.

Kretzmann, J. P., & McKnight, J. L. (1993). *Building communities from the inside out: A path toward finding and mobilizing a community's assets.* Evanston, IL: Center for Urban Affairs and Policy Research.

Leffert, N., Benson, P. L., & Roehlkepartain, J. L. (1997). *Starting out right: Developmental assets for children.* Minneapolis, MN: Search Institute.

Leffert, N., Benson, P. L., Scales, P. C., Sharma, A. R., Drake, D. R., & Blyth, D. A. (1998). Developmental assets: Measurement and prediction of risk behaviors among adolescents. *Applied Developmental Science, 2*, 209–230.

Leffert, N., Scales, P. C., Vraa, R., Libbey, H., & Benson, P. L. (2001). The impact of developmental assets on adolescents' academic achievement. Minneapolis, MN: Search Institute (paper under review).

Lerner, R. M. (1982). Children and adolescents as producers of their own development. *Developmental Review, 2*, 342–370.

Lerner, R. M. (1986). *Concepts and themes of human development* (2nd ed.). New York: Random House.

Lerner, R. M. (1992). Dialectics, developmental contextualism, and the further enhancement of theory about puberty and psychosocial development. *Journal of Early Adolescence, 12*, 366–388.

Lerner, R. M. (1995). *America's youth in crisis: Challenges and options for programs and policies.* Thousand Oaks, CA: Sage.

Lerner, R. M., Fisher, C. B., & Weinberg, R. A. (2000). Toward a science for the people: Promoting civil society through the application of developmental science. *Child Development, 71*, 11–20.

Luthar, S. S., Cicchetti, D., & Becker, B. (2000). The construct of resilience: A critical evaluation and guidelines for future work. *Child Development 71*, 543–562.

Masten, A. S., & Curtis, W. (2000). Integrating competence and psychopathology: Pathways toward a comprehensive science of adaptation in development. *Development and Psychopathology, 12*, 529–550.

McKnight, J. (1995). *The careless society: Community and its counterfeits.* New York: Basic Books.

Norris, T., Ayre, D., & Clough, G. (2000). *Facilitating community change.* San Francisco: Grove Consultants International.

Pittman, K., Irby, M., & Ferber, T. (2001). Unfinished business: Further reflections on a decade of promoting youth development. In P. Benson & K. Pittman (Eds.), *Trends in youth development: Visions, realities and challenges* (pp. 3–50). Norwell, MA: Kluwer Academic Publishers.

Putnam, R. D. (1996). The strange disappearance of civic America. *American Prospect, 24*, 34–50.

Roehlkepartain, E. C. (1998). *Building assets in congregations: A practical guide for helping youth grow up healthy.* Minneapolis, MN: Search Institute.

Roehlkepartain, J. L., & Leffert, N. (2000). *What young children need to succeed: Working together to build assets from birth to age 11.* Minneapolis, MN: Free Spirit.

Roth, J., & Brooks-Gunn, J. (2000). What do adolescents need for healthy development? Implications for youth policy. *Social Policy Report, 14*, 3–19.

Saito, R. N., Sullivan, T. K., & Hintz, N. R. (2000). *The possible dream: What families in distressed communities need to help youth thrive.* Minneapolis, MN: Search Institute.

Scales, P. C., Benson, P. L., Leffert, N., & Blyth, D. A. (2000). Contribution of developmental assets to the prediction of thriving among adolescents. *Applied Developmental Science, 4*, 27–46.

Scales, P. C., Benson, P. L., & Roehlkepartain, E. C. (2001). *Grading grown-ups: Adults report on their real relationships with kids.* Minneapolis, MN: Search Institute and Lutheran Brotherhood.

Scales, P. C., & Leffert, N. (1999). *Developmental assets: A synthesis of the scientific research on adolescent development.* Minneapolis, MN: Search Institute.

Seligman, M. E., & Csikszentmihalyi, M. (2000). Positive psychology: An introduction. *American Psychologist, 55*, 5–14.

Starkman, N., Scales, P. C., & Roberts, C. (1999). *Great places to learn: How asset-building schools help students succeed.* Minneapolis, MN: Search Institute.

Zigler, E. (1990). Preface. In S. J. Meisels & J. P. Skonkoff (Eds.), *Handbook of early childhood intervention* (pp. ix–xiv). Cambridge: Cambridge University Press.

Zigler, E., Taussig, C., & Black, K. (1992). Early childhood intervention: A promising preventative for juvenile delinquency. *American Psychologist, 47,* 997–1006.

Part II

Promoting Positive Youth Development through Community Building

Indeed, when the first author made much the same point in his 1995 book *Greater Expectations*, he encountered initial skepticism from critics who believed that young people need less, not more, responsibility and challenge in their everyday lives. Such skepticism has largely passed, and the phrases "personal responsibility" and "high standards" have been universally adopted by professionals and policy makers of all ideological persuasions.

Peter Benson from the start has included in his scheme of developmental assets the notions of responsibility, service, and expectations. For example, Benson considers the following two assets to be critical for "youth empowerment": (1) Youth as resources: young people are given useful roles in the community; (2) Service to others: young people serve in the community one hour or more per week (Benson, 1997, p. 32).

In the category Boundaries and Expectations, Benson lists six assets, including High expectations: both parents and teachers encourage the young person to do well (Benson, 1997, p. 32). Although some of this may sound like common sense from our vantage point now, when Benson first assembled his 40 developmental assets, the conventional wisdom was a world apart. The excessively child-centered perspective that had come to dominate the field was adverse to holding children to anything resembling objective standards, placing its emphasis instead on subjective feelings such as self-esteem (Damon, 1995). Benson's work, among other like-minded efforts, has led the way to a more balanced view of children's developmental needs.

The Role of Moral Values and Religious or Spiritual Faith

One of the categories of internal assets that Benson lists is Positive Values, with an unmistakable moral dimension: caring, equality and social justice, integrity, honesty, responsibility, and restraint. One of the "external assets" that Benson identifies is religious community, indicated by a young person's participation in the activities of a religious institution (Benson, 1997, pp. 32–33). The proposition that deeply held moral convictions and religious faith can provide young people with crucial resources for their development flies in the face of our secular social science traditions, but it has been supported by the all-too-rare research that takes such variables into account. Garmezy (1983), for example, reported longitudinal data showing that sincere religious faith was the personal characteristic most likely to keep at-risk youth out of trouble. Hart and Fegley (1995) found that the major difference between disadvantaged adolescents who were exemplars of prosocial behavior and those who were frequently antisocial was the presence of a strong moral sense.

As along each of the other three fronts, we have seen significant movement in the field of youth development in this area. Professionals have been increasingly willing to use a moral language when working with young people and to draw upon community religious institutions for support. The old idea that it is necessary to be "value neutral" out of respect for the child's autonomy has been pretty much discarded, in recognition of children's undeniable need for moral guidance. The field is now prepared to help young people with one of their primary developmental challenges, namely, acquiring a moral identity.

Much of our own work has been dedicated to this challenge, through a community-based moral education approach that we have termed "the youth charter" (Damon, 1997). This approach differs from previous moral education efforts in all of the ways that the field of youth development has changed generally. That is, the youth charter approach reflects the shifts in the field that we have discussed above, in the same directions and along the same four fronts— a positive vision of youth strengths, a use of community as the locus of developmental action, an emphasis on expectations for service and social responsibility, and a recognition of the role of moral values and religious or spiritual faith. We turn now to an account of this approach, along with a description of some related community youth initiatives that we are now attempting.

The Youth Charter Approach

Although modern-day moral education programs are usually delivered in the classroom, the older tradition was to base moral education in communities instead of schools. The classic Aristotelian view, for example, was that all citizens—children and adults alike—were educated into a life of virtue through their active participation in the laws and mores of their communities. During premodern times in Westerns societies, moral education of the young was shared among the home, the neighborhood, the workplace (for the many children who either labored or did apprenticeships), and the church. Of these contexts, the church was the ultimate authority, with the sacred texts of Jews and Christians providing the sources of moral instruction and guidance. In many non-Western societies, religious traditions retain their authoritative role in moral education (see, for example, Jessor, Colby, & Shweder, 1996). In our own society, when formal schooling first became available to multitudes of children, there was a tight connection between the community's values and those of the teaching staff—a staff that was largely composed of parents and local adults (Cremin, 1964). Only with the increased professionalization of teaching during the latter part of the twentieth century did the school become a separate, and in many ways primary, source of instruction for the young.

Such separation makes little sense in the moral domain, and it especially makes no sense to think of school as a privileged context in this regard. When sources of moral guidance become separated from one another, they often fall into conflict. They then can provide only confusion and disillusionment for the young, rather than coherent moral guidance. It is essential to locate moral education in the entire community rather than in a collection of separate contexts.

But this is not easy in modern times, since so many communities have become polarized around matters of belief. In order to accomplish moral education in times of society-wide discord, communities must make special efforts to identify their common values, at least with respect to their hopes and expectations for their young. What Durkheim (1961) assumed comes naturally to societies—an almost transcendental sense of unifying belief—now must be worked at. Otherwise, as Etzioni (1993) has written, we shall live in aggregations rather than true communities.

Is it possible consciously to create—or at least to discover—the kinds of shared beliefs that are essential for community and for the moral identities of the young? We believe that it is possible, and that it is readily within our reach to do so. The fractiousness of public discourse has created a widespread yearning for common values. In this sense, we believe that Durkheim (1961) was right about the inevitable ideational foundation of any society. One sign of the widespread yearning, in fact, has been the avid receptiveness of many people to fundamentalist doctrines that have rushed to fill the contemporary void. But fundamenalist approaches are too authoritarian and too exclusionary to be sustainable. They mesh poorly with the pluralism and egalitarianism inherent in democratic societies, creating further conflict. To build common community values in modern times, we need procedures that draw on the unique qualities and virtues of a democratic society rather than reacting against them.

Another present limitation is a negative bias in the overall message conveyed by many of today's moral and character education programs. Most often, the focus is exclusively on bad behavior and how to deter, defuse, or repair it (Lickona, 1996; Oser, 1996). The solutions are preventive in nature. If people follow society's rules, abide by proper values, develop virtues, respect traditional codes, understand principles of right and wrong, and rely on fair negotiation procedures, they will avoid conflict, resist temptation, and stay out of trouble. The overwhelming thrust of moral and character education is to show children how to stay within societal bounds by regulating their antisocial impulses.

Behavioral regulation is certainly important for every young person to learn, but it is not the sum total of a moral life. In fact, preventive proscriptions cannot provide young people with the motivation they need to form moral goals, construct a moral identity, and build enduring moral commitments. The key motivational element is a belief system that transcends everyday behavioral regulation. As Nisan (1996) has written, "Identity-based motivation . . . includes expressing and affirming one's identity—performing positive acts."

If young people are to dedicate themselves to moral goals, they need to acquire beliefs that provide them with a sense of higher purpose for the creation of their moral identities. They must encounter moral ideas that they find inspiring, not merely constraining. In the Colby and Damon (1992) study, virtually every one of the moral exemplars identified an early discovery of an inspiring moral purpose—charity, justice, peace, human rights, global protection—as the source of their enduring moral commitments. The exemplars reported that their beliefs in a higher moral purpose not only inspired their dedication to sustained moral action throughout life but also defined the essence of their self-identities.

The shortcomings in present-day moral education programs that we have noted have a common, indeed a cumulative, effect: they conspire to demoralize young people who are subject to them (see Damon, 1995). In this context, demoralization has two meanings. First, it means a debilitating loss of purpose (as in the familiar military use of the term). Second, and closer to the word's original root, it refers to a cynical attitude toward moral values. Young people become demoralized by conflicts and confusion among those to whom they look for direction; they become demoralized by vague, empty assertions that fail to connect meaningfully to their own life choices; and they become demoralized by messages that are overwhelmingly negative and discouraging in tone. These, of course, are precisely the moral education shortcomings that we have noted; their co-occurrence makes for an unholy combination because they reinforce one another's demoralizing influences.

One solution to the shortcomings of present-day approaches is to use the community rather than the school as the primary point of entry. In this approach, a community determines the methods and substance of moral education, and the school is one of many sites where the action takes place. This creates the necessary condition for coordination among the sites, thus avoiding many of the problems we have cited. With proper communication and a general sense of agreement, conflicts can be avoided, confusions can be clarified, and young people can be offered many contexts in which they can turn abstract ideas into moral acts. Moreover, in a whole community, it is possible to find many people who can introduce young people into the positive, inspirational possibilities of moral commitment. Similarly, an entire community affords many opportunities for authentic service activities, such as helping those in need, that can provide young people with a chance to experience the psychological rewards of moral commitment.

One such procedure is a "youth charter." A youth charter is a consensus of clear expectations shared among the important people in a young person's life and communicated to the young person in multiple ways. In times and places in which there is a strong sense of community, a youth charter is implicit. It may be given voice by an educational leader or emphasized in a religious sermon; but by and large the consensus of expectations is widely accepted without much articulation. In 17th-century New England, for example, it was taken for granted that children would be raised to respect their elders, perform household duties, study the Bible, obey the Ten Commandments, acquire proper manners, learn skills, find a calling, work hard, and establish a family. Achieving consensus on such standards was not considered to be a problem worth discussing. The standards permeated every setting where children spent time, were internalized as children grew up, and were passed along to the next generation without hesitation.

Some communities have implicit youth charters, some have partial or uneven ones, and some have none that can be detected. Those that have implicit youth charters arrive at them spontaneously, through frequent communication among people who are in a position to influence the young. Francis Ianni, the sociologist who originally coined the term "youth charter," found evidence of cohesive youth charters in a range of American settings, including large cities, suburbs, towns, and rural areas (Ianni, 1989). But Ianni found an ever larger number of American settings in which there was little or no sign of a youth charter.

Not surprisingly, young people growing up in communities with youth charters show stronger signs of moral identity than do young people who grow up in places without them. After a 12-year study of American youth, Ianni concluded that the best predictor of an adolescent's social conduct—better than economic background or other social indicators—was the extent to which the people and institutions in the child's life shared a set of common standards for the youngster's behavior. "We soon discovered that the harmony and accord among the institutions and what their adolescent members heard from them *in concert* was what scored the adolescent experience" (Ianni, 1989, p. 20; emphasis in original).

Yet Ianni found that harmony and accord were the exception rather than the rule in much of American society. He looked at how schools, families, peer groups, local institutions, the media, and the job market sent messages to youth. He found that often these messages clashed rather than harmonized. Ianni noted that this lack of coherence had created a fragmented and confusing context for youth development.

Ianni concluded that for positive identity formation, every young person needs coherent structure, "a set of believable and attainable expectations and standards from the community to guide movement from child to adult status"

(Ianni, 1989, p. 267). When disparate institutions such as the family, school, and other public and private agencies offer a young person coherent guidance, her or his identity is not a "collection of isolated experiences" but rather an "organization of experiences and exposures in the various social worlds of the community" (Ianni, 1989, p. 279).

In places that operate like true communities, there are many ways in which families, schools, workplaces, agencies, and peer groups connect with one another through their contact with youth. For example, schools are influenced by the values and attitudes that students pick up in their families. Students' family lives are in turn influenced by their quest for academic achievement, which fills their after-school time with homework—and which in turn is supported on the home front. A young person's identity formation, rooted initially in the family, is shaped by a sense of belonging in the community, including sports teams, media, clubs, religious institutions, and jobs. In such communities, there also is concordance between the norms of the peer culture and those of adults.

In places where the sense of community has waned, young people are often faced with conflicting demands and messages from each of these sources. The problem, as Ianni wrote, is that many communities have lost the traditional social networks that once guided youth into adulthood. Without these networks, role models are lacking, intergenerational guidance is rare, and isolation prevails. The institutions within the community blame one another for all the problems of its youth. Ianni concluded that such fragmentation is injurious to adolescent development.

To provide a clear, firm, and consistent set of behavioral and social standards and expectations for adolescents, Ianni advocates development of a network of social institutions by a community: "A well-integrated and consciously developed pattern of relationships can provide a stabilizing transformational structure that produces equally integrated identities as workers and citizens and parents; no single institution has the resources to develop all of these roles alone" (Ianni, 1989, p. 279). Ianni's name for this stabilizing structure is a "youth charter," a term we borrow here. Ianni proposed several suggestions for developing a successful youth charter in communities that do not already have them. First, the community must work toward a consensus of values and standards in order to coordinate expectations. Second, all members of the community must be invited to participate; outside imposition of a charter will not be successful. Third, young people must be involved in the process of developing the charter. Finally, the charter must be open and adaptable to change.

The Development and Implementation of Youth Charters

We have expanded upon Ianni's notion of a youth charter in order to develop a process through which a community can build its own consensus of shared understandings concerning its expectations for youth development. A youth charter is usually not formalized in a written document; rather, evolving sets of records are kept about areas of agreement and resolutions for action. To build a youth charter, community members go through a process of discussion, a movement toward agreement, and the development and implementation of action plans. Elements of the process include special town meetings sponsored by local institutions; constructive media coverage on a periodic basis; and the formation of standing committees that open new lines of communication among parents, teachers, and neighbors.

In our procedure, we begin with discussion among the adult members of the community; then, after a common language and agenda are established, we invite young members of the community to participate. A youth charter may be revised as circumstances dictate, and it can vary from community to community. The essential requirements of a youth charter are that (1) it must address the core matters of morality and achievement necessary for becoming a responsible citizen; and (2) it must focus on areas of common agreement rather than on doctrinaire squabbles or polarizing issues of controversy. A youth charter guides the younger generation toward fundamental moral virtues such as honesty, civility, decency, and the pursuit of benevolent purposes beyond the self. A youth charter is a moral and spiritual rather than a political document.

Youth charters are communication devices. They can help young people anticipate and understand the reactions of others to their behavior. When a teacher is disappointed in a student's performance, or when a neighbor calls the local police on a miscreant teenager, a youth charter can turn the youngster's shame or outrage into a constructive developmental experience. A youth charter can define high moral standards for adolescent conduct throughout the entire community. It can provide a conduit for regular feedback between young people, their friends, and the adult world. It is the multifaceted and yet coherent nature of this feedback that enables it to facilitate the formation of a young person's moral identity.

In our early pilot work with the youth charter procedure, we have conducted meetings in a small number of towns and cities. The focus of the discussions has varied widely among the different settings. In one setting, community members were mainly concerned about a rash of cheating incidents at the local high school. In another setting, a recent pair of teenage suicides and some widespread (and perhaps related) drug use among the town's young people dominated the conversations. In a third, parents were upset about an epidemic of binge drinking, especially at teen parties. Other town meetings have traversed a range of issues, from racial and ethnic conflict to disrespect of authority in academic and work settings.

In some of these settings, the large- and small-group discussions have identified core values that provide a basis of response to the problem or crisis. For example, following an afternoon of intense discussion, adults and students in the high school community with the cheating problem agreed that cheating was wrong because (1) it violates trust between teacher and student, (2) it gives students who cheat an unfair advantage over those who do not, (3) it encourages dishonest behavior, and (4) it undermines the integrity of the school. This agreement was apparently a change from prior sentiments, which reportedly were ambivalent about moral issues surrounding cheating. (For example, one teacher had said publicly that it was hard for him to hold students to a non-cheating standard in a society in which people cheat on taxes, spouses, and so on.) Based on the newfound agreement, it became possible to create more widely supported codes and sanctions in the school. It also became possible for teachers and parents to clearly explain, in unambiguous terms, why they expected young people not to cheat. From the adolescents' perspectives, their new understanding of the moral purposes of anticheating codes may prepare them to accept this societal standard as part of their own moral identities. They may become more likely to assert, as one teenager phrased it, that "I don't not want to become the kind of person who cheats all the time . . . to think of myself as a sneaky cheater."

In another community, a coalition of local institutions and people, originally formed to reduce the use of drugs and alcohol among youth, invited us in to help them develop a youth charter. The coalition was made up of private and public school staff, the police force, parents, an interfaith council, local colleges, the business community, human service agencies, the town council, and other concerned citizens. A subcommittee of the larger coalition organized a townwide forum. With the hopes of gathering a substantial cross-section of the community, the organizers launched a large-scale publicity of the forum. The publicity efforts included sending articles to the local newspaper and notices to the parents of students, posting flyers, and giving presentations to community groups, such as the Rotary Club, the police department, and senior centers. In the local high school auditorium, the forum was held on a weekend afternoon for three and a half hours. Large and small groups covered a series of topics that related to how young people were spending their time after school. From the forum arose a number of resolutions, action plans, and task forces, mostly dedicated to resolving the following issues: (1) the need for alternative town settings that provide young people with more opportunities to participate in constructive, safe, and purposeful activities; (2) youth sports in the community—the scheduling conflicts between sports and religious services, the pressures of competitive sports on young people, and the standards and expectations held by coaches, players, and referees; (3) the development of a community service program; and (4) the heavy use of drugs and alcohol by young people from all parts of town.

Over the next year, task forces made up of the town's various constituencies, including youth themselves, set about tackling the many issues raised at the town forum. Addressing concerns about competitive sports, one task force drafted a player code of conduct. Athletes from all different types of sports were asked to sign an agreement that they would uphold positive behavior on the playing fields. A youth-led group, concerned that there were few athletic opportunities for nonvarsity players, worked with the school administration to keep gyms open during after-school hours. The need for alcohol-free evening events resulted in an organizing effort to bring a movie theater back to the town and to build a coffee house where young people could congregate. An interfaith group arranged a series of speakers to discuss various challenges of parenting. With leadership from a parent, a group of high schoolers established an ongoing editorial series in the local paper, in which they expressed their own perspectives about "hot topics," such as reasons why youth drank heavily during social gatherings.

A challenge to the community members spearheading this youth charter was to create regular opportunities to involve new people in building the youth charter. It was considered important to maintain an open process that felt welcoming for all to join. They were determined to head off any sense that task force members were making whimsical plans without input from the community. Cycling in new cohorts of committed participants, whether they were parents, youth, senior citizens, or business owners, was essential in building a truly community-based initiative. Similarly, organizers took seriously the need to periodically open up dialogue with large sectors of the community about the youth charter and various "action plans." Drawing on local resources—the paper, a town Web site, and a community television station—they solicited feedback about the best and most agreed upon directions to proceed. They knew it was crucial to hold regular town forums in order to identify the changing needs of the community and redirect the efforts of the youth charter.

Another community took a slightly different approach as it initiated its youth charter. During their first community-wide meeting, citizens representing the far-ranging constituencies of the town decided that before they could proceed they needed to draft a written statement that would direct future actions of the charter. Using the brainstorming conducted at the first community-wide meeting, a group carefully constructed a written charter that could be upheld by the town. In a poster-like format, the charter read that their community endorsed five "ethical ideals," such as respect, responsibility, and compassion. Each ideal was followed by a well-crafted and concrete definition. From all community members, they sought both feedback about these ideals and support to use them as a guide for the community as a whole. They then scheduled another community-wide meeting to consider what concrete actions both individuals and institutions could take to promote such ideals.

Guidelines for Implementation of a Youth Charter

A youth charter begins with an initial meeting in a community center, a school auditorium, or any other accessible location that can accommodate a large group. The meeting is sponsored by a local organization that also takes responsibility for widespread publicity of the meeting. An effort should be made to draw out as many people as possible from different sectors of the community in order to guard against misrepresentation or exclusion. Publicity efforts could include flyers sent home with students, announcements in the local press and radio, and a banner hung in a visible location.

An initial meeting is the first step of opening up dialogue among community members about their concerns regarding youth development. This meeting requires at least three or four hours. After a brief introduction of the goals of the meeting, the participants break into small groups. The small groups should be made up of individuals representing different organizations and interests in order to open new lines of communication across constituencies. Group facilitators, who are volunteers from the community, are trained in advance. With the guidance of these facilitators, the small-group discussions cover a series of topics. First, the groups list their collective concerns for young people and the community. Next, the groups clarify and identify the expectations and standards that are currently being held for young people. They then list the standards and expectations for young people that can be agreed upon and implemented by the community as a whole. Grounded by these standards and expectations, "next steps" are derived to address the collective concerns listed earlier. These next steps could include identifying task-oriented subcommittees, possible solutions, or previously underutilized strengths within the community. Overall, the small-group discussions should end with a concrete list of identified needs for youth and the community, and ways to resourcefully address those needs.

All of the participants then reconvene to hear summaries of the small-group discussions as presented by the facilitators. Out of all the small-group summaries comes a clear list of areas that need to be addressed by future task forces. In the final hour, these task forces hold their first meeting with participants who have volunteered for more sustained involvement. The task forces discuss their goals and determine future meeting times.

At this point it is important to involve young people in the development of the youth charter. Each task force must recruit several youth to be active members. The young people should be integral members of each group whereby they contribute their own ideas and concerns to the development and implementation of action plans.

A youth charter should be renewed periodically, at least yearly, to adapt to the changing needs of the community. Large community town meetings can occur annually to encourage reflection on the achieved progress and the future challenges.

Evaluating a Youth Charter

Many challenges are inherent in evaluating community-wide interventions (Hollister & Hill, 1995). An assessment of change would hope to capture not only individual efforts but also the potentially synergistic effect of the multiple components of a large-scale intervention, like the youth charter. Measuring such synergism, as opposed to summing the effects across each institutional intervention, is a complex task. Furthermore, it is quite difficult to establish whether changes in the community can be attributed to the impact of the intervention, or if such changes are a product of other forces. For instance, significant change in the community may be misattributed to the intervention when, in fact, such change was due to shifting demographics transforming the neighborhoods or to economic growth resulting in lower unemployment. Even when drawing on comparison data from a similar community—one in which the intervention is not being implemented—evaluators cannot rely on the fallible assumption that once matched on a set of characteristics, the comparison and intervention communities would have changed over time in the same way with respect to the outcome variables.

A look back at large-scale interventions reveals how evaluators have fallen short of overcoming many of the challenges discussed thus far (O'Conner, 1995). In the mid-1960s, eight case studies of the Community Action Agencies (CAA), under Johnson's War on Poverty, were not taken seriously due to the lack of uniformity in conducting these studies. Another study of 100 CAAs included multiple surveys, personal interviews, and observations. They focused on local institutional change (based on number of referrals by CAA, areas served by agencies, and composition of community boards). Their findings that the CAA affected institutional change were criticized because of their reliance on correlation findings rather than causal analysis. Evaluations of the Community Development Corporations (CDC), in the early 1970s, included statistical measures of job creation and resident attitudes. They found that the CDCs had little effect on outcome indicators. Evaluators concluded that in the future they must take into account external political and economic forces. More recently, evaluation in the mid-1980s of 130 CDCs has been called into question for not capturing the synergistic effects of the intervention in their measurement of housing production, commercial real estate, and small business development. Decades of experience reveal that there is no easy solution to the difficulties of evaluating community-wide interventions. In fact, history shows that any evaluation, like the large-scale interventions themselves, must be comprehensive and multifaceted.

As of yet, there has been no such comprehensive evaluation conducted on a youth charter initiative. However, an ideal evaluation would include both a process evaluation and a product evaluation (Scriven, 1991; Stufflebeam, 1983). A process evaluation would involve an ongoing cycle of reflection concerning both organizational operations and implementation of the youth charter. For instance, reflections on the degree of collaboration, open dialogue, and efficiency during town meetings and task force sessions could provide crucial information to ensure the long-term viability of the initiative. Assessments of leadership, participation, decision making, conflict resolution, and productivity of each meeting could refine the mechanisms shaping the charter. Youth charter action plans and implementation of those plans could also be evaluated. A process evaluation would be integral to refining and redirecting the youth charter. At the same time, it is important to keep in mind that assessing "process" should not preclude assessing "product"—the larger goal of fostering the healthy development of youth and their community.

The product (or outcome) evaluation of the youth charter would ideally utilize a pre-post design using time series (Hollister & Hill, 1995). In other words, data concerning community-wide indicators (e.g., completed hours of community service, alcohol- or drug-related accidents, citizens' sense of community cohesion) would be collected at multiple time points—most importantly before and after the youth charter was initiated. An ideal evaluation would also involve selecting a sociodemographically similar community that was not within close proximity of the intervention community (so that residents were less likely to overlap in the intervention and comparison community). The two communities should also have similar rates of the outcome variables as well as other variables that would be considered exogenous to the intervention (Weiss, 1998). In addition, interviews with key informants in the comparison community would help assessors stay abreast of new initiatives, legislation, or economic swings that may affect the comparison's post-measures.

Implementing such a multifaceted evaluation design would likely be well worth the additional resources. Such a comprehensive approach, which includes a focus on the process of developing and implementing the charter, could strengthen the youth charter itself. In fact, the evolving nature of the youth charter and its responsiveness to updated concerns and needs make this community-wide initiative well suited to effectively utilize evaluation feedback.

References

Benson, P. (1997). *All kids are our kids: What communities must do to raise caring and responsible children and adolescents.* San Francisco: Jossey-Bass.

Colby, A., & Damon, W. (1992). *Some do care: Contemporary lives of moral commitment.* New York: Free Press.

Colby, A., & Damon, W. (1993). The uniting of self and morality in the development of extraordinary moral commitment. In G. Noam & T. Wren (Eds.), *The moral self* (pp. 149–174). Cambridge, MA: MIT Press.

Council of Program Directors in Community Research and Action (2000). Society for Research and Action—American Psychological Association, Division 27, www.apa.org/divisions/div27/.

Cremin, L. (1964). *The transformation of the school: Progressivism in American education.* New York: Knopf.

Damon, W. (1995). *Greater expectations.* New York: Free Press.

Damon, W. (1997). *The youth charter: How communities can work together to raise standards for all our children.* New York: Free Press.

Durkheim, E. (1961). *Moral education: A study in the theory and application of the sociology of education.* New York: Free Press.

Etzioni, A. (1993). *The spirit of community: Rights, responsibilities and the communitarian agenda.* New York: Crown.

Hart, D., & Fegley, S. (1995). Prosocial behavior and caring in adolescence: Relations to self-understanding and social judgement. *Child Development, 66,* 1346–1359.

Hollister, R. G., & Hill, J. (1995). Problems in the evaluation of community-wide initiatives. In J. P. Connell, A. C. Kubisch, L. B. Schorr, & C. H. Weiss (Eds.), *New approaches to evaluating community initiatives: Concepts, methods, and contexts.* Washington, DC: Aspen Institute.

Ianni, F. (1989). *The search for structure: A report on American youth today.* New York: Free Press.

Jessor, R., Colby, A., & Shweder, R. (Eds.). (1996). *Ethography and human development: Context and meaning in social inquiry.* Chicago: University of Chicago Press.

Lerner, R. M., Fisher, C. B., & Weinberg, R. A. (2000). Toward a science for the people: Promoting civil society through the application of developmental science. *Child Development, 71,* 11–20.

Lickona, T. (1996). Eleven principles of effective character education. *Journal of Moral Education, 25,* 93–100.

Nisan, M. (1996). Personal identity and education for the desirable. *Journal of Moral Education, 25,* 75–83.

O'Conner, S. (1995). Evaluating comprehensive community initiatives: A view from history. In J. P. Connell, A. C. Kubisch, L. B. Schorr, & C. H. Weiss (Eds.), *New approaches to evaluating community initiatives: Concepts, methods, and contexts.* Washington, DC: Aspen Institute.

Oser, F. (1996). Learning from negative morality. *Journal of Moral Education, 25,* 67–74.

Redl, F., & Wineman, D. (1951). *Children who hate.* New York: Free Press.

Scriven, M. (1991). Beyond formative and summative evaluation. In M. W. McLaughlin & D. C. Phillips (Eds.), *Evaluation and education at quarter century* (pp. 121–144). Chicago: University of Chicago Press.

Steinberg, L. (1996). *Beyond the classroom.* New York: Basic Books.

Stufflebeam, D. (1983). The CIPP model for program evaluation. In G. Madaus, M. Scriven, & D. Stufflebeam (Eds.), *Evaluation models* (pp. 117–141). Boston: Kluwer-Nijhoff.

Weiss, C. (1998). *Evaluation* (2nd ed.). Englewood Heights, NJ: Prentice Hall.

4 Youth Participation: A Critical Element of Research on Child Well-Being

Brian Chan, Mary Carlson, Barbara Trickett, and Felton Earls
Harvard Medical School

The social scientific study of children is an evolving discipline, a fact that benefits society in that our knowledge about the lives of children presumably improves with every refinement of the scientific method. Among the latest and most important innovations to appear is Search Institute's methodology of developmental assets, which offers a "set of benchmarks" for families and communities to follow to help ensure "positive child and adolescent development" (Benson, Leffert, Scales, & Blyth, 1998). The framework of developmental assets represents a huge step forward in social science because it studies positive youth development, not merely negative actions such as delinquency or drug use, and strives to characterize both "external assets" in the community and "internal assets" held by children themselves.

As powerful as this model is, we believe that there are significant limitations in its design and application. Essentially, we contend that this approach does not go far enough in utilizing children as full participants in creating and applying these new benchmarks. Unless children's own interpretations and perspectives are garnered, social scientists will necessarily obtain only an adult-centered interpretation of their lives. To create a more complete picture, children themselves should be involved in the research process so that their subjective interpretations can be put to a critical test and incorporated into research design. The universality of the developmental assets measure, which Search Institute points to as a desirable characteristic, masks the diverse opinions and motivations of children as well as the importance of context. In other words, by pointing to developmental assets as a universal benchmark, Search Institute ignores the possibility that certain assets might be more or less important in different contexts, or even that there might be other assets that have not been included. This is precisely the sort of problem that could be addressed by eliciting the input of youths speaking from their own experiences in their particular communities. Thus, the importance of respecting children's participatory rights can hardly be overemphasized. This, we believe, is a necessary next step in the progression of research on children. We challenge the developmental assets approach, not in a negative spirit, to debunk or scrap the work done by Search Institute, but to build on it and spur a dialogue that we hope will advance social science and ultimately benefit all children.

In part I, we examine the recent evolution of the social science of children and how this evolution reflects changing understandings and interpretations of children and childhood. At least in Western societies, perceptions of difference between adults and youths dissipated at the same time that movements to establish children's rights to protection and provision (e.g., shelter and food) helped entrench the idea that children's best interests should be a primary societal goal. In time, in addition to children's best interests, the notion that children should participate in decision making and initiate actions for themselves became increasingly valued. This was manifested perhaps most definitively in the inclusion of "participatory rights" in the groundbreaking United Nations Convention on the Rights of the Child (CRC), adopted by the General Assembly in 1990. Social science has paralleled these societal changes, with Search Institute's work a prime example of research that has moved away from traditional views of children. However, the developmental assets approach and social science in general have yet to reflect the idea that children have participatory rights, a deficiency that prevents researchers from fully obtaining youths' perspectives and interpretations and addressing the issue of context.

In part II, we introduce the theoretical basis for a methodology that both acknowledges and utilizes children's ability to participate. We believe that the CRC can serve as an essential set of guidelines to measure the extent to which researchers take into account children's participatory rights. To translate the CRC into practical action, we have looked to the writings of Jürgen Habermas, whose theory of communicative action provides a method for engaging children's opinions and putting them to a critical test. In short, dialogue between youths and adults on as equal a basis as possible allows researchers to come to conclusions that reflect reasoned and nuanced interpretations from children themselves.

In part III we describe our efforts to put this theoretical model into practice with the Young Citizens Project (YCP). Initially conceived in 1997 by Earls and Carlson (in press) as an adjunct to the work done by the Project on Human

Development in Chicago Neighborhoods, a longitudinal study of child development in the urban context, the YCP was founded to examine how youths assess their quality of life and well-being, as well as their ability as research collaborators to contribute a perspective that would complement and challenge the ideas of adult researchers. In the summer of 1999, a group of six teenagers from Cambridge, Massachusetts, came together in the latest incarnation of the YCP to produce knowledge on issues that affect their lives, using a framework of dialogue sessions designed to bring about shared understanding among participants. Despite significant obstacles, the YCP was able to ensure a reasonable level of equal participation, providing a practical justification for collaborative social science. Although we do not necessarily espouse the YCP model as a panacea, we do believe it demonstrates both the feasibility and the desirability of participatory research with children.

Finally, in part IV, we examine the future directions of the social science of children, drawing on the lessons learned from the YCP. We believe that many aspects of the YCP can be used to inform the idea of developmental assets such that this paradigm can become a richer and more nuanced tool for researchers. The participation of youths in the research process adds a valuable perspective that otherwise would be unavailable to adult researchers. Moreover, a higher level of participation from children can enhance the ability of an assets-centered approach to reflect specific community characteristics and thereby produce data immediately useful for informing action. Of course, participatory research with children is not without its limitations, such as the relatively lengthy amount of time it can take. On balance, however, these limitations would appear to be outweighed by the benefits of enhanced validity and contextuality offered by collaborative research.

I. Developmental Assets and the Evolution of the Social Science of Children

The ongoing evolution of the social scientific study of children reflects fundamental changes in the way in which society as a whole thinks about and interprets children and the phenomenon of childhood. Traditionally, society treated the differences between youths and adults as both inevitable and unalterable. In other words, common notions of children as incompetent and incomplete individuals were seen as basic truths rather than as interpretations grounded in societal norms and conventions. For example, in the traditional view, the actions, beliefs, and traits of children were essentially important only in how they affected their socialization into the "real" adult world (Bardy, 1994; Blitzer, 1991; Shamgar-Handelman, 1994). Similarly, children were assumed to be unable to think critically about their environment and interactions with others (Qvortrup, 1994). Children needed to be protected and sheltered rather than granted the right to participate in shaping their communities (Ennew, 1994; Morrow, 1995; Suransky, 1982). Furthermore, as children could not provide information and knowledge pertinent to adults, they were to learn from adults, and not vice versa (Qvortrup, 1994).

The net effect of these kinds of beliefs was that youths were seen as "human becomings" rather than "human beings" (Qvortrup, 1994). The term "human becomings" is itself enormously illustrative. Although children are human, and thus deserving of protection (food, shelter, and the like), their "becoming" status casts them as distinctly incomplete—"preadults" or "precitizens." In other words, children are defined and treated in terms of what they are not and what they are striving to be. This conception turns childhood from being merely the "state of being a child" to a developmental pathway with a definite beginning and end, upon which children march inexorably toward adulthood.

Unsurprisingly, the prevailing attitude toward youth in society strongly influenced social scientists' perceptions. The study of children was chiefly framed in terms of children's development or socialization into adulthood (i.e., how the social order is reproduced) (Frones, 1994; Qvortrup, 1987, 1991). Traditionally, this meant a propensity to define the child either in negative terms, as what adults are not, or as limited in the sense of lacking what adults possess (Alanen, 1988). Moreover, development was thought of as an individualized phenomenon (Bardy, 1988; James, Jenks, & Prout, 1998). That is, youth were rarely thought of in groups, especially in terms of how they might influence each other. Instead, youth were thought to become socialized essentially in isolation, with "vertical" rather than "horizontal" influences from parents, teachers, and so forth. Jean Piaget's voluminous writings influenced these developments (Corsaro, 1997; Tesson & Youniss, 1995). At least in the way that he was understood by many, Piaget was unduly inattentive to context or children's experience, ignoring children's cultural environments and children's subjective sense of the world around them (Graue & Walsh, 1998; Silvers, 1976; Speier, 1976). All in all, the development framework tended to treat children as comprising a rather monolithic category and as essentially devoid of agency (except in a negative sense, in their tendencies to engage in antisocial and delinquent behavior) (Corsaro, 1997).

At least in developed societies, however, the view of youths as inferior and incompetent individuals has become less tenable. Writers such as Philippe Ariès (1962) have pointed out that the status of children in society is not a natural consequence of biology, but is in large part socially constructed. Moreover, several factors, including the movement of women to the workplace and the growth of professionalized day care, have created an ever-growing spatial and temporal gap between adults and youths (Sgritta, 1987; Suransky, 1982). This trend, combined with information becoming more readily available to broader segments of the population (e.g., through television and the Internet), has lessened the "cultural gap" between adults and youths: children increasingly have had to take care of themselves and become savvier to the "adult world" at an earlier age (Corsaro, 1997; Postman, 1994; Qvortrup, 1994). Accompanying these broad trends have been movements to advance the idea of children's best interests as a compelling societal goal, especially through efforts to establish children's rights to protection and the provision of food, shelter, education, and the like (Edelman, 1977; Freeman, 1983; Hegar & Hunzeker, 1988; Shamgar-Handelman, 1994). In addition to advocating children's best interests, efforts have been initiated to popularize the notion that youths should have agency, the ability to initiate ideas and plans and participate in decision making (Bardy, 1994; Blanc, 1994; Ladd, 1996). Youth empowerment groups, for example, have attempted to channel children's energies and talents to benefit themselves, their schools, and their communities (Gibson, 1993; Parsons, 1989; Petoskey, Van Stelle, & De Jong, 1998). Increasingly, then, youths have been seen as true "human beings" who are capable of thinking critically about their relationships and environment, initiating action in more than just negative ways, and participating in decisions that affect their own lives.

The evolving place of youth in society has been reflected in social science; increasingly, the idea that children are "human becomings" on a universal developmental pathway and devoid of agency has been seen as providing only one particular, incomplete picture of children's lives (Alanen, 1988). No longer is the view of a youth as a "solitary scientist" making discoveries for him- or herself (a single actor unaffected by "horizontal linkages" with peers) viewed as a paradigm that reflects all of children's reality (Graue & Walsh, 1998). Piaget has been increasingly criticized: His developmental stages have not been supported empirically; his view that the child is essentially egocentric has been discredited; he underestimated children's cognitive abilities; and his universality ignored children's unique social and cultural contexts (Graue & Walsh, 1998).

Although the traditional approach to children still lingers, more researchers now treat children's peer cultures, language routines, motivations, and actions as important in and of themselves. This especially means not automatically studying children in the context of their family or schools (Alanen, 1988). New methodologies focus on the "whole child," with qualitative research (e.g., ethnography) forming an important area of research (Blanc, 1994). Furthermore, research now tends to avoid painting the child as only a victim or a perpetrator (Alanen, 1988). Social science traditionally concentrated on the activities of youth that threaten to divert them from the correct "path"—hence research concentrated on pinpointing the characteristics that contribute to making an "innocent" child susceptible to antisocial tendencies. The evolution of social science has meant a more nuanced framing of issues such as teen pregnancy and violence in the larger context of children's lives, especially in terms of examining "positive" as well as "negative" tendencies (Corsaro, 1997; Graue & Walsh, 1998).

How can social scientists ensure that their research reflects a balanced interpretation of children's lives? Fortunately, a powerful set of guidelines for research exists in the United Nations Convention on the Rights of the Child (CRC). Societal trends toward respecting children's agency were strongly affirmed by the CRC, adopted by the General Assembly in 1990 and signed and ratified by all member nations except the United States and Somalia. The CRC is an expression of the idea that children are citizens, politically complete individuals who should be consulted in matters concerning them (Bardy, 1994; Earls & Carlson, 1999; Head, 1998). For this reason, "the Convention can be regarded as a historic milestone. On the one hand, it is the culmination of a difficult struggle over a decade, aiming at improving children's situation in society, on the other, it is the beginning of a new way of dealing with children, enshrined in hard law by the international community" (Verhellen, 1997, p. 9). In other words, the groundbreaking feature of the CRC is that it has both confirmed the societal trend toward recognizing children as competent agents and committed signatory nations to continuing that trend.

To that end, the CRC guarantees rights not only to protect youths and to provide for their needs, but also to encourage their participation (Boyden, 1997). The rights included in the CRC can be roughly divided into three categories: rights of protection, rights of provision, and rights of participation. The first two categories are obviously important and relatively uncontroversial (e.g., the right to protection from harm and the right to be provided education, shelter, and so forth). The third category, on the other hand, includes rights that are pioneering in their application to children. For example, the CRC provides for children's rights of association and expression (Table 1). By doing so, the CRC goes beyond ensuring a child's survival to the promotion of her or his physical, mental, spiritual, and moral well-being (Ben-Arieh, 1999). Thus, the CRC has opened up "as never before in history the way to provide children with positive rights" (Qvortrup, 1991, p. 39).

Just as the CRC has reflected—and reinforced—changing views of youth in society, so can it provide a useful set of parameters for social scientists. Casas

Table 1. CRC Participatory Rights

Article 12: The Child's Opinion

The right to express an opinion, and to have that opinion taken into account, in any manner or procedure affecting the child.

Article 13: Freedom of Expression

The right to obtain and make known information, and to express his or her views, unless this would violate the rights of others.

Article 14: Freedom of Thought, Conscience, and Religion

The right to have ideas and think freely, and to choose what he or she believes is the right thing to do, unless this would endanger the child or violate the rights of others.

Article 15: Freedom of Association

The right of children to meet others and to join or set up associations, unless the fact of doing so violates the rights of others.

(1997, p. 283) argues that "both in a sociological and in a psychosocial sense the CRC even starts a 'new childhood,' a new image of what children are as a social group or as a social category." The utility of intertwining the CRC with social scientific research has been demonstrated in a few cases. Johnson et al. (1995), for example, used the CRC to frame their view of the Nepalese children they studied, which prompted them to include both traditional and untraditional research techniques such as listening to children's songs, interviewing children, and having children rank tasks that they liked or disliked.

When placed against the benchmark of the CRC, traditional social science has done rather well in examining the extent to which children are protected or provided for. But children's agency and participation were much less frequently taken into account. This omission occurred on two levels. First, on a topical level, social scientists infrequently framed their investigations to measure children's ability or opportunity to participate. Second, on the level of process, social science has rarely engaged children as partners in the development and conceptualization of research. That is, social scientists have not use children's agency in a manner that could help shape and enhance investigations.

It is in this context that we can understand the progress exemplified in Search Institute's work on the 40 developmental assets. The asset approach is painted as an alternative to approaches that focus only on children's basic needs (e.g., food and shelter) or on the risks and deficits that can hinder children's development (Benson, 1997). This alternative calls attention to the positive developmental "building blocks" that can add up to healthy and happy children. Thus, Search Institute's asset approach is meant to provide balance to a discipline that had previously focused too heavily on deficits. Moreover, Search Institute's work reflects a relatively newfound emphasis on the role of community in child development (Benson et al., 1998). The asset approach moves beyond the family or school environment and implies a degree of communality among youths (rather than a treatment of children as individuals in a vacuum). For Search Institute, important actors in building child-friendly communities include not only policy makers, academics, and professionals, but also "neighbors, coworkers, employers, congregation members, teachers, coaches, and youth group leaders—and our children and adolescents" (Benson, 1997, p. xiv).

Importantly, Search Institute includes both external and internal assets. The four categories of external assets are Support, Empowerment, Boundaries and Expectations, and Constructive Use of Time, whereas the four categories of internal assets are Commitment to Learning, Positive Values, Social Competencies, and Positive Identity. External assets are those assets that the community can provide, whereas internal assets are assets that young people develop within themselves over time (Benson et al., 1998). Search Institute does not, however, address a critical question: How do external assets and internal assets affect each other? As conceptualized by Search Institute, external assets and internal assets appear to exist in a vacuum, such that the presence of one group is not necessarily connected to the presence of the other. The integration of internal and external assets, then, is notably absent in Search Institute's methodology. Presumably in the "real world," however, this is not the case.

At the very least, the inclusion of internal and external assets represents an important advance in that it suggests that Search Institute has moved beyond issues of protection and provision. But does the assets approach take the "next step" and address participation? In one respect, Search Institute does acknowledge children's agency, both in external and internal assets. The Empowerment category of external assets includes "Youth as resources: Young people are given useful roles in the community" and "Community values youth: Young person perceives that community adults value youth." A number of internal assets imply the importance of children's motivations and actions, such as "Peaceful conflict resolution: Young person seeks to resolve conflict nonviolently" and "Personal power: Young person feels he or she has controls over 'things that happen to me.'" Additionally, Benson (1997) champions youths as community builders and leaders, and even admonishes adults to be aware of power differentials between adults and youths that can prevent children from serving as leaders. Thus, at least on a topical level, the asset framework would appear to pay attention to issues of children's agency as laid out by the CRC.

However, on the level of process—input into the development and structure of the research project—children's participation seems absent. According to Search Institute, the developmental assets framework represents a synthesis of knowledge from social scientists and child professionals. Not surprisingly, this synthesis has required some "tweaking." In its first incarnation, the list consisted of 30 developmental assets, which, as Search Institute later acknowledged, over-represented the experiences of white, middle-class communities. The later version has 40 developmental assets; to better conceptualize the experience of minority, lower-income, and inner-city youths, Search Institute initiated "dialogues, workshops, and focus groups" involving "about 150 youth, educators, parents, social service providers, and policy makers" (Benson, 1997, p. 29). Despite the inclusion of these varied groups, it is clear from Benson's description of the genesis of developmental assets that the ultimate decision regarding content and methodology rested with Search Institute. The extent to which the institute's decision making accurately reflects the experiences of diverse communities remains debatable.

Children's input, then, apparently did not play a substantial role in forming the developmental assets approach. Benson (1997) does encourage communities to enlist youths as partners in information gathering, but this is a limited partnership, indeed. In essence, youths would be recruited to use a research tool developed entirely by adults. Children, then, would have virtually no say in determining what needs to be understood and what questions should be asked. It is true that the 40 developmental assets chosen reflect the expertise of adults. But that expertise is exactly that—not gospel, but the perspective of adults. The viewpoints of children might be different in subtle or not-so-subtle ways, and to ignore them or otherwise prevent them from contributing to the research instrument would seem to limit understanding of children's lives.

It is critical, then, that we emphasize a point that Benson (1997) concedes: by choosing 40 assets that are meant as universal, some other potential assets important for particular communities might be overlooked. In many ways, Search Institute has done society an immense service by presenting this innovative and unifying approach to the social science of children. But we must caution social scientists and communities not to fall into the trap of measuring children's experiences exclusively with this framework. The 40 developmental assets do not form a perfect and universal definition of children's well-being. Notions of rights and well-being can and do differ among communities, families, and children. Moreover, they can evolve over time—a reality that Search Institute does not appear to address. Even the CRC must be interpreted with an eye toward flexibility; as our experiences with the Young Citizens Project have shown us, different groups of children experience rights in different ways and value certain rights more than others. Whereas the CRC, for example, is universally endorsed but can be translated locally, Search Institute's methodology appears to be both diagnostic and prescriptive. Our concern is that in the quest for universal applicability, the assets approach risks silencing dialogue within communities by presenting a seemingly all-encompassing "definition" of well-being.

In addition, although the aggregative nature of the developmental assets survey (the idea that well-being can be measured with a scale) is easy to understand and useful for comparison purposes, it does not allow for communicative exchange among individuals. That is, we caution communities from measuring their progress over time or vis-à-vis other communities with numbers that could obscure complex phenomena. Although the 40 developmental assets may serve as a good starting point, we hope that both social scientists and "ordinary" individuals would want to challenge them and spur dialogues within particular communities. These dialogues would allow the construction of a more particularized list of assets, not to mention the redefinition of assets or the selection of specific assets for close study.

The inclusion of children and their unique perspectives in these dialogue sessions would be especially valuable. After all, youths are equipped to understand the motivations and opinions of their peers without the potentially distorting lens of adulthood. For example, children could help address the interplay of external and internal assets. As beneficiaries of external assets and holders of internal assets, children would seem to offer important insight into how the two sets of assets affect each other. Thus, as dialogue partners, children can play an especially valuable role in determining the path of study for social science.

Although this may sound appealing (or at least reasonable) in principle, turning principles into coherent theory and, ultimately, action is not a straightforward task. This is a fact that we have discovered through our work with the Young Citizens Project, perhaps the best example to date of a social science project that has engaged children as research collaborators. Before discussing the practical aspects of research projects like the YCP, we examine their theoretical underpinnings.

II. Toward a Collaborative Model of Research

As we argued in the preceding section, the developmental assets framework represents progress in the move of social science toward a more balanced view of children that takes into account their agency. The next step, we believe, is a methodology that not only focuses study on children's participation but also actually allows children to participate in the research process. As we hope to demonstrate, this approach provides a means by which youths' own perspectives on their own lives and cultures can be used to produce useful knowledge. By using discursive processes to lend "intersubjective" rigor to interpretations of social phenomena, this model of the social science of youth attempts to provide a more complete picture of children's lives than that made available by more traditional conceptions of the study of youth.

As previously noted, the CRC can be a helpful benchmark for measuring how well researchers take into account children's participatory rights. The principles of the CRC require a set of actions to guide their implementation, however, and for this purpose we have searched for a philosophical and practical basis for involving youths as citizens in our research. This led us to study the writings of Jürgen Habermas and his theory of communicative action. Habermas helps solve the dilemma of including children's perspectives while putting them to the critical test—in essence, allowing research to be both inclusive of people's subjective opinions and legitimate in testing the veracity of these opinions.

Habermas criticizes both the universalism and positivism exemplified by the traditional approach to children (which, he believes, unjustifiably ignores human volition and subjectivity) and the interpretivism trumpeted by some of the "reformed" social scientists of youth (which neglects the possibility that ideology and other social institutions can distort people's views) (Habermas, 1987, 1988, 1995; McCarthy, 1994). Habermas puts forth a third type of "critical" social science that seeks to retain the best characteristics of positivism and interpretivism by using discourse among persons in a community to validate subjective interpretations and thereby produce "intersubjective" knowledge (Habermas, 1973, 1992; McCarthy, 1994). In Habermas's view, this research process is emancipatory for participants because the knowledge produced is immediately accessible to them, allowing them to understand their particular situation and to take steps to improve it (Dryzek, 1995; McCarthy, 1994). Moreover, the act of dialogic research itself encourages people to think of themselves as capable initiators who can think critically about their own lives and spark positive action (Christiano, 1997; Warren, 1995). Thus, the line between researcher and researched, as well as the line between research and action, is redefined in Habermas's critical social science.

According to Habermas, if all parties in a dialogue are allowed to participate equally, subjective interpretations can be tested critically and a "valid" conclusion reached. He puts forth several especially important procedural rules for ideal dialogue:

> Every subject with the competence to speak and act is allowed to take part in a discourse.

Everyone is allowed to question any assertion whatever.
Everyone is allowed to introduce any assertion whatever into the discourse.
Everyone is allowed to express his attitudes, desires, and needs.
No speaker may be prevented, by internal or external coercion, from exercising his [dialogic] rights. (1990, p. 89)

A group of individuals can engage in a discursive process designed to achieve an intersubjective "truth" that comprehends the influence of the "system" (e.g., ideologies and practices ingrained within the whole of society) (Habermas, 1973). Any interpretation is, in a sense, "rational" in that the person attempting to gain understanding must appeal to standards of rationality that he or she assumes would be applicable to all persons (Habermas, 1990). Yet these standards are all subjective; discourse is a way to introduce intersubjectivity into these rational norms. In the ideal speech situation, subjects' arguments and the norms on which they are based are treated as hypotheses that are tested by other members of the group (Warnke, 1995). Speakers and listeners may legitimately (and inevitably) have norms, emotions, and desires that influence their reasoning, but it is the role of discourse to combine reason and personal experience in a manner that will critically test this adherence to what might be called the "irrational." As John Rawls argues, in the formalized speech context that is discourse, speakers must make explicit what is latent in their argumentation (see Bohman, 1996). The stance of listeners in a dialogue is not to accept blindly what another says as valid, but to challenge it in order to reach a mutual understanding. When biases and "tradition" that underlie "common" understandings are made explicit, they become less convincing. Dialogue, then, makes clear that one's view may be "a part of the whole story" and that it is just one possible perspective among many (Young, 1997). Indeed, discourse allows differences in biographical experiences and histories to become assets for each member of a group; distinct and new perspectives on issues can be presented that can challenge established norms (Cohen, 1997). People from different backgrounds can add their "situated knowledge" to the larger pool of knowledge now available to the group; this is especially important for garnering the perspectives of the disempowered, who would otherwise not be able to have their voices heard (Young, 1997). As long as participants look out for the "public interest" of group truth (rather than employing strategic actions, e.g., pushing some unspoken agenda), decision making ought to improve (Cohen, 1986). As John Stuart Mill contends, the critical back-and-forth of ideas hones the group's argumentation until a consensus that represents the "truth" can be achieved (Christiano, 1997).

This concept of critical social science based on dialogue has been manifested "in the real world" in the form of participatory action research (PAR), which seeks to transfer production of knowledge from academia to the people who would normally be "under study" (Rahman, 1993; Smith, 1997). In this model, purely "objective" research is an impossibility; academics who attempt to obtain an objective view of social phenomena in actuality project their own political biases into their subjective interpretation (Rahman, 1991; Tandon, 1988). In contrast, PAR strives to have people speak for themselves. Dialogue between "common people" and academics, who become partners in the research, allows subjective interpretations to be tested and revised such that intersubjective knowledge can be produced.

In a handful of projects in locations ranging from Colombia to England, PAR research has been used in the context of child-centered social science (e.g., Alder & Sandor, 1990; Atweh & Burton, 1995; Atweh, Christensen, & Dornan, 1998; Campbell, Cook, & Dornan, 1995; Park & Dolph, 1997; Salazar, 1991). In these projects, engaging children as research partners proved feasible, although the issue of equality between adults and youths proved critical. Because of its strong emphasis on the idea of youth-adult collaboration on an equal basis, the Young Citizens Project (YCP) offers perhaps the best glimpse to date of participatory research with children. Next, we examine how the YCP put the theoretical model of collaborative research into practice.

III. Collaborative Research in Action: The Young Citizens Project

For the last three years, the Young Citizens Project has attempted to adhere to a participatory model in its research with urban youths in Chicago, Illinois, and Cambridge, Massachusetts. The YCP has been deeply informed and in part inspired by the Convention on the Rights of the Child (CRC). Using the theoretical underpinnings of dialogue as we outlined in the preceding section, the YCP strives to put into practice as well as validate the rights of participation that the CRC details. In this section, we examine the functioning of the latest version of the YCP, including both its successes and its missteps. By doing so, we hope to illuminate the kinds of measures that need to be taken to make such projects both feasible and genuinely collaborative. In particular, we want to demonstrate that a reasonable level of equality between adults and youths, though difficult to attain, can indeed be achieved and maintained.

Before discussing the 1999 YCP, let us examine briefly the group's history. In its first two years of existence, the YCP broke significant new ground in validating the research model of adult-youth collaboration. Groups of teenagers (young citizens, or YCs), numbering 6 to 10, from around Chicago, representing myriad ethnicities, cultures, and socioeconomic statuses, successfully used dialogue with adults to learn about their own lives and the lives of all youths, especially in relation to the Convention on the Rights of the Child. The first two YCPs demonstrated that despite inherent power differentials between adults and youths, cooperation on a reasonably equal level was possible. The YCP's heavy emphasis on the ideals of equal participation, shared trust, and commonality, especially as expressed through the CRC, created a scenario in which youths could feel comfortable in expressing their views and in monitoring violations of these ideals by adults or by fellow youths. In the process, the first two YCP groups created two research projects that aimed to produce knowledge that would incorporate the viewpoints and needs of children themselves.

The second YCP group was particularly successful. For the 10 YCs in this group, the concept of authority figures, specifically parents, teachers, and the police, seemed to have the greatest impact on their day-to-day well-being and reflected their understanding of the CRC's Article 27, the right to an adequate standard of living. The YCs decided to survey their peers about their feelings on this topic and, with our assistance, developed a questionnaire. During the last week of the project, they interviewed roughly 50 youths participating in summer programs in the Chicago Park District. Analyses of the completed surveys revealed what they had hypothesized to be the case—that adult engagement, support, and protection in many areas of young people's lives decreased as youths got older. This result is similar to that obtained by Search Institute, which found that both external and internal assets diminish with increasing age.

After two years in Chicago, the latest incarnation of the Young Citizens Project involved youths from Cambridge, Massachusetts. Six teenagers, aged 14 to 17 and representing a diversity of genders, races, and socioeconomic classes, came together with adults (the authors) to engage in collaborative research. As the YCs were informed, the project was designed not only to impact the lives of youths in Cambridge but also to demonstrate the ability of youths to take part in research and, indeed, to take part in constructive projects requiring critical understanding in general. The aim was to engage youth in a 6-week project in which they would agree to work from 4 to 5 P.M. each day.

The group began with an introduction to the YCP and more generally the concepts of child rights and child participation. We (the authors) first established the principle that the YCs' ideas were valuable and that there should be a level of equality among adults and youths that would ensure that everyone's opinions were equally respected. We explained what had happened with previous years' groups as examples of what types of projects this group could undertake. As in the previous year, we introduced Roger Hart's "Ladder of Participation" (Figure 1), which details the continuum of roles that children can play when adults and children collaborate on a project. The Ladder of Participation, as we explained, was a way in which participants could continuously measure the level of equality and cooperation in the group. We emphasized that projects that were both child-initiated and adult-supported, not merely child-initiated, were at the top of this ladder. In our view, this was what differentiated child participation from an unrealistic notion of child "liberation" from all adult influence and support. Child participation, marked by cooperation with and assistance from adults, stood a better chance of yielding successful and sustainable endeavors.

The youths were then asked to develop their own mission statement that would guide their work. When completed, the mission statement read as follows:

> Our mission is to explore the diverse issues of importance to young people, examining both their positive and negative experiences. Through our explorations, we hope to increase awareness of the rights of youth for

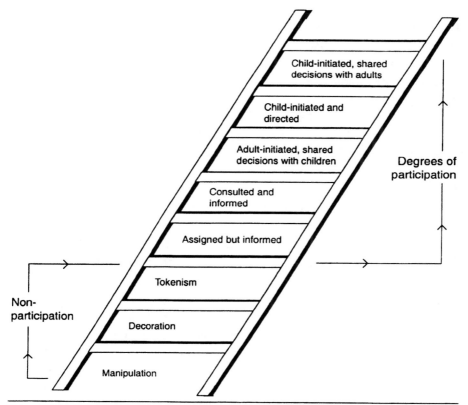

Figure 1. The Ladder of Participation (adapted from Hart, 1997)

ourselves personally and for all youths and adults. We want to make positive changes in the lives of youth, but more importantly, we want to show how changes can be made. Ultimately, we would like to produce something real which will give us a feeling of accomplishment.

The next step was to introduce the CRC. After reading the text of the CRC, the YCs were asked to think about which articles they felt were most important to well-being, and which were most frequently violated in their own lives and communities. As in the previous years, the examination of the CRC was meant to have at least two effects. First, the rights of participation detailed by the CRC were supposed to govern the functioning of the group itself. By understanding this framework, the youths could be more certain of their rights to participate fully and have their opinions heard within the group. Second, studying the CRC would allow the YCs a new perspective on how to measure youths' quality of life and well-being, as well as a tool to focus their area of research. The group also held a session intended to have the YCs think about the notion of well-being. This session included word association exercises to see what came to the YCs' minds when words such as *well-being* and *healthy* were used. Additionally, the YCs were asked to create pictorial representations of health or well-being. The wide variety of responses and images that resulted suggested that the ideas of well-being and health held many different meanings for the YCs. Afterward, the YCs discussed what they felt were the most significant threats to their well-being and that of all young people. Among the answers put forth by the YCs were violence, hate, discrimination, lack of education, oppression, and the restriction of opportunities. This session, then, gave the YCs an opportunity to think critically about the issue of well-being.

As the YCs received a grounding in child rights and youth participation, they simultaneously began developing the project they would undertake. The group deliberated and decided at the outset that the project would focus on an issue that affected youths in Cambridge in particular, rather than youths in general. Given the option, then, the group chose to pursue knowledge important for themselves and their own community. After several days of deliberation, the YCs seized upon the idea of "detachment" as an important concept to examine. The YCs all believed that a significant number of adolescents in Cambridge were or had been detached from school or their family and friends. Additionally, most of the YCs had personally felt the effects of detachment, as they considered either themselves or their close friends to be or to have at one time been detached. Besides the general topic of detachment, other potential subject areas such as the problem of gangs surfaced. After further deliberation, the group decided that detachment was a broad enough concept that it could incorporate more specific issues such as gangs.

Having chosen the topic of detachment, the YCs now had to develop a methodology. How would the group learn more about detachment, and how would it present its findings? We began with the expectation that the YCs would elect to create a survey. After all, the previous year's group had created a survey; such an instrument was "scientific" because it yielded quantifiable results, and it was relatively easy to administer. At the outset of the YCP, we suggested a survey as a possibility, noting our skill and experience using this approach. Furthermore, we suggested the use of another potential instrument related to the traditional survey, the Internet-based "Delphi process," in which each respondent's answers to open-ended queries are shared with all other respondents until a consensus is reached after several rounds of questioning. In addition to surveys and Delphi, we also presented in-depth interviewing as a research method. Besides being an important source of information, interviews with peers about detachment could serve as a preliminary instrument to other methods: They could unearth some general themes that could be investigated further (e.g., with a survey). The YCs agreed to practice interview techniques, taking turns interviewing each other using questions they devised themselves.

From the beginning, however, the YCs expressed more interest in a method that would reach a "broader" (i.e., nonacademic) population. Eventually, several of the YCs pushed for a video project. Despite our expressed concern about the group's collective lack of equipment and expertise in videomaking, the YCs believed that a video would be the most interesting way to explore the issue of detachment and an especially effective way to present it to their peers. The video could also include footage from interviews, a technique that the group had already practiced. We agreed that the group should proceed, but we also asked the youths to keep open the option of conducting a more traditional social science project, such as a survey, after the video's completion. The YCs agreed to this.

In addition to practicing video and interview techniques, the YCs began using dialogues to develop for themselves the concept of detachment. To begin this process, the YCs brainstormed about the effects detachment had on youth. They agreed that detachment could result in violence, isolation from family and peers, low self-esteem and depression, drug and alcohol use, bad grades, criminal behavior, and in general, worsened opportunities for the future (e.g., college and employment). The YCs then deliberated over what could cause detachment. The resulting answers were diverse and multifaceted. Peer influence, negative experiences at school (including bad teachers or poor grades), marginalization, mental disorders, and even poor physical health were seen as factors that could cause any youth to become detached. Especially important in the eyes of the YCs was the influence of adult role models such as parents, police officers, and teachers. According to the YCs, adults could make youths detached in many different ways. The YCs especially thought that adults created "self-fulfilling prophecies" (a phrase we introduced to capture their own sentiments) by unduly expecting youths to be failures and troublemakers. Moreover, some factors were seen as specific to particular groups (e.g., immigrants, minorities, girls, and youths from working and lower classes).

Next, the YCs determined what questions they wished to address in their project: What is the cause of detachment? How do detached youths view the future? Do they feel that they would ever "reattach"? However, in addition to asking "negative" questions, the YCs began to think that detachment could also be perceived positively: Are detached youths happy being detached? Was detachment a coping or defense strategy? In this way, the YCs began to construct for themselves a more balanced view of the issue, such that detachment was not necessarily an automatically bad thing that had to be fixed. In time, after further dialogue and upon our suggestion, the YCs' view became even more nuanced when they reached the conclusion that if there existed a concept such as detachment, there could also be a concept known as attachment. Thus, they began to perceive that youths did not somehow go astray from a "normal" path and "fall" into detachment, but rather that factors could influence youths to become relatively attached or detached.

At this point, the YCs decided to try to "operationalize" the variable of detachment. In the end, five main areas (school, family, criminal behavior, interests, and friends) were agreed on and questions developed for each area. After developing these questions, the YCs listed the nine important areas that an interview about detachment would have to address: school, health, family, crime, drugs and alcohol, authority figures, friends, interests, and prejudice.

As the YCs finished their dialogues in preparation for beginning their video, we wanted to revisit the issue of the more "traditional" social science project that we hoped the YCs would pursue. We especially pushed the YCs to consider the new Delphi process, which we felt had the potential to be an innovative tool to gain knowledge. Furthermore, we began to think that the YCs were becoming too task oriented and were not paying enough attention to the child rights and social justice aspect of the work. We thus asked the YCs to consider these issues before continuing ahead to the video. The YCs seemed to consent, and the group proceeded to form dialogue sessions to address these issues.

A few days later, however, the YCs made it clear that the Delphi was not a project that interested them, and that in general they felt that inequality in the group between adults and youths had to be addressed. They were willing to continue work on Delphi because they felt obligated to do so (as a job), but they believed that the idea was being forced on them. They thought that we did not really support studying detachment and that the work on Delphi was leading them away from the project they really wanted to work on, the video. The YCs agreed that there seemed to be different expectations now, in that they seemed obliged to do what we suggested, than there were at the outset, when true equality between adults and youths seemed to be the ideal. One of the YCs noted that the group was "slipping down the ladder of participation." The YCs also felt that we tended to dominate conversations, and consequently the group was not "doing" things (in the sense that there was a feeling of progress toward a certain end) but was simply speaking about things. This seemed to be a function mostly of our superior abilities at articulation as well as our general verbosity. Thus, there needed to be a discussion about the quality of discourse itself. Reestablishing norms of equality in discussions was necessary, after all, because these norms were the foundation for equality in general, including deciding what projects to pursue.

Upon hearing these concerns, we encouraged the YCs to continue to speak out and assured them that we were genuinely interested in achieving a measure of equality (i.e., their job security would not be jeopardized by their articulating their grievances). We realized the need to establish the limits to equality for the group. We expressed appreciation for the YCs' candor and reemphasized our desire to see a group characterized by equalized interaction, mutual trust, and perspective taking. At the same time, we did make explicit (perhaps for the first time) the requirements that could be seen as necessarily restricting the YCs' autonomy. We had initially conceived the YCP most importantly as an affirmation and exercise of child rights as well as a means to study child well-being. In our view, then, there was a need to ground the youths' work with explicit discussions about child rights and well-being. Furthermore, we had all envisioned the YCP as fundamentally a social science project; there was thus an expectation of a more traditional scientific method. However, we also expressed our support for the YCs' plan to produce a video on the topic of detachment. We agreed to shelve the Delphi idea and simply asked, as we had before, that the YCs keep in mind the possibility of a survey after the video's completion. As a group, we clarified among ourselves that the video was not to be a substitute for research, but would be a means (perhaps unorthodox) of obtaining qualitative knowledge. This commitment, in fact, was one of the reasons why the YCs felt strongly about making their video as thorough and as professional as possible: Producing a good-quality video and producing good-quality "data" were synonymous.

In addition to inequality between youths and adults, the YCs addressed inequality in participation among themselves, encouraging the two youngest members to speak more. Their relative lack of participation seemed to be more a function of their less outgoing natures than of their ages per se. To ensure that the opinions of the more reticent YCs were heard, prompting became a more or less institutionalized method for the group. While arguably an "artificial" means of pushing for equality, it succeeded in maintaining at least a minimal amount of participation from all group members.

It would not be hyperbolic to claim that this forthright discussion fundamentally altered the project's trajectory. We explicitly reaffirmed our commitment to equality, but with qualifications that had always been present but insufficiently articulated. Despite their feelings of intimidation, the YCs were still able to call attention to what they considered a faulty situation and receive a substantive and meaningful response from us. Of course, whether the group would move beyond the rhetoric of change and actually operate differently was another matter entirely. Nevertheless, the YCs at this point felt more confident that they could speak their minds and not be reprimanded, but rather congratulated. Indeed, their action had achieved immediate results: They had succeeded in scrapping the Delphi plan. Furthermore, the YCs received a definite go-ahead on their video project on detachment—until they began to rethink their topic entirely.

One of the dialogue sessions we had to prepare for the ill-fated Delphi idea centered on the topic of segregation and racism as a violation of youths' rights. The YCs found this topic extremely engaging, and the discussion was lengthy, heated, and thought-provoking. This was one of the first instances of the YCs being able to ground child rights in something that they faced in their daily lives. For the Cambridge YCs (unlike the Chicago YCs before them), explicit racism was not the chief problem; rather, they saw a less blatant but perhaps equally pervasive form of segregation, which they called "self-segregation," as more important. As the YCs defined it preliminarily, self-segregation was the voluntary separation of youths by race, whether in schools, in peer groups, or in any other situations that youths faced. The YCs agreed that although Cambridge was a progressive city and that their high school was ostensibly racially balanced, self-segregation was a serious issue but one that people often pretended did not exist. The YCs theorized that self-segregation was the result of many factors, including economics, location of people's homes, and just simply the commonalities that people of the same race might share. The YCs also agreed that self-segregation might be necessary as a way to feel comfortable, but that in general it was not a good thing because it encouraged prejudices and an artificial feeling of comfort. Finally, the YCs noted that self-segregation was based not just on race but also on socioeconomic status, and that the two factors were intertwined. They felt that a video could produce information that could be helpful in taking action on this issue. In particular, there had been some talk of restructuring the local high school to restore greater equality among its "houses" (i.e., schools within the school to which all students belonged). The video could contribute to this discussion, demonstrating that youths could hold and express "sophisticated" opinions about this issue and encouraging other youths to think about it, talk about it, and make their feelings known.

To understand better the phenomenon of self-segregation, the group undertook many exercises. First, we encouraged the YCs to think about how self-segregation tied into child rights and well-being. In regard to rights, the YCs individually examined the CRC and selected the articles that were applicable to self-segregation. Second, they interviewed each other, focusing on personal experiences with self-segregation. Not only did this produce additional knowledge about self-segregation, it also increased their knowledge of each other (thus enhancing their perspective-taking ability) and it gave them further practice at interviewing. Third, the group read some background literature about the topic, including articles on the Internet and Beverly Daniel Tatum's (1999) *Why Are All the Black Kids Sitting Together in the Cafeteria?* Fourth, the group spoke with Gary Orfield, a professor from the Harvard School of Education who is an expert on school desegregation. He noted among other things that "self-segregation" was not necessarily an accurate term, as the structural influence of socially ingrained discrimination made the phenomenon less than completely voluntary. This helped them to understand the multifaceted causality of self-segregation, which would become an important part of the final project. The professor also proposed a host of potential ways to reduce self-segregation, which the YCs would also incorporate in their project.

After exploring the issue in these ways, the YCs decided to make a preliminary list of the possible effects of self-segregation. The list included the ingraining of particular attitudes toward other groups, especially in terms of stereotypes and fears of "the other." At the same time, self-segregation could also yield feelings of attachment to one's own group and a sense of a shared culture. Furthermore, it was postulated that self-segregation could have an effect on youths' education, especially in that students (at least at their school) were "tracked." Some groups, it was thought, might do better in school than other groups because of teachers' expectations, internalized norms regarding achievement, or other reasons. Finally, self-segregation possibly constrained youths' choices in that they might follow the group rather than pursue an activity or express a thought that seemed to fall outside of the group. Through dialogue sessions (both with and without outside participants), mock interviews, and background research, then, the YCs were able to build a base of knowledge that could be used to create a research method that would produce yet more knowledge about self-segregation.

By this time, there were only three weeks remaining in the summer to complete the project, which meant that the group had to act expeditiously. While dialogue sessions ideally require the equal participation of all group members, the task-oriented nature of producing the video required the YCs to split apart at times to take care of individual responsibilities. This included obtaining a suitable camera and finding editing equipment. One of the first tasks was that each of the group members had to recruit one or two classmates to interview. After discussing the logistics at some length, the group decided that each interview would ideally be conducted by two YCs, one to do the bulk of the interviewing and one to run the camera and ensure that all questions had been posed. The YCs recruited a diverse group of fellow students representing a variety of ages, genders, races, and classes.

After recording shots of their school and popular hangouts, the YCs set about developing their interview questions. Initially, the group planned to create general question areas first and then specific questions for each of the areas. This approach was quickly abandoned, however, in favor of brainstorming individual queries, followed by the organization of these questions into sections and removal of those questions deemed less important by the group. As the YCs noted, the professor from Harvard had introduced an important issue: namely, whether self-segregation was truly a personal choice or was in a way forced by society. Furthermore, the YCs wanted to investigate the importance of the influence of teachers, counselors, and other faculty in the perpetuation of self-segregation. In the end, the YCs' list of questions (Table 2) covered these two issues, as well as interviewees' personal experiences with self-segregation and thoughts about its prevalence, causes, effects, future, and potential solutions. In our opinion, the sophistication and thoroughness of the YCs' questions offer compelling evidence for the efficacy of the collaborative approach.

After recruiting their interviewees, the YCs split into small groups to conduct their interviews. They seemed especially to enjoy this element of the project and clearly relished the role of interviewer. This role allowed them to apply the knowledge they had already produced to obtain yet more knowledge from different people without direct constraints from adults. While interviews were being conducted by one group of YCs, the other YCs would work on the video's narration, which served to introduce the video, to "signpost" its structure, and to

Table 2. Questions for Students about Self-Segregation

---

1. **Background**
   Tell me a little about yourself—your name, grade, house.
2. **What do you think self-segregation is?**
   Do you think we segregate ourselves at Cambridge Rindge and Latin? Have you ever thought about this as a kind of self-segregation? Have you ever thought about it this way before?
3. **Where do you see or notice self-segregation at the school?**
   At lunch?
   After school?
   In classes?
   In sports?
   In school houses?
   In clubs (like NHS, Black Student Union, AHORA . . .)?
   In different Cambridge neighborhoods?
   Social life, when you hang out or get together after school?
4. **Do you think of yourself as self-segregated? As more comfortable with people of the same background or race?**
5. **What do you think are some of the effects of self-segregation—do you think there are both positive and negative effects?**
   For example, does self-segregation affect the kind or quality of education one gets? Do the advantages and disadvantages in education split down the color line?
   Another example: How does self-segregation affect your social life or the social lives of those around you?
6. **Are teachers part of the problem? If so, how?**
7. **Is the faculty integrated? Is this an issue? Should the faculty be more integrated?**
8. **Are there enough counselors? Do all people get counseled equally, or do you feel that some students, because of race or background, tend to get different advice or kinds of support?**
9. **Do you have any ideas about why self-segregation occurs? What causes it? Does it have to do with racism? Does some of it have to do with personal identity?**
10. **What do you think should be done to deal with self-segregation at our school? Or more generally?**
    What should youth do?
    What should faculty do?
    What about the administration?
    Is there enough talk in our school, in our houses, in our classes about racism and about self-segregation?
    What do you think about restructuring the house system? Would it solve some of the problems of self-segregation?
11. **What do you think will happen in the future? Do you think there will be self-segregation?**

mark transitions between interviewees' comments. It was difficult to compose this narration, as it had to include an extremely succinct explanation of the project's history and goals. Nevertheless, after extensive deliberation and numerous revisions, the group was able to agree on a final version. The YCs also had to discuss other proposed components of the video, including the background music.

After all of the footage was shot and transcripts made, the YCs developed a complete script, although this script was subsequently altered as the editing process progressed. Furthermore, after the interviews were complete, it was realized that like any other instrument of knowledge, the video was not without "biases" introduced by its producers. Thus, it was deemed necessary to introduce the project and the YCs at the beginning of the video so that viewers would understand its purpose and rationale. To this end, a dialogue of group members discussing their thoughts and experiences with self-segregation was taped to provide footage for the introduction of the video. The script was revised accordingly, and the last week and a half of the project was thus filled with the technical tasks needed to complete the video. A rough cut of the video was completed just as the project was scheduled to come to a close. After obtaining input from fellow students, a final copy was completed several weeks later.

In addition to the video, however, the YCs came to believe that a survey was a necessary next step. One of the YCs explained that she realized that one person's opinion was exactly that—one particular subjective view out of many possible views: "A survey, I think, gets people to talk, and it reaches a bigger audience ... in the video, we only interviewed, I don't know, seven kids, eight kids? . . . I just really felt like I was misrepresenting the students' voice . . . , and I just realized that there are so many more opinions out there." Thus, the YCs spent extra time after the completion of the six weeks, not only to finish the video, but also to craft the survey. Having demarcated question areas and specific questions for the video, as well as having discussed the issue of self-segregation in countless dialogues, it was not difficult for the YCs to compose questions for the survey.

Through their work on the video, the YCs had improved their group dynamic in that each person's contributions became better recognized. Moreover, as it turned out, the survey was a natural next step because it could assess opinions on questions and issues raised in the video. In creating the video, the YCs obtained in-depth information from a variety of sources and then deliberated over these "data" in the editing process to come to nuanced conclusions. The production of the video, then, built a qualitative base that enhanced the quality of the survey and resulted in the creation of still more knowledge.

It took only an afternoon for the YCs to come together and compose a survey that addressed and built on all areas of the video. In addition to questions about self-segregation, in accordance with our advice, the survey included questions on each respondent's age, grade, gender, house affiliation, home neighborhood, elementary school, race, and socioeconomic class. The YCs agreed that closed-ended, quantitative questions would be the simplest and most effective way to measure students' opinions. The majority of the questions therefore were scaled assessments of people's levels of agreement to statements regarding self-segregation. The YCs also believed, however, that perhaps the most difficult question to answer about self-segregation was how it could be "solved." Because of this, in addition to scaled questions, the YCs left space for respondents to come up with their own solutions.

Based on advice given by the project's adults, as well as other interested adults, the wording and format of the survey instrument were revised on several occasions. By the time the school year began for the YCs, both the video and the survey were essentially complete. The YCs had succeeded in producing two distinct but complementary ways to explore, increase knowledge about, and take action on the issue of self-segregation. The next step was to share the video and survey with the rest of the school. Although the video and survey could exist alone, the group agreed that they would be most effective together. The video could introduce the topic of self-segregation and generate thought and discussion, whereas the survey could assess students' feelings.

The YCs agreed that showing the video in smaller settings (i.e., in individual classrooms) would be most effective. Additionally, showing the video during classes would be conducive both to engendering discussions among students and to distributing surveys afterward. The YCs ended up distributing their videos and surveys to 9th- and 10th-grade advising groups at the high school. The logistics involved in sharing the video and survey with youths at the school were more complicated than anyone in the group had imagined, and 92 completed surveys were eventually collected, fewer than had been hoped for. Still, the results of the surveys that were returned proved intriguing, and the video was distributed successfully throughout the school.

After the project's completion, the group members came together to reflect on their work. This was a chance for the YCs to share their opinions on how the project went, what was learned, and what could be changed. As a group, we began by summarizing our work creating the video and the project. They recalled the experiences that had compelled them to choose self-segregation as a topic, and how the video and survey had altered their opinions. Additionally, at this time, we discussed the feedback the YCs had begun to hear from classmates, family, and friends.

As the YCs made clear, producing a video rather than just a survey or other instrument was especially important in that they felt it was a medium that would reach youths in their community most effectively. At the same time, after having completed the video, they became aware of the need for a survey to garner the opinions of many more individuals. It was also important for the youths to be able to choose a topic that they felt was important to them.

Perhaps most important, the YCs discussed equality within the group. They noted first how in the initial weeks of the project, they had felt a certain degree of manipulation. The YCs recounted the controversy over the proposed survey and Delphi process and the way in which they were able to assert their own desires and needs. Although they acknowledged possible discrepancies early on between our rhetoric of equality and the reality of constrained action, the YCs expressed appreciation that we responded to their concerns and acted to improve equality between adults and youths. They agreed that the project demonstrated that meaningful and constructive interaction with adults who were not typical authority figures was possible. One of the YCs spoke for the rest of the youths when she stated that she still thought that "adults are the hardest people to interact with"; thus, a "cultural gap" remained between us and the youths. At the same time, the YCs did think that dialogue was a valuable tool to help bridge gaps, not only between us and them, but among the youths as well. In synthesizing a shared understanding from disparate viewpoints, dialogue proved valuable as preparation for action.

One of the YCs made a remark that was probably the most validating for the group's legitimacy: "[The adults] didn't treat us like kids; they treated us like adults, or not total equals, but equals nonetheless . . . They tried to talk to us like we were their friends, and not talking down to us because we were kids. And that's what I really liked about it." Despite the occasional pitfall, then, the project was able to establish a relationship in which adults and youths were "not total equals, but equals nonetheless." Perhaps this is the best possible summary of the way in which adults and youths can overcome inherent power imbalances to create a truly collaborative relationship.

In the end, then, the Young Citizens Project demonstrated that children can—and should—help shape the research process. Using a dialogic process, youths' perspectives on social issues important to them can be both obtained and critically tested. Although there exist obstacles to achieving equality between adults and youths (especially in terms of participation in dialogues), the success of the YCP shows that these obstacles can be overcome. In this way, the expertise of adult social scientists can be combined with the practical knowledge of youths to provide a well-rounded picture of youths' lives.

IV. Future Directions in the Social Science of Children

We introduce the YCP not as a panacea for all social science research but as an example of how youths can successfully contribute to research and offer a nuanced and particularized view of children's lives. In essence, we believe that social science must acknowledge children's agency in order to obtain the "complete picture." This entails not only focusing study on children's participation with others and in the world around them but also engaging their participation in the research process. This is not to say that we endorse a vision of child "liberation" in which youths are expected to act completely independently of adults. Rather, we believe that by working together, children and adults can contribute their own unique strengths and insights to the scientific study of children.

In this respect, Search Institute's developmental assets approach falls short. To be fair, the asset approach represents a major advance in child-centered social science. Perhaps most laudable, it eschews the traditional paradigm of concentrating exclusively on children's deficits. Moreover, it assumes that children can be agents rather than just objects on a developmental pathway. However, in the conception and development of the asset approach, children's participation seems to have been nearly absent. In neither its original form nor its subsequent expansion, did children apparently play a meaningful role in determining which assets would be included.

We would like to pose questions to Search Institute that we also ask ourselves in our work:

- How is the child conceived in your work? How is agency defined and what capabilities are emphasized?
- How have children been involved in the institute's work? Have they developed any of the assets or survey questions? Have they helped design any community initiatives?
- Is there a theory that integrates internal and external assets?
- How do you deal with diverse populations? What about children who are not in school? How do you address diverse value systems?
- How do you deal with secular changes? Do you modify the survey as you encounter children or communities that do not fit?

We believe that children's input would enrich the asset approach tremendously. As it stands, Search Institute's methodology risks imposing an aggregative and universalized notion of well-being that may not in fact represent the diversity of communities in which children live. Involving children in collaborative research would permit social scientists to move beyond the adult perspective to a greater understanding of children's own unique perspectives. Soliciting the input of youths and other community members would allow for a more particularized understanding of children's lives—for the local translation of the universal asset framework and flexibility over time and locale. This could include the selection or emphasis of particular assets, the redefinition or restructuring of assets, and an examination of the interplay between external and internal assets.

There are some important limitations to consider when undertaking collaborative research with children. Perhaps the foremost limitation is the amount of time such research can take. In general, although dialogues may produce more or better information, it takes time to establish an equitable and comfortable environment for discussion and to come to a consensus on any issue. And in the case of dialogues with youths, overcoming problems of inequality and difference between adults and youths can be an especially involved process. Another limitation is that adult researchers might be confronted with youth researchers' personal problems and be forced to intervene. In the case of the YCP, one of the youths experienced personal difficulties that required the adults to step in for his safety and well-being.

Nevertheless, these are not insurmountable obstacles. Although it was not a simple process, the YCs skillfully defined issues of importance to them, came to consensus about the important dimensions of these issues, and devised strategies to measure other people's perspectives and present them in a critical and informative manner. The YCP demonstrated that children in a particular community might have their own, unique ideas about their well-being and the well-being of their peers. The YCs began with the Convention on the Rights of the Child, a universal document meant to address all facets of children's lives, and applied it to their specific community, critically examining it to determine which aspects were most important to their lives. After deliberation, the YCs determined that the issue of self-segregation was crucial to well-being. Starting with a simple definition and focusing on its negative effects, the YCs found out more about the subject and through dialogues came to a more nuanced understanding that associated self-segregation with a variety of other issues both positive and negative. To learn about the topic and present their findings in a manner accessible to their fellow youths, the YCs used both a traditional scientific technique, a survey, and a more unorthodox medium, a video. Overall, we believe that the quality of the knowledge produced by the YCP, and the fact that its unique features reflect the input of children who might otherwise not have been represented in scientific research, provide a powerful rationale for collaboration between adults and youths—in particular, for investigations into children's well-being. After all, in focusing on self-segregation, much like the previous year's YCs had focused on relations with authority figures, the YCs determined central aspects that enhance or constrain their achievement of well-being.

The universality of principles of the process of dialogue and community involvement has allowed us to use this kind of approach not only with the YCP but also with groups such as elementary school students in Costa Rica. In the future, we plan to apply what we have learned to expand our efforts, most notably with AIDS orphans in Tanzania. We invite Search Institute and other social scientists to consider how children's participation can broaden their efforts to understand children's lives. In time, we hope that the inclusion of children's participation will enhance all child-centered social science and become a powerful tool in our collective efforts to ensure the health and well-being of all children.

The authors gratefully acknowledge the generous support of the Turner Foundation for making the Chicago and Cambridge Young Citizen Programs possible. We also thank Barbara Holecek, for her direction in the making of the video production *Chillin*, and the Task Force for Child Survival and Development for support of the Delphi and video projects. Portions of this paper were taken from Brian Chan's senior thesis at Harvard College, and he acknowledges the mentoring of Professor Christopher Winship.

References

Alanen, L. (1988). Rethinking childhood. *Acta Sociologica, 31*, 53–67.

Alder, C., & Sandor, D. (1990). Youth researching youth. *Youth Studies, 9*, 38–42.

Ariès, P. (1962). *Centuries of childhood* (R. Baldick, Trans.). New York: Vintage Books.

Atweh, B., & Burton, L. (1995). Students as researchers: Rationale and critique. *British Educational Research Journal, 21*, 561–575.

Atweh, B., Christensen, C., & Dornan, L. (1998). Students as action researchers: Partnerships for social justice. In B. Atweh, S. Kemmis, & P. Weeks (Eds.), *Action research in practice* (pp. 114–138). London: Routledge.

Bardy, M. (1994). The manuscript of the 100-years project: Towards a revision. In J. Qvortrup et al. (Eds.), *Childhood matters: Social theory, practice, and politics* (pp. 299–318). Aldershot: Avebury.

Bardy, M. (1988). Childhood as a cultural concept and phenomenon in the West and its implications for child welfare policy. In K. Ekberg & P.-E. Mjaavatn (Eds.), *Growing into a modern world: Proceedings of an international interdisciplinary conference on the life and development of children in modern society.* (3 Vols., pp. 264–280). Trondheim: Norwegian Centre for Child Research.

Ben-Arieh, A. (1999). The international effort to measure and monitor the state of children. In A. B. Andrews & N. H. Kaufman (Eds.), *Implementing the U.N. Convention on the Rights of the Child* (pp. 33–46). Westport, CT: Praeger.

Benson, P. L. (1997). *All kids are our kids: What communities must do to raise caring and responsible children and adolescents.* San Francisco: Jossey-Bass.

Benson, P. L., Leffert, N., Scales, P. C., & Blyth, D. A. (1998). Beyond the "village" rhetoric: Creating healthy communities for children and adolescents. *Applied Developmental Science, 2*, 138–159.

Blanc, C. S. (1994). Some comparative urban trends: Street, work, homelessness, schooling, and family survival strategies. In C. S. Blanc (Ed.), *Urban children in distress: Global predicaments and innovative strategies* (pp. 311–374). Luxembourg: UNICEF/Gordon and Breach.

Blitzer, S. (1991). "They are only children, what do they know?" A look at current ideologies of childhood. *Sociological Studies of Child Development, 4,* 11–25.

Bohman, J. (1996). *Public deliberation: Pluralism, complexity, and democracy.* Cambridge, MA: MIT Press.

Boyden, J. (1997). Childhood and the policy makers: A comparative perspective on the globalization of childhood. In A. James & A. Prout (Eds.), *Constructing and reconstructing childhood: Contemporary issues in the sociological study of childhood* (pp. 184–215). London: Falmer Press.

Campbell, J., Cook, A., & Dornan, L. (1995). Empowerment through student-initiated action research: Exploring tertiary paths in a multiply disadvantaged school. *Education, Research, and Perspectives, 22,* 80–89.

Casas, F. (1997). Children's rights and children's quality of life: Conceptual and practical issues. *Social Indicators Research, 42,* 283–298.

Christiano, T. (1997). The significance of public deliberation. In J. Bohman & W. Rehg (Eds.), *Deliberative democracy: Essays on reason and politics* (pp. 243–278). Cambridge, MA: MIT Press.

Cohen, J. (1986). An epistemic conception of democracy. *Ethics, 97,* 26–38.

Cohen, J. (1997). Deliberation and democratic legitimacy. In J. Bohman & W. Rehg (Eds.), *Deliberative democracy: Essays on reason and politics* (pp. 67–92). Cambridge, MA: MIT Press.

Corsaro, W. A. (1997). *The sociology of childhood.* Thousand Oaks, CA: Pine Forge Press.

Dryzek, J. S. (1995). Critical theory as a research program. In S. K. White (Ed.), *Cambridge companion to Habermas* (pp. 97–119). Cambridge: Cambridge University Press.

Earls, F., & Carlson, M. (1999). Children at the margins of society: Research and practice. In M. Raffaeli & R. W. Larson (Eds.), *Homeless and working youth around the world: Exploring developmental issues* (No. 85, pp. 71–82). San Francisco: Jossey-Bass.

Earls, F., & Carlson, M. (in press). Adolescents as collaborators: In search of well-being. In M. Tienda & W. J. Wilson (Eds.), *Urban youth—asset or burden? Successful mediators of normative development in comparative perspective.* Cambridge: Cambridge University Press.

Edelman, M. W. (1977). We are failing the children. In R. Gross & B. Gross (Eds.), *The children's rights movement* (pp. 109–114). Garden City, NY: Anchor Books.

Ennew, J. (1994). Time for children or time for adults. In J. Qvortrup et al. (Eds.), *Childhood matters: Social theory, practice, and politics* (pp. 125–144). Aldershot: Avebury.

Freeman, M. M. D. (1983). *The rights and wrongs of children.* London: Frances Pinter.

Frones, I. (1994). Dimensions of childhood. In J. Qvortrup et al. (Eds.), *Childhood matters: Social theory, practice, and politics* (pp. 145–164). Aldershot: Avebury.

Gibson, C. M. (1993). Empowerment theory and practice with adolescents of color in the child welfare system. *Families in Society, 74,* 387–396.

Graue, M. E., & Walsh, D. J. (1998). *Studying children in context: Theories, methods, and ethics.* Thousand Oaks, CA: Sage.

Habermas, J. (1973). *Theory and practice* (J. Viertel, Trans.). Boston, MA: Beacon Press.

Habermas, J. (1987). *The theory of communicative action: Vol. 2. Lifeworld and system: A critique of functionalist reason* (T. McCarthy, Trans.). Boston, MA: Beacon Press.

Habermas, J. (1988). *On the logic of the social sciences* (S. W. Nicholsen & J. A. Stark, Trans.). Cambridge, MA: MIT Press.

Habermas, J. (1990). *Moral consciousness and communicative action* (C. Lenhardt & S. W. Nicholsen, Trans.). Cambridge, MA: MIT Press.

Habermas, J. (1992). *Postmetaphysical thinking* (W. M. Hohengarten, Trans.). Cambridge, MA: MIT Press.

Habermas, J. (1995). *Justification and application* (C. P. Cronin, Trans.). Cambridge, MA: MIT Press.

Hart, Roger A. (1997). *Children's participation: From tokenism to citizenship.* Florence, Italy: UNICEF/ International Child Development Centre.

Head, A. (1998). The child's voice in child and family social work decision making: The perspective of a guardian *ad litem. Child and Family Social Work, 3,* 189–196.

Hegar, R. L., & Hunzeker, J. M. (1988). Moving toward empowerment-based practice in public child welfare. *Social Work, 33,* 499–502.

James, A., Jenks, C., & Prout, A. (1998). *Theorizing childhood.* Oxford: Polity Press.

Johnson, V., et al. (1995). *Listening to smaller voices: Children in an environment of change.* London: Action Aid.

Ladd, R. E. (1996). *Children's rights revisited: Philosophical readings.* Belmont, CA: Wadsworth.

McCarthy, T. (1994). *The critical theory of Jürgen Habermas.* Cambridge, MA: MIT Press.

McCarthy, T. (1976). Translator's Introduction. In J. Habermas, *Communication and the evolution of society.* Boston: Beacon Press.

Morrow, V. (1995). Invisible children? Toward a reconceptualization of childhood dependency and responsibility. *Sociological Studies of Children, 7,* 207–230.

Park, P., & Dolph, G. (1997). Youth engaged in urban neighborhood development through participatory research. Association Paper. Knoxville, TN: Society for the Study of Social Problems.

Parsons, R. J. (1989). Empowerment for role alternatives for low income minority girls. *Social Work With Groups, 11,* 27–45.

Petoskey, E. L., Van Stelle, K. R., & De Jong, J. A. (1998). Prevention through empowerment in a Native American community. *Drugs and Society, 12,* 147–162.

Postman, N. (1994). *The disappearance of childhood.* New York: Vintage Books.

Qvortrup, J. (1994). Childhood matters: An introduction. In J. Qvortrup et al. (Eds.), *Childhood matters: Social theory, practice, and politics.* Aldershot: Avebury.

Qvortrup, J. (1991). *Childhood as a social phenomenon—An introduction to a series of national reports* (2nd Ed.). Eurosocial Report 36/0. Vienna: European Centre for Social Welfare Policy and Research.

Qvortrup, J. (Ed.). (1987). Special issue on "The Sociology of Childhood." *International Journal of Sociology, 17.*

Rahman, M. A. (1991). The theoretical standpoint of PAR. In O. Fals-Borda & M. A. Rahman (Eds.), *Action and knowledge* (pp. 13–23). New York: Apex.

Rahman, M. A. (1993). *People's self-development.* Dhaka: University Press Ltd.

Salazar, M. C. (1991). Young laborers in Bogota: Breaking authoritarian ramparts. In O. Fals-Borda & M. A. Rahman (Eds.), *Action and knowledge* (pp. 54–63). New York: Apex.

Sgritta, G. B. (1987). Childhood. Normalization and Project. The Sociology of Childhood. *International Journal of Sociology, 17,* 38–57.

Shamgar-Handelman, L. (1994). To whom does childhood belong? In J. Qvortrup et al. (Eds.), *Childhood matters: Social theory, practice, and politics.* Aldershot: Avebury.

Silvers, R. J. (1976). Discovering children's culture. *Interchange, 6,* 47–52.

Speier, J. (1976). The adult ideological viewpoint in studies of childhood. In A. Skolnick (Ed.), *Rethinking childhood: Perspectives on development and society* (pp. 168–186). Boston: Little, Brown.

Suransky, V. P. (1982). *The erosion of childhood.* Chicago: University of Chicago Press.

Tandon, R. (1988). Social transformation and participatory research. *Convergence, 21,* 5–15.

Tatum, B. D. (1999). *Why are all the black kids sitting together in the cafeteria?* New York: Basic Books.

Tesson, G., & Youniss, J. (1995). Micro-sociology and psychological development: A sociological interpretation of Piaget's theory. *Sociological Studies of Children, 7,* 101–126.

Verhellen, E. (1997). *Convention on the Rights of the Child: Background, motivation, strategies, main themes.* Leuven/Apeldoorn: Garant.

Warnke, G. (1995). Communicative rationality and cultural values. In S. K. White (Ed.), *Cambridge companion to Habermas* (pp. 120–142). Cambridge: Cambridge University Press.

Warren, M. E. (1995). The self in discursive democracy. In S. K. White (Ed.), *Cambridge companion to Habermas* (pp. 167–200). Cambridge: Cambridge University Press.

Young, I. M. (1997). Difference as a resource for democratic communication. In J. Bohman & W. Rehg (Eds.), *Deliberative democracy: Essays on reason and politics* (pp. 383–406). Cambridge, MA: MIT Press.

5 Enhancing the Assets for Positive Youth Development: The Vision, Values, and Action Agenda of the W. T. Grant Foundation

Karen Hein
W. T. Grant Foundation

National tragedies become galvanizing moments for nations to look both back and forward through a new lens. It is too soon to know the full implications of the events of September 11, 2001, as this book is being finalized just as the aftermath is taking shape. However, the impact of these tragic events on children and youth, and concern about them in terms of their sense of safety, were early considerations across the nation. This chapter focuses on the ways in which we might think of them not merely as the recipients of adult attention but also as resources for adults. The voices of young people are vitally important for us to hear, understand, and incorporate into our thoughts, research, and action.

This has become all the more apparent in light of the tragedy in Littleton, Colorado in April, 1998. The problems that incident illustrates have no simple solutions, since they had no simple cause. At first, media coverage focused on the young people and defined them in terms of antitheses: the good versus the bad, the innocent versus the guilty, the benign versus the treacherous. Quickly, the scope of the discussion widened, drawing on factors well beyond any one high school or community. Debate ranged from our ability to identify and help youngsters at risk to the influence of the media and the impact of easy access to means of destruction such as bombs and guns.

The story of the teenagers who were caught up in this event highlights the

This chapter summarizes material presented in the William T. Grant Foundation's annual reports for 1999 and 2000.

dilemmas and complex life situations faced by all young people in America. The focus on this tragedy has shifted the discussion from the life experiences of individuals to a consideration of the experiences of the whole group of young people. The discussion should include an understanding of our role in shaping the lives of young people and a reexamination of their role in our society. The question is not whether or not there will be another incident like that at Columbine High School, but what we can do to ensure different outcomes for other young people in this country.

Interpreting the events at Columbine is like looking into a kaleidoscope. With each twist, the pieces reassemble to form new patterns that exaggerate different parts. The viewer ultimately interprets the pattern. Impressions change over time as the kaleidoscope turns. Similarly, the nation's view of young people is based on events at a particular moment. Sometimes the pieces produce a picture of the positive contributions of young people, their strengths, energy, creativity, and idealism. At other times, the pieces present a more troubling image: danger, tensions, and alienation. The Colorado events caused viewers to reinterpret the images. As the kaleidoscope turns and the pieces settle, the viewers see new sides, different angles. Interpretation of the patterns determines individual and collective actions.

When William T. Grant established the foundation in 1936, his view of young people was influenced by his own life experiences and his interpretation of the kaleidoscopic patterns in place at the beginning of the twentieth century. He described his intentions by saying, "What I have in mind is to assist, by some means, in helping people or peoples to live more contentedly and peacefully and well in body and mind through a better knowledge of how to use and enjoy all the good things that the world has to offer them" (Cahan, 1986, p. 10). He mentioned several features of his own adolescence as being pivotal in forming his approach to managing his business and setting up the foundation.

Grant reports that he was never a good student and felt bullied by employers who would "drive and criticize and browbeat their employees with the deliberate purpose of striking fear into their hearts." A memorable event occurred while he was a young man working at the Houghton-Dutton department store in Boston. The owner placed a hand on Grant's shoulder and said, "Good boy!" causing him to decide, "Maybe I can amount to something after all." He went on to build a chain of more than 1,100 W. T. Grant stores as a way to bring affordable household goods to people. He set up the foundation to "further the understanding of people . . . that individual potential be more surely realized." He wanted the foundation to support the accumulation and application of usable knowledge.

A new kaleidoscopic view with different images of young people and their potential has emerged in the second half of the 20th century. My views have been shaped by the experiences I have had doing research and developing programs in adolescent medicine since the 1970s, working in the HIV/AIDS pandemic in the 1980s, writing health-care-reform legislation in Washington, D.C., in the 1990s, and, most recently, in shaping health policy as executive officer of the Institute of Medicine at the National Academy of Sciences. During the early years of my career, as the baby boomers became more visible, the special problems of youth gained prominence in research, policy arenas, and media coverage. More recently, researchers have linked youth development to the influences and context in which young people are growing up.

When the perspective is narrowed to the problem behaviors of young people, individuals are often the focus of interventions. But if the view is enlarged to encompass the role of adults in helping young people or the contributions that young people can make to society, possibilities for interventions grow. For example, to use a garden metaphor, if people think of a troubled adolescent as a weed, then the options may be narrowed to ways of removing that individual. Alternatively, if the image is one of a garden with a variety of plants, then the options for promoting growth would include consideration of soil quality, opportunities for light, added nutrients, and adequate space, water, and care. Some of the images and metaphors that will reflect our views of young people as we move through the next century are already visible, but the kaleidoscope is turning once again. During my time at the Grant Foundation, conversations with its board and staff, with colleagues in philanthropy, and with others around the country, such as Peter Benson and his colleagues at Search Institute, have contributed to what I believe will become a new shared vision—one with a focus, one in which the parts or pieces are arranged in a coherent picture of how we might foster innovative research and programs to encourage the nation to value young people as a resource.

Why Focus?

The overall mission of the W. T. Grant Foundation is to help people live up to their potential through the accumulation of usable knowledge. During the 65 years of its existence, the foundation has supported research in infant, child, and youth development, as well as other areas involving the social, medical, and behavioral sciences. The results of this work have contributed to the knowledge on which evidence-based policies can be constructed. Policies, laws, and regulations related to youth, however, are often not in sync with this knowledge. Public perceptions of this age group and the amount and type of supports available and resources expended are forces that ultimately shape the outcomes for this generation of young people.

In view of the fact that resources in philanthropy are growing, the strategic use of these resources is even more important. Foundations in the United States are growing in number and in financial resources. Among private foundations, the total value of assets grew more than 24% in one year—from $227 billion in 1996 to $283 billion in 1997. The total number of foundations is also growing, doubling from 22,088 to 44,146 since 1980 (Blum, 1999). Our assets have grown beyond $270 million to mark the point where our expenditures in program are in the range of $15 million per year (see Figure 1). A coherent sense of purpose and a programmatic focus are now essential elements of successful philanthropic investment (Prager, 1999).

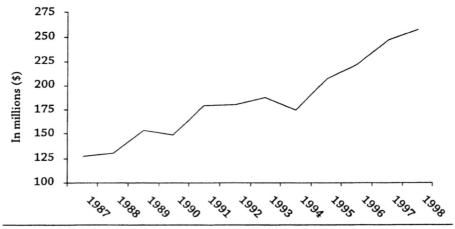

Figure 1. William T. Grant Foundation Assets, 1987–1998

The impact of our investment and our ability to track progress will, we hope, increase as the foundation focuses its program. By stimulating new knowledge, encouraging multidisciplinary work, evaluating and analyzing current policies and perceptions, and understanding and helping change the public's opinions of young people, William T. Grant's goal of fostering human potential will continue to be realized.

Why Focus on Youth?

At the beginning of the 21st century, both the role and the place of adolescents in our society are changing. There are four reasons why we have selected a focus on youth. First of all, there are more of them than ever before. In the United States, there are presently more young people between the ages of 14 and 25 (puberty to adulthood) than there were at the peak of the baby boom. Although adolescents comprise a smaller proportion of the population than the elderly, their absolute numbers are growing and will continue to do so for the next few decades. By the year 2005, there will be more than 40 million young people in their second decade of life, roughly half between the ages of 10 and 14 and another half between the ages of 15 and 19 years (Figure 2).

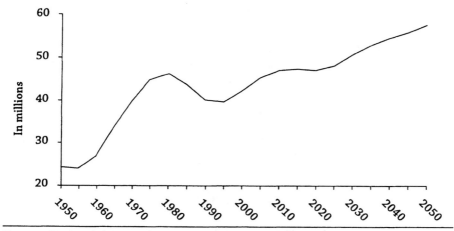

Figure 2. U.S. Youth (Ages 14–24), 1950–2050 (Source: U.S. Bureau of the Census, Current Population Reports)

Second, the teenage population of the United States is already more ethnically diverse than the adult population, and as young people age, the adult population will become increasingly diverse (Figure 3). We have an opportunity now, while they are still young, to learn about, and possibly influence, the ways different groups in a diverse population interact with each other. By listening to this generation, we may all learn how to value differences, instead of allowing differences to contribute to conflict.

Third, fostering the healthy development of young people should include efforts to help them become engaged citizens who are both economically and socially productive. Investments in young people will benefit them as well as the elderly, who will increasingly depend on the young as the ratio of retirees to workers grows. Yet, as a nation, we are not analyzing and approaching our investment in youth with the degree of care it merits.

Fourth, the time of transition from childhood to adulthood has expanded. Youth are maturing earlier and thereby engaging in some adult behaviors at earlier ages, while at the same time, the age for assumption of meaningful adult responsibilities, such as economic independence, is being delayed. Thus, the nature

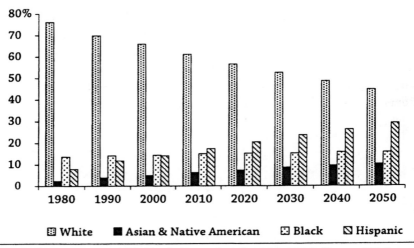

Figure 3. Ethnic Diversity of U.S. Youth (Ages 10–24), 1980–2050 (Source: U.S. Bureau of the Census, Current Population Reports)

and place of youth as a developmental period in the life course are undergoing profound change.

When William T. Grant was growing up at the end of the 19th century, hundreds of thousands of immigrants were coming to America. As they flooded the factories and schools, it became clear that the problems of poverty and of children working under terrible duress could no longer be ignored. It seemed to him that charity would alleviate only the immediate effects of "social dysfunction," manifested in poverty and sickness. To Grant, scientific research promised to uncover the causes of maladaptation rather than simply to relieve some of its symptoms. When the causes were better understood, the maladaptation could be prevented, and the foundation's work would contribute to human betterment and social progress. A focus on youth from this perspective is consistent with William T. Grant's concept and with his interest in gaining a scientific understanding and useful application of the factors that help young people live up to their potential.

Why Focus on Youth as a Resource?

Rather than concentrating exclusively on the problems of young people, the foundation's program will focus on promising ways to give young people a meaningful role in society. The idea is to capitalize on their fresh approach, talents, and energy. Until the recent downturn in 2001, the United States enjoyed a robust economy and its lowest overall unemployment rate in 25 years. But high rates of unemployment among our "forgotten half" of non-college-bound young people have persisted, although they have been ameliorated somewhat (Halperin, 1998). Many young people who should be facing the future with optimism and hope are alienated, separated by the growing "digital divide," and regarded by some as a threat to the well-being of others. In short, young people's needs for emotional security and stability, for a relevant education, and for a successful launch into adulthood are not satisfied in our flourishing economy.

Youth are not benefiting fully from this rosy economy, in part because they are not allowed to be full participants in it. Prolongation of dependency and progressive segregation of young people from the adult world without a meaningful role in society may contribute to the public resentment and suspicion that is too often exhibited against our young people. Paradoxically, at the very time youthful dependency is prolonged, puberty is starting earlier, with physical maturation beginning as early as age eight. This means that young people can spend close to two decades making the transition to adult status. Mid to late 20s is now the typical age for establishing independence from family. The median age of marriage in the United States is now 26 for young women, compared with 21 just two decades ago.

Since the baby boom peaked in the 1960s, researchers have concentrated on the ways in which adolescents differ from younger children or adults. These differences have been cast as problems that are unique to or characteristic of youth. Categorical approaches and programs devoted to each problem (e.g., adolescent suicide, unintended pregnancy) evolved, each with separate funding streams. Emphasizing the problems related to youth brought attention to the age group, but the results of this attention have been mixed. In some cases, increased awareness has led to amassing resources to lessen problems facing youth. In other cases, the focus on youth has led to a sense that problems are inherent in their age group and therefore not amenable to intervention. In yet other cases, reactions have led to demonization, or blaming young people for these problems.

Currently, we are experiencing a shift in the role of young people from one of producers to one of consumers. Corporations' investments in advertising to young consumers speak to their recognition of their buying power. For example, adolescents represent a $230 billion annual consumer market for advertisers. Although many people bemoan the large sums of money being spent on brand-name items or music or videos, the nature, extent, and impact of this phenomenon have not been fully elucidated. The diffusion of innovation from young people to adults is even less well understood.

For example, it is accepted that jazz and blues arose early in the 20th century from ethnic minority cultures that have greatly enriched our culture as a whole.

Currently, inner-city youth are prominent trendsetters in music and style, extending their influence to middle-class suburbs and international arenas, as hip-hop culture has spread globally. The relationship between young people and the market economy, the diffusion of innovation from young people to adults, and the growing disparity of access to some resources and to the levers of success in today's economy are important areas for further study.

During the past decade, a movement has grown to look more holistically at youth development. If a problem or challenge faced by young people is tied to a likely solution or intervention, communities may be persuaded to see what they can do to contribute to youth development rather than further alienating young people from the very supports that will be critically important in the long run. The concepts of developmental assets and asset-building community pioneered by Benson and his colleagues at Search Institute (e.g., Benson, 1997, and chapter 2) are particularly helpful in both defining the supports youth need from comunities and assessing how well comunities deliver these resouces. Among the findings emerging from this body of work are the differences between adults' and young people's views of these supports. Adults frequently report that their communities offer opportunities or resources, whereas young people from the same communities report a dearth of options, supports, and resources.

When adults are asked about their community, up to 80% view it as supportive of teens, while only 20% of teens in the same community agree with the adults' positive perception. Seeing youth as a resource for the community also raises other opportunities for them. If they are to be a resource, they need outlets for expressing their energy and talents. If they are a resource to be nurtured, they need encouragement, skills, and opportunities to build on. If they are a resource, they have value and should become the focus of investment.

Why Focus on Research on Youth Development?

For many years the main focus in developmental research was on infancy; this applied to the W. T. Grant Foundation's program until the 1980s. Recent research in brain development has fueled renewed interest in infancy and early childhood in many institutions. Although brain development continues through adolescence, more important to successful adolescent development is the array of current social forces that affect youth, creating an urgency for research and policy attention comparable to that for early development. Research has broadened from a consideration of early adolescent development to include late adolescence, when transition to independent living occurs. Researchers now study the larger context in which adolescents are developing: families, schools, peer groups, as well as the influence of political forces, the media, and new technologies, including the Internet.

Adolescents must acquire a different set of skills to succeed in making the shift from a manufacturing to a service and information-based economy. Societal views, expressed through laws, regulations, and policies, the amount or proximity of deadly conflict and consequent migration and disruption, and the development of new modes of communication, are all major forces molding youth. Encouragement of healthy youth development depends on understanding this wider circle of influences. When we lived in an agrarian society, children and youth were full participants in the household and family economy. As industrialization progressed, youth spent their days in factories and their nights in boarding houses. As a reaction to the exploitation of children, laws to prevent cruelty to children, the juvenile justice system, and public education evolved, accompanied by a dramatic alteration in our view of young people. Historians have described this change as a move from viewing children as economic assets to seeing them as economic liabilities, but emotionally priceless.

However, our affection for younger children does not extend to adolescents, it appears. Their transition to meaningful and productive roles in society has been increasingly delayed. The information-technological revolution is likely to have an impact on society as great as that of industrialization. It may provide opportunities for a new view of, and role for, youth. Clearly, young people are embracing new technologies, and some are participating in the creation of new opportunities in the new global economy. The discrepancies in access to new technologies and the tension between the use of the World Wide Web for public versus private interests are two pivotal issues that have arisen in the past decade that the foundation plans to explore.

Why Focus on the Systems Affecting Youth?

Welfare, education, juvenile justice, health, and workplace policies are all undergoing major changes. These changes will have a profound effect on the life experiences of young people. Research on youth should be the basis for constructing these reforms. But policies, laws, and regulations are influenced by forces that often have little to do with the results of rigorous empirical research. Adult perception of young people is one example. Balancing the rights of the individual with the needs and constraints of the community is difficult when adolescents are the center of discussion. If adolescents' immaturity or need for protection is emphasized, then restrictive approaches make sense. If, on the other hand, the emphasis is on adolescents' growing independence, their need for exploration, and acquisition of skills, then granting them adult rights and responsibilities seems reasonable.

Examples of this dichotomy include debates about punitive approaches to juvenile crime versus an emphasis on prevention, punishing minors who use tobacco versus restricting the promotion of and access to tobacco products, and passing laws that restrict gun purchases versus limiting or changing weapon manufacture. Clearly, policies will continue to be formed and reformed based on a variety of factors, of which evidence-based research is only one consideration.

Societies invest in social or human capital through their laws, policies, and allocation of resources. California, Texas, and New York are currently spending more on prisons than on secondary education. Although decisions to increase expenditures in one area (e.g., incarceration) are not necessarily directly linked to decreases in another (e.g., education), the impact on young people is nonetheless inarguable. Research and policy analyses are needed to examine the effect of these allocations and investments on youth, so that we can monitor the consequences, both intended and unintended, of these systems reforms.

Why Focus on the Public?

Analyses of media depictions of teens, especially of minority teens, indicate that they are usually painted in negative terms. Research suggests that the widely broadcast representation of youth as "superpredators" has had a substantial effect, especially on adults without adolescent offspring. In a recent study, adults were asked what first came to mind when they thought about teens. Adults with teenagers of their own spoke of their personal frustrations in raising adolescents, while those without teen children spoke about young hoodlums in trouble. This negative image also affects young people. In a 1994 survey by Children Now, youngsters reported that the way the media pictured them was upsetting, making them feel angry or sad. For youth to be portrayed positively, they felt they had to perform an extraordinary feat, such as winning an Olympic medal or a national contest.

It would be preferable if adults had an accurate picture of the real issues facing young people and a clear sense of what they might do to improve their lives. As a step toward understanding adult perceptions and possibly providing alternative ways in which adults might think about young people and support youth development, the W. T. Grant Foundation will explore the following activities. First, we will support analyses of current polls and surveys to better understand the basis of adults' and policy makers' views of young people. We will investigate the current "frames" and metaphors used by the media and the public, and devise and test new frames that emphasize the ways in which we can help or support youth and the ways in which they are an asset and contribute to society, while recognizing the considerable barriers they face. Shaping messages that help connect adults to young people is another appropriate way to create a "tipping point," encouraging more adults to think and behave in ways that are more supportive of young people.

We hope to increase the scientific understanding of how to change the way adults view young people, using evidence-based approaches and market-testing new frames. We will also support the development of scientific indicators that describe a range of supports as well as problems experienced by youth. Scientific indicators of the status of youth would be more useful if they went beyond the usual indicators of morbidity and mortality as expressions of health, or grade completion as a measure of educational achievement, for example, to include such dimensions as economic security, access to community resources, and other social-environmental factors. Indicators that look at both positive and negative outcomes, put into a meaningful framework of youth development, could contribute to the efforts to shape the public's perception of youth as a resource.

Assembling the Pieces to Reflect Change

William T. Grant developed retail stores that offered people goods at an affordable price. His employment philosophy was to create a family-like atmosphere that recognized the contributions of employees.

The foundation's work builds upon his notions of usable knowledge contributing to our understanding of human potential. The foundation will continue to support research and the scholarly pursuit of knowledge, but will now also invest in bringing good ideas, developed through research, to the public through the work of its grantees and scholars. But the ideas require more than the supply of well-conceived research, carefully crafted ideas, and thoroughly analyzed data. Getting the results of promising approaches out to the world of service providers, policy makers, and the public, engaging the energy and creativity of young people, allowing for the exchange of ideas among researchers, cross-fertilizing fields, creating new ones, and encouraging discussion and debate are vitally important roles for the foundation to play as well. Grant making alone cannot accomplish this. Convening meetings and providing leadership, technical assistance, means and strategies of communication, and a gateway for information about youth, are all appropriate roles for the foundation to play. Over the centuries marketplaces have been where people congregated to exchange goods as well as information and ideas.

At the beginning of a new millennium, we hope that the foundation will create a marketplace of ideas and information as well as a source of financial support. As we enter the new millennium, the kaleidoscope will continue to turn. The basic elements, however, will remain. Interpretation of the complex pattern that emerges will depend on the beholder. We hope to encourage a view, informed by research and evidence-based decisions, that will select a configuration of pieces that helps the nation value its young people and focus on the image of youth as a resource.

An Action Agenda for the New Millennium

> It is not possible for civilization to flow backwards while there is youth in the world.
>
> Helen Keller

Despite the celebrations at the end of the 20th century, an era does not end or begin on one day. Rather, the decades, centuries, millennia flow from one to the other. Our view may focus on a moment or slice of time, but events flow, like a river. We see only a segment of the river, but the flow continues and therefore our perception captures only a passing instant. Our view of young people is similarly limited if we consider only what is in our direct line of vision.

Adolescence is not an entirely discrete or separate phase of life. We arbitrarily separate this stage because of its special characteristics, but this is not meant to imply a sharp disjuncture between childhood and adulthood. We view adolescence as we view the part of the river within our gaze at the moment. As with flowing water, the lives of young people are directed by forces, both apparent and hidden, that they encounter. In turn, young people have an effect on those around them, much as flowing water sculpts and molds the land as it passes through: The land and the river are shaped by each other.

Visible forces shaping the life course of young people today include the rosy economy, generally low levels of unemployment, and a quiet, peaceful national scene. But beneath the surface are boulders and diversions shunting some off to marginal, stagnant backwater areas where egress is not apparent and flow halts.

The success of the U.S. economy has amazed everyone. By the end of 1999, the stock market had set new records. Similarly, the economy helped create 4.8 million millionaires, 250,000 decamillionaires, and 140 billionaires in the United States. Not all people benefited from the rosy economy, however. According to the U.S. Census Bureau:

- The poverty rate for 1998 stood at 12.7%—virtually the same as at the peak of the last expansion in 1989.

- Average income for families in the bottom fifth of the income scale fell 5% after adjusting for inflation between the late 1970s and the late 1990s.
- New York was one of nine states in which the richest 20% of households earned at least 11 times the income of the poorest 20%.

Further evidence of this point derives from a study of the most recent wave of the National Longitudinal Survey of Youth (NLSY). More than 9,000 12–16-year-olds were surveyed, and early findings were released at a conference sponsored by the W. T. Grant Foundation:

- Many families of these youngsters reported little or no net worth or financial wealth. Many families don't have checking or savings accounts; but, compared to teenagers in 1979, these young people reported higher expectations about going to college.
- Similarly, according to the Federal Reserve Bank's latest survey of consumer finances, the average net worth of families earning less than $10,000 a year has fallen by $6,600 over the past 3 years, while households earning more than $100,000 a year have seen their wealth jump by more than $300,000.

Some parts of the river are flowing fast. Teenage entrepreneurs, start-up Internet companies, and the power of youth as trendsetters and consumers have made some businesses focus exclusively on this segment of the population, spending $230 billion annually on advertising to them, marketing products such as clothing, entertainment, and sports equipment.

Attempts to channel youth have varied over the past decades. Some, taking the approach used by the Army Corps of Engineers, have promoted a containment or diversionary approach to controlling the forces thought to be destructive. During this decade, particularly in the juvenile justice arena, mandatory sentencing, treating young people as adults, "adult crime/adult time" and "zero tolerance" policies, and "abstinence only" funding restrictions all reflect attempts to contain and control young people. This approach is being questioned as data highlight the unintended consequences of these policies. Two examples are the lack of positive effects—or the destructive effects—of youth boot camps, and the implications of having one in three African American males involved with the prison system.

Juvenile violent crime soared in the 1980s, peaked in 1994, and has been declining since, yet the policies resulting from the punitive approaches crafted in the early 1980s persist. Currently 5,000–6,000 young people under age 18 are treated as adults by the criminal justice system. Kip Kinkel was sentenced to life imprisonment at age 17 for crimes committed when he was 15 years of age. Yet, often a wider set of considerations and perspectives is presented when news coverage persists after a tragedy involving young people. In the months following the Columbine tragedy, successive waves of coverage changed in character and emphasis. For example, the 1999 back-to-school edition of *Time* magazine featured a week in the life of high school students, giving a more balanced portrayal of the issues facing the majority of young people in the country. This shift in perspective from problems created by youth to the range of their life experiences and influences gives a wider view of the types of resources and investments that can help young people develop.

Shifting the gaze downriver gives quite a different view of youth development. Fight Crime: Invest in Kids, an organization supported by the foundation, has focused on disseminating research that indicates that the peak hours of juvenile crime occur after rather than during school (Figure 4).

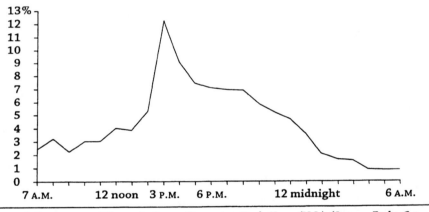

Figure 4. Percentage of Juvenile Crime Occurring Each Hour (U.S.) (Source: Fight Crime: Invest in Kids)

Communication studies demonstrate that the messenger as well as the message is critical in getting the attention of policy makers and the public. Thus, when law enforcement officials say that prevention is a good investment and explain the rationale for investing in prevention and after-school activities, policy makers and the public respond by putting more resources into safe spaces and programs. The combined efforts of people in research and credible messengers speaking about prevention have contributed to the increase in federal after-school funds from $17 million in 1997 to $200 million in 1998 and then to $450 million in the FY 2000 federal budget. The flow we witness is more complex than it might appear. The mixing and confluence of streams is revealing. I note here three examples.

Civic Development

Many young people are engaged in their communities, but voting may not be a measure of their commitment to contributing to a "civil society." The foundation's notion of civic development encompasses a wider view of ways in which young people participate.

For example, 73% of college students report doing volunteer work. Areas in which such volunteering occur are helping the homeless, teaching, religious service, or work related to the environment, health care, or social work.

Mixing School and Work

We often separate aspects of youth development into distinct categories, as if they were separate rivulets. We speak of the transition from school to work or the transition from living with one's family of origin to living independently. Schooling is not confined to adolescence, nor does work begin at the end of the teenage years for the majority of young people. Today the concept of lifelong learning has replaced the older notion of a specific school-age population. Most adults consider their learning to be ongoing as they acquire new computer skills or get training or attend classes that provide skills to bolster new roles or interests.

Similarly, the age of entry into the workplace is declining: The National Longitudinal Survey of Youth reports that two-thirds of 15-year-olds have freelance or institutionally based work experience. The balance between school and work, then, becomes a promising area of research that will promote the understanding of the real-life experiences of young people.

Lengthening the Adolescent Phase

We must also look at other, more distant rivers to gain a fuller view of youth. Most Western industrialized nations, along with the United States, have experienced a lengthening in the transition to adulthood. In 1999, the W. T. Grant Foundation partnered with the Jacobs Foundation in Switzerland to convene a group of scholars who looked at recent adolescent trends in various countries. They identified areas of congruence and divergence among and between these European countries and the United States across four areas:

- School and work;
- Living independently;
- Problem behaviors; and
- Civic engagement.

In Europe today, young people well into their 20s and 30s experience conditions traditionally associated with youth rather than with full-status adulthood.

In countries like Spain, Italy, and Poland, for example, young people tend to live at home with their parents for an even longer period of time than do their U.S. counterparts. In southern Italy, the average age to leave one's parents' home is now 34 years.

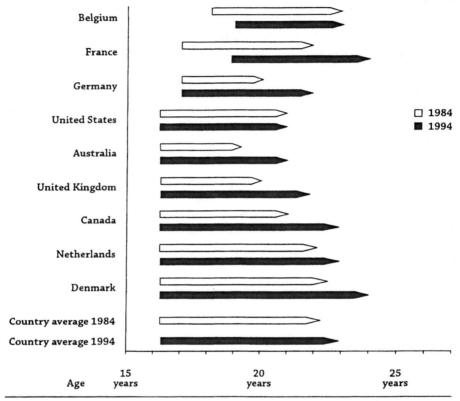

Figure 5. Length of Transition: Age Range of Transition from School to Work, 1984–1994 (Source: Organisation for Economic Co-operation and Development, 1996)

It is common throughout Europe for formal schooling to continue until youths are in their late 20s. This is partially due to the high cost of housing and the low wages associated with young people with lower educational attainment. The results? Delayed age of marriage and childbearing, as well as low fertility rates. For example, Italy's fertility rate for young adults, currently at 1.7, is below replacement level.

The prolongation of the transition from school to work is apparent when comparing 1984 and 1994 for nine countries. All nine countries showed an increasing prolongation of this transition, with some extending the average time of the transition well into the mid 20s, according to data provided by the Organisation for Economic Co-operation and Development (Figure 5).

Unemployment for youth who are not in school is surprisingly high for many European nations. In most countries, the rates of youth unemployment are higher for 15–24-year-olds, compared to 25–29-year-olds. Some countries, like Italy and France, report that at least 30% of the younger group were unemployed in 1996.

Poverty after taxes is another indicator of the status of young people. When compared to the total population in their respective countries in the mid-1990s, 18–24-year-olds did poorly, even in the Scandinavian countries, which are usually thought to be supportive of all citizens. For example, according to the Luxembourg Income Study, in Denmark the percentage living in poverty was 20% for 18–24-year-olds and only 8% for the total population (Figure 6).

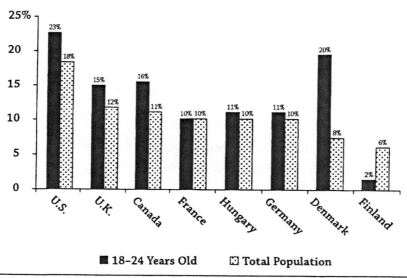

■ 18–24 Years Old   ▨ Total Population

Figure 6. Poverty after Taxes: Young Adults 18–24 Years Old Compared with Total Population, Mid-1990s (Source: Luxembourg Income Study)

Migration patterns had altered significantly by the end of the 20th century. Countries that used to be sources of migration are now recipients. For example, today Italy receives many Croats. Countries in Europe thought to be quite homogeneous in terms of cultural traditions and populations are already confronting issues related to the recent infusion of cultural diversity. For example, inner-city London now has a majority of youngsters from other cultures enrolled in its schools. In New York City, the borough of Queens is reportedly the most culturally diverse area in the United States, with the greatest number of people of different nationalities represented per square mile. Moreover, throughout the world, there has been a significant migration within countries of young people from rural to urban settings. It is projected that there will be 300 million more young people living in cities than in rural areas by the year 2025 (Figure 7).

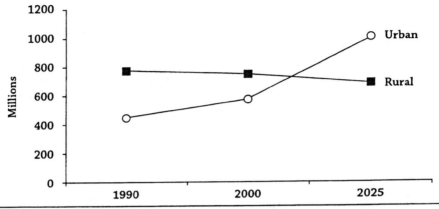

Figure 7. Youth Population Living in Urban and Rural Areas in Developing Countries, 1990–2025 (Source: UNICEF, World Assembly of Youth, 1995)

Whether we invest in or exploit young people as they are buffeted about by these trends and currents is a pressing question.

Innovations in Programs for Youth

An understanding of the flow patterns involving young people is leading to innovative approaches. The creation of a cabinet-level Unit for Social Exclusion in the United Kingdom is one example. Recently the unit was instructed by the prime minister to work with other departments to assess how many 16–18-year-olds are not in education, work, or training, analyze the reasons why, and reduce the numbers significantly. This is in contrast to the categorical approach to problems and problem behaviors that tend to be the focus of U.S. funding in past years.

The federal budget for youth programs in the United States is revealing in several ways. There is a fragmentation of both funding streams and offices, agencies, and congressional committees responsible for these resources. At a time of devolution, when states are being asked to consolidate programs, the federal picture is, indeed, a complex one. The federal government is now asking (or requiring, in some cases) that states combine funding streams for categorical problems (like sexually transmitted diseases and unintended pregnancies) to create more holistic programs and approaches. However, federal funding and the structure for appropriating resources continue to be highly fragmented. The 1995 Institute for Educational Leadership Policy Exchange Report, *Who Controls Major Federal Programs for Children and Families,* is subtitled *Rube Goldberg Revisited,* and refers to the effects of "trickle-down fragmentation" on families and communities. Moreover, some of the new initiatives that are meant to help the nation invest in youth have stipulations or unintended consequences that may, ironically, reduce rather than expand opportunities. For example, Department of Labor initiatives like the Youth Opportunity Grants and Workforce Investment Act of 1998 contain new restrictions for summer school employment requiring year-round job availability on the part of the employers. In New York City, given the way in which summer jobs are currently constructed, the number of opportunities may, as a result, decrease from 45,000 to 5,000.

Let us expand our view beyond a single stream or river and consider the collective presence and force of this age group. Young people viewed globally are an important part of the world's human and social capital. As with rivers, we must strike a balance between exploiting and preserving youth's productive potential.

The Convention on the Rights of the Child is one expression of the wider view of the potential value and force of this age group. The convention has strong international support. Only the United States and Somalia have yet to ratify the overall agreement. The proposed revised convention calls for raising the minimum age of volunteer soldiers above 15 years, the convention's current standard, and would prohibit drafting children younger than 18. There has been a recent compromise on the strict age limit that would prohibit recruiters from signing up 17-year-olds who today can join the military with parental consent. Last year, 49,900 enlistees were 17 when they joined the U.S. armed services, but only 2,500 had not turned 18 by the time their training was complete. Experts have estimated that as many as 300,000 children are fighting in wars, from Africa to Chechnya to Latin America. Many of them have been drafted against their will.

Conclusions

The history of the William T. Grant Foundation is also one of flow, not discontinuity. Our current focus, "helping the nation value young people as a resource through innovative research and programs," builds directly on our long tradition of research and evidence-based approaches to current societal issues.

The foundation's historic flow was broadened and quickened this year. The "value" of the foundation can be viewed in several ways. Our assets continue to grow. We enter the new millennium with assets of $280 million, roughly twice the amount we had a decade ago. We are joined by a growing number of new individual and institutional partners in philanthropy.

In the United States, giving from individuals increased by nearly 10% in 1998 to nearly $135 billion, and foundation giving increased by 22% over the previous year to a record $17 billion (Figure 8). Our value must extend beyond the roughly $10 million we give annually in grants. Our role in helping others value young people—through convening meetings, disseminating research-based findings, and helping people find ways to engage with and invest in young people—generates values beyond grant making.

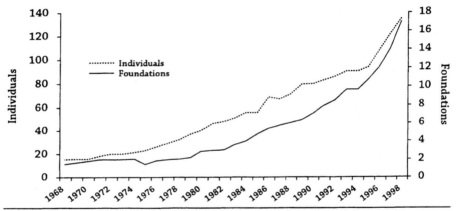

Figure 8. Giving by Individuals and Foundations, U.S., 1968–1998, in billion $ (Source: Philanthropy, *November–December, 1999)*

The nature of the flow of ideas from scholars' research to public policy and public understanding has been an area of recent discussion at the foundation. The need to focus on the interplay of people and ideas is encapsulated in the term "strategic communications." Because we recognize the need for new expertise, both internally and from advisers, we have created a new officer-level position, vice president, strategic communications, to develop a vision for this aspect of the foundation's work and to direct it.

The program of the foundation flows from the "blueprint" developed and approved by the board in April 1998. It is the chart we are using to navigate our course. Our work is not solitary. It flows along and commingles with the efforts of others. We are actively forming partnerships with other foundations. Examples include the Markle Foundation in the area of the impact of new technologies on youth; the Jacobs Foundation in understanding the transition from adolescence to adulthood; and the Kellogg, Ford, Edna McConnell Clark, DeWitt Wallace,

Surdna, Annie E. Casey, Robert Wood Johnson, and Henry J. Kaiser Family foundations regarding both youth development and strategic communications.

As we allow our gaze to shift from that part of the river directly before us to that part downstream where the river is heading, we gain new perspectives. Babies born in 2000 will be ten in 2010, 20 in 2020, and 30 in 2030. It is their journey that we are now following. Their experiences will be channeled by the current set of contours and forces we have helped to create in their lives. They will have their impact on us and on each other as they progress. We will become more skillful in our use of technology because of them, as they act as teachers and mentors for us. We will have new technologies because they will invent them. We might reconsider some of the artificial barriers and constraints to their flow that we have constructed over past decades. We might, instead, look at the landscape as it fits with the flow of the river—guiding, not containing it. By understanding the nature of mixing and pressures, we can provide outlets, bridges, and intake valves as needed, always recognizing the power and value of the forward flow.

Observing the flow of young lives can be a passive experience that we watch from the shore. Or, we can play a more active role and swim into the river, recognizing our connection as adults with young people. We can look ahead, intent on anticipating our shared fate, watching for evidence of turbulence in the current, always aware of our collective powers to use the creative force of flow.

References

Benson, P. L. (1997). *All kids are our kids: What communities must do to raise caring and responsible children and adolescents.* San Francisco: Jossey-Bass.

Blum, D. E. (1999, April 22). Foundation giving rose 22% in a year, report says. *Chronicle of Philanthropy, 11,* 14.

Cahan, E. D. (1986). *The William T. Grant Foundation: First fifty years, 1936–1986.* New York: William T. Grant Foundation.

Halperin, S. (Ed.). (1998). *The forgotten half revisited: American youth and young families, 1988–2008.* Washington, DC: American Youth Policy Forum.

Prager, D. J. (February 1999). *Raising the value of philanthropy: A synthesis of informal interviews with foundation executives and observers of philanthropy* (pp. 6–7). Washington, DC: Grantmakers in Health.

Part III

Building Families and Communities Serving Youth

6 Building Assets in Real-World Communities

Raymond P. Lorion and Harris Sokoloff
University of Pennsylvania

For more than a decade, scientists at Search Institute have committed them-selves to identifying, assessing, and documenting the developmental implica-tions of human "assets" (Leffert et al., 1998). As Peter Benson explains in chap-ter 2, assets represent psychosocial resources that have been linked conceptually and empirically to optimal development in youth. The resources identified thus far include environmental qualities (i.e., the 20 external assets) and individual characteristics (i.e., the 20 internal assets; see Chapter 2, Table 1). These 40 as-sets have been identified through a systematically scientific investigatory se-quence. A reasonably comprehensive analysis of relevant developmental, psy-chological, and social science literature (Scales & Leffert, 1998) informed the construction of a paper-and-pencil survey measure that, over the past decade, has been administered across a relatively wide range of ages and grade levels (grades 6–12) across economic and cultural subgroups. Aggregating survey re-sponses across hundreds of settings with hundreds of thousands of children, Search Institute investigators have produced an encouraging and heuristically exciting body of evidence linking measured asset levels with selected develop-mental outcomes. Specifically, Scales, Benson, Leffert, and Blyth (2000) report significant positive correlations between asset levels and desirable developmen-tal outcomes (i.e., "thriving behaviors" such as "succeeds in school," "delays gratifi-cation," and "overcomes adversity") and negative correlations with undesirable outcomes (i.e., "high-risk behaviors" relating to substance involvement, anti-social behavior, and school problems). Table 1 lists the two categories of develop-mental outcomes (i.e., thriving indicators and high-risk behaviors) considered by Search Institute investigators.

In a recent discussion of assets with community parents, the authors likened youth development to a flower. The audience was asked to consider past ef-forts to shape youth behavior toward desired outcomes through the repetitive

Table 1. Indexes of Health and Risks

Thriving Indicators	High-Risk Behaviors
Succeeds in School	Alcohol Use
Helps Others	Tobacco Use
Values Diversity	Illicit Drug Use
Maintains Good Health	Sexual Intercourse
Exhibits Leadership	Depression/Suicide
Resists Danger	Antisocial Behavior
Delays Gratification	Violence
Overcomes Adversity	School Problems
	Driving and Alcohol Use
	Gambling

recitation of rules; nagging about unmet responsibilities, incomplete tasks, and missed opportunities; and even verbal and physical intimidation as similar to attempting to hasten a flower's growth by pulling on its stem. The preferred alternative among gardeners is to prepare the soil in a way that maximizes the growing conditions for the flower. In a sense, assets represent the soil conditions, nutrients, moisture, and available sunlight. Challenges to growth, such as inclement weather, threaten the outcome but can be mitigated by an optimal and, as necessary, protective growing environment. Creating such environments represents the defining purpose of building assets. An important, indeed primary, quality of the assets is their assumed mutability—their responsiveness to efforts to change their presence, intensity, availability, and effectiveness. Assets below capacity level presumably can be increased; when absent, they presumably can be established.

The authors' discussions with colleagues and community members suggest that assets may be nonorthogonal and that changes in some appear likely to reverberate in others simultaneously or sequentially. As we measured asset levels in youth, presenting and explaining findings and their implications to the community (including youth, their parents, and local policy makers), the systemic quality of the assets structure became increasingly clear. Their inherently "social" nature became apparent as we reflected on the likelihood that changes in assets can be targeted at the individual, family, setting (e.g., school), neighborhood, or community levels. Yet, we speculated that lasting change was unlikely if limited to either the individual or the family. Intuitively, it seemed to us that family-level changes were needed to promote as well as sustain individual change. Similarly, changes in family support seemed hardier if echoed by neighbors, by those in developmentally significant settings, and ideally by local norms and values. If valid, this line of reasoning implies that changes in one or more levels may be necessary but not sufficient for lasting positive changes in developmental trajectories.

Our discussions led us to consider how external and internal assets were related. Again, it seemed reasonable to assume that these categories were related, perhaps transactionally such that changes in either enhanced the likelihood of changes in others. Presumably, such transactions would occur both within (i.e., external or internal) and across (i.e., external and internal) asset categories. As noted for levels of change, perhaps lasting developmental change requires enhancements of both external and internal resources. In effect, each is a necessary but insufficient condition for achieving desired improvements in youth's lives. As we will discuss later, we are convinced of the heuristic merit of such intuitions and speculations and intend to pursue a series of these questions in future research. Ideally, readers of this chapter and this volume will be similarly encouraged to expand their understanding of assets and their implications for optimal development of youth. Benson supports this line of inquiry in his reference to "asset-building" communities as potential components of "asset-building culture."

Unquestionably, work completed to date on assets represents only the tip of the iceberg in terms of its potential contribution to our understanding of positive and negative development in youth. A critically important next step in research on the developmental assets is to establish through longitudinal prospective studies an understanding of the nature and level of the causal linkages between assets and developmental outcomes. One would also seek to determine whether specific assets, solely or in combinations, are more or less relevant to increases in certain thriving behaviors and decreases in certain risk behaviors. One must also identify which assets are best changed at which level of intervention (i.e., the individual, family, neighborhood, or community), and how the resulting change radiates across levels.

It should be noted, however, that assets are not the only elements that may change. After all, reported relationships among assets, thriving indexes, and risky behaviors suggest bi-directionality of influence. A transactional-developmental perspective (Sameroff, 2000; Sameroff & Chandler, 1975; Sameroff & Fiese, 1989) would reasonably predict that the presence of thriving indicators has a positive impact on an individual's responsiveness to changes in assets and that risky behaviors negatively affect receptiveness. Moreover, one needs to determine how assets vary across time, setting, and circumstance. Are they ever-present once they exceed some to-be-determined threshold level, or does their potential positive impact vary similar to risks (Bell, 1986)? Assuming that the aforementioned linkages can be untangled, and that assets, thriving indexes, and risky behaviors respond to intervention, Search Institute investigators have opened a most important door to the enhancement of youth and, consequently, to their preparation for adulthood. The implications of such effects for altering the social fabric have, to date, resided in wishful thinking.

Toward a New Developmental Paradigm?

In the authors' view, the program of research undertaken thus far and seemingly within reach has the potential to move the developmental and mental health sciences toward a paradigmatic shift (Kuhn, 1974). As Kuhn explains, such shifts do not occur often or easily. Nor should they. Paradigms, after all, encompass far more than merely a dominant conceptual perspective on how phenomena under its aegis operate. A paradigm identifies which aspects of those phenomena merit attention, how that attention is to be applied methodologically, and in what sequence questions about the phenomena are to be addressed. The work of science may be likened to gathering and organizing bits of information until, in jigsaw puzzle fashion, one has accurately reproduced a picture of how some aspect of the natural world operates (e.g., human development generally or the evolution of aggression and aggressive acts specifically). A paradigm represents assumptions about how the "picture" will look when complete. This picture is shared by members of the relevant scientific disciplines and by those who apply their knowledge bases. A paradigm contains within it the methodological rules by which pieces are sought, identified, and connected. It informs scientists regarding which parts of the puzzle are ready to be integrated into the current puzzle and which should be held back until other pieces or sections are complete. In that way, a paradigm offers, at least implicitly, a chronology for the investigatory sequence. In that sense, it determines when the "time is ripe" for the field to recognize "new" discoveries and locate them within the assumed framework of discovery.

Paradigmatic dominance also explains why important additions to knowledge may be rejected or simply ignored. Findings discovered too early (i.e., before their adjacent surroundings have been organized) may, for a short or long time, be "orphaned." A part of the puzzle, even an important part, may not be appreciated until adjacent pieces have been found and put into place. Alternatively, the new knowledge may belong to an alternative picture of the phenomenon.[1] The

---

1. Kuhn refers to such pieces as "anomalies" and to such alternative pictures as competing paradigms. A paradigm shift occurs when the alternative replaces the dominant set of assumptions about how the phenomenon of interest develops, operates, and changes.

circumstances for a paradigmatic shift occur when an increasing number of pieces are identified that do not fit the expected picture but, when combined with other seemingly orphaned parts, suggest an alternative picture of the phenomenon. The shift occurs when there is agreement that the alternative requires little, if any, shifting of existing completed sections while allowing for the placement of the heretofore orphaned pieces. Understandably, shifts generate considerable scientific excitement and activity. As the previously unused pieces are placed together, sizable portions of the puzzle take shape and confidence grows in the accuracy of its presumed final image.

As noted, we do not believe that the work completed by Search Institute justifies at this point a paradigmatic shift in the developmental and mental health sciences. Many questions remain and much has yet to be done to establish causal links and confirm that reported findings can be generalized across settings, populations, and time. What does seem clear is that the institute's work is sufficiently innovative in its methods, findings, and implications to stir the kind of excitement described by Kuhn (1974) as antecedent to a paradigmatic shift. It is also evident that the excitement has scientific and well as political implications at multiple levels. This chapter identifies and examines some of those implications for the relevant human sciences, human services, and, importantly, day-to-day life of youth, families, and the communities in which they live.

Into the Fray

Our sensitivity to the political implications of Search Institute's work emerged within our ongoing efforts (our initial independent efforts soon became collaborative) to assist two local communities in understanding and responding to the needs of their youth. One of the authors (H.S.) joined a committee of educators, service providers, policy makers, and citizens of a nearby affluent suburban community. The committee's concern was catalyzed by the events at Columbine, Jonesboro, and other suburban-rural locations at which school-based shootings had occurred. Acknowledging its demographic similarity to many of these tragic settings, the local community sensed that it could no longer simply assume its capacity to protect its children. Deciding to "do something," they chose to conduct a community-wide assessment of youth to inform the design and targeting of selected or created programs responsive to identified needs. After considerable discussion and examination of alternatives, the committee was impressed by Search Institute's focus on positive development rather than pathology and on its optimistic assertion that its findings could readily be linked to positive change efforts.

In 1999, the community contracted with Search Institute to assess youth enrolled in grades 7 to 12 in public and private schools throughout the community.[2] As reported below, the resulting survey *(Search Institute Profiles of Student Life: Attitudes and Behaviors)* gathered information about the external and internal assets, risky behaviors, and thriving indicators of nearly 3,000 middle and high school youth. Given the community's leadership in acknowledging its concerns, in organizing sources to fund the resulting assessment, and tireless efforts to effectuate data collection, all involved were optimistic about the benefits of the anticipated open discussion of "the problem" and its solution. The community's initial response to the positive and negative results was most encouraging. Not only was feedback provided to many segments of the community, including policy makers, educators, and youth, but that feedback appears to have prompted substantive discussions of what the data reveal and what needs to be changed, by whom and in what priority.

Concurrently, the other author (R.L.) was assisting an elementary school in a densely populated, generally impoverished, and predominantly minority urban neighborhood. His involvement was a response to the school's attempts to understand the bases for significant academic and behavioral problems presented by its students and to introduce strategies for their resolution. As expected, the team of university faculty and graduate students of which he was a member invested significant time initially in gaining the trust of the school and its surrounding community. Based on past experiences with such settings, the team anticipated and encountered considerable hesitancy and some negative reactions from neighborhood families to its expected recommendation that the team, community representatives, and school personnel (including faculty, staff, students, and parents of students) collaborate on the design, administration, and analysis of a survey to assess their youth in terms of risks and resources. That process of negotiation continues and now includes the expectation that the resulting consortium will assess and improve the general learning and behavioral climate within the school prior to conducting the survey. In effect, the consortium appears to be saying that enough is known currently about areas in need of intervention that some steps must be taken both to improve the quality of the setting immediately and as evidence of "good faith" on the part of the university team. Most recently, the school's leadership and faculty have identified steps to be taken. Specifically, they have requested programs to (a) reduce the disruption created throughout the school by 10–12 problematic students;

2. The survey organizers justifiably took considerable pride in their capacity to forge an unprecedented partnership between the public and private educational sectors. Doing so was essential if the results were to represent the community's economic and ethnic diversity and, most important, were to be used subsequently as the basis for identifying areas for community change.

(b) calm the turmoil experienced daily as 800–900 children move back and forth in an aging three-story building between lunch and recess within a two-hour period; and (c) deliver support and discipline to students unable to remain in classrooms because of academic or behavioral difficulties, respectively. The seeming intransigence of such problems has so overwhelmed and demoralized staff and students that further studies of youth and their needs seem "academic" (in the worst sense of the term) without relief in each of these areas. Essentially, we must show results or be shown the door.

This demand relates directly to the authors' expectations about the political obstacles to be encountered and overcome in this and comparable urban neighborhoods. We have assumed that resistance to yet another study would reflect the frequency with which urban families and communities feel they have, at best, limited opportunity to participate in the planning and conduct of research on "them." Residents of such communities often have little influence on decisions about what to measure and how to do so. That does not, however, protect them from being "blamed" for the developmental deficits and behavioral transgressions of their youth identified with the selected methods. Nor does it alter their expectation that they will be abandoned by those who measure and report such findings (Lorion & Hightower, 2001). Thus, the care with which the work had to evolve was anticipated by the university team and in retrospect (as explained below) was perhaps complicated by that expectation. Rather than resistance to our involvement, the concern was expressed about the caution with which we seemed prepared to act. The school and its families sought *immediate* interventions and, as we have noted, set that as the quid pro quo for data collection. That any intervention would influence and potentially bias the data was, as stated explicitly by one school administrator, "not their problem." One parent wryly noted that one cannot study the prairie until the fire is out. Politically, we had to comply if we wanted to stay long enough to assess the developmental assets of their children.

Similar political complications arose from our failure to anticipate the responses of our suburban community partner. Based on their enthusiastic involvement in selecting, planning, and implementing the survey, we did not expect these highly educated, affluent, and youth-oriented community residents to respond as they did when presented with the survey's results. We expected them to challenge evidence of problem behaviors and asset deficits by raising questions about the scientific qualities of the measure and the accuracy of the analyses. We expected defensiveness and, in some ways, heard indifference at times and a sense of impotence at other times. As Alice experienced in her travels in Wonderland, we found ourselves out of balance as partners in the suburbs became protagonists and presumed urban reluctance became irritation at the slowness of our efforts. As we will explain in some detail, we found ourselves confronting the results of a Search Institute survey whereby assets seemed transformed into risks; risks seemed transformed into thriving indexes; resources seemed to obstruct optimal development and responsible maturation; and the youth who responded to the survey seemed, among all of those involved, most able and willing to understand the results of the survey and the reactions of those who had sought and sanctioned the survey.

Prior to describing the survey results and ongoing planning, we offer our perspective on how an orientation toward human resources and positive functioning challenges extant scientific and professional emphases. That shift in orientation appears to have the same "Wonderland" quality for raising uncertainties about the relative meaning of positive and negative, health and pathology, and helping and harming. In the process of our work, we have increased our already emerging appreciation of the essential complementarity of quantitative and qualitative methods in understanding how wellness and pathology surface in youth and their communities (Sullivan, 1998). Of particular value has been the emergence of "deliberative conversations" as an effective and welcome tool for deciphering a community's code for its expectations for youth and the consequences and rewards of transgressing or meeting those expectations.

Collaborative Research and Action through Deliberative Conversations

Our communities were understandably wary of the seemingly automatic response of social scientists to conduct and report on the results of a survey. Prior encounters with that approach had left each community feeling somewhere between "so what?" and "what's next?" Each admitted feeling uneasy about which questions to ask and, most important, how to proceed with the answers. They also appreciated their need for information and for new ways of looking at how to help their youth. One of the authors (H.S.) introduced the qualitative method of "deliberative conversations" as a response to their concerns.

From the outset, it became evident that both the communities with which we were working, and the developmental, educational, health, and mental health disciplines to which we belonged and on whose knowledge bases we relied, struggled with reaching agreement on defining concepts such as "health," "wellness," and "successful" development in youth. However committed all involved were in optimizing the development of youth, improving their educational performance, and enabling their successful adaptation to the challenges of adolescence, clear, unambiguous answers were not available to guide our work. Developmental psychopathology has merged insights and findings from many disciplines to solidify the realization that human development is a transactional process that occurs within and across behavior settings that themselves are shaped by social and cultural forces (e.g., Rutter, 2000; Sameroff, 2000; Sroufe, 1997). Since each discipline within the aforementioned behavioral health consortium has slightly different normative structures, their respective definitions of "health" and "wellness" differ in important ways. Similarly, the two communities with which we were working differed in their criteria for developmental success of their youth.

The reality of these differences complicated the likelihood of reaching consensus within and across each community on identifying and resolving the needs of youth. Negotiation and mediation techniques are often used to work through such disagreements and try to build bridges among stakeholders. Old styles of working on such challenges (e.g., debate and negotiation) are frequently inadequate for this task. Rooted in opposition, each presents the opportunity for "winning" and "losing" (Yankelovich, 1991, 1999). Debates, for example, start with the assumption that there is a "right" answer and that someone has it. Each side in a debate argues the strengths of its position and the weaknesses of the opponent's position. In a debate, each side listens intently for flaws and weaknesses in order to assert the validity of one view over the other. Albeit less concerned with "right" and "wrong," negotiators are no less concerned with winning and losing. In a traditional negotiation, each side focuses on getting as much as it can for itself and its adherents. This is true both for labor contracts and for international peace treaties, as well as our current discussions with local communities. The goal is to give as little as possible and to gain as much as possible. Right or wrong (or true or false) is less important than one side's net gain relative to the other's net loss.

To move beyond the frequently unavoidable impasses that arise from debate and negotiation, Fisher, Ury, and Patton (1992) offer an alternative form of negotiation. Their process modifies traditional negotiation strategy by shifting the focus from "positions" to "interests." In positional bargaining, "each side takes a position, argues for it, and makes concessions to reach a compromise" (p. 3). This is inefficient, produces bad agreements, and endangers ongoing relationships. The alternative, variously called "principled negotiation" or "interest-based negotiation," goes beneath public positions to focus on the interests, or human needs, that underlie those positions.

Adding deliberation, which is a collaborative process, potentially enables participants to appreciate common interests and how collaboration can contribute toward achievement of shared interests. Deliberation assumes that each participant has something to contribute to solving the question before the group. That outcome depends on listening to each other, on understanding rather than countering the bases of arguments and positions, and on finding points of shared or proximal agreement. Listening deliberatively allows participants to enlarge, and perhaps change, their point of view. Ideally, this result occurs because participants submit their best thinking so that other people's reflections may improve rather than destroy that thinking. This listening process involves weighing pros, cons, and potential trade-offs in order to find areas of common ground for action toward the achievement of shared interests (Gutmann & Thompson, 1996; Mathews, 1999; Mathews & McAfee, 1999; McCoy, Emigh, Leighninger, & Barrett, 1996; Yankelovich, 1999).

Unlike informal discussion, deliberation has a structure to support its goals. That structure includes the following components:[3]

1. *Opening*, in which the issue or topics to be discussed are presented and the group is charged with the work it has to accomplish;
2. *Personal stake*, in which participants are asked to share at least one of their concerns about the topic to be discussed. Here, participants typically tell stories of how this issue affects them or someone they know;
3. *Deliberation*, in which participants weigh different ways of looking at the issue, discuss major directions for action or policy, the pros and cons of each, the trade-offs they are and are not willing to make, and the underlying values that drive their opinions and beliefs on the issue. Here, participants, perhaps with the assistance of a moderator, will ask each other questions for clarification and offer constructive comments for the group to consider. For example, the following kinds of questions will be helpful:
   - questions that connect the issue to people's real lives and concerns;
   - questions that ask people to weigh the costs and consequences of each choice until they have begun to hear others' perspectives and to acknowledge conflicting values (both within themselves and between each other);
   - questions that ask people to weigh the costs they are willing to accept in order to achieve the results they want;
   - questions that probe each person's statement until others can under-

---

3. The work of the National Issues Forum Institute (www.nifi.org) and the Study Circles Resources Center (www.studycircles.org) provides two different, but related, structures for deliberative conversations.

stand what he or she believes should be done and why (avoid letting people end with "ain't it awful" or "if only" statements);

- questions that encourage the speaker to make a connection between the actions he or she would advocate and what is important to him or her;
- questions that promote interaction between participants;
- questions that invite others to respond to what has just been said; and
- questions that give people an opportunity to identify what they have heard that reveals a shared understanding of the problem, a new option they have created, or costs the group cannot accept; and

4. *Reflections*, in which participants think back over the deliberative conversations to review their own thinking and the thinking of the group, as well as next steps. Typical questions here might include: How has your thinking about X changed? How has your thinking about the thinking of other people change? Have you detected any common ground for action through the course of the deliberations? What trade-offs do you think people were and were not willing to make? What tensions still need to be addressed? What can you/we do with what you/we now know?

Deliberative conversations thus involve one or more guided considerations of an issue that includes as many stakeholders as possible. For our purposes, it was apparent to us from the outset that defining health, wellness, and community goals for the development of youth could not be left to professionals, whether in health, mental health, or education. For the work to have salience, and for substantive changes to be initiated, it was essential that the public, including parents, students, and policy makers, be engaged in discussions of what questions were to be raised, how they were to be raised, and how responses were to be interpreted.

Support for our position comes from Heifetz's (1994) discussion of the role of experts in addressing three different problematic situations. Regardless of the kind of fracture (simple or compound), a broken arm fits into Heifetz's Type 1 situation in which the problem is clear and has a technical (although not necessarily simple) solution. In such a case, the primary locus of responsibility for the work would be with the technician (e.g., the physician) who applies the solution with little or no additional learning on the part of the service provider or recipient. By contrast, bipolar disorder represents for Heifetz a Type 2 situation. The problem is clear insofar as it meets diagnostic criteria, but the solution or treatment requires additional information on the part of all involved. To understand and solve the problem, the provider needs to view the problem from the recipient's perspective, especially within the context of the recipient's lifestyle and social ecology. In turn, the recipient needs to learn about the problem and solution options from the perspective of the provider. Since both have learning to do, they share the primary locus of responsibility for work that is both technical and adaptive.

We believe that defining and pursuing health, wellness, and successful human development fit into Heifetz's Type 3 situation. Neither the problem nor its solution is clear or easily or neatly defined. The provider and the recipient together must learn more about the situation, the problem, and possible solution(s) to identify the problem. The solution and its implementation also require learning, and often that learning means that the primary locus of responsibility for the work—which is more adaptive than technical—sits with all the parties. Deliberative conversations are ideally suited for the adaptive work we need to undertake in our respective communities (presented later here as case studies) as they identify stakeholders and invite them to participate in a collaborative examination of the health and welfare of their youth.

Veering toward Health and Wellness

We must acknowledge that both communities seemed somewhat surprised by our discussions of assets, health, and wellness. They expected us to focus on problems, provide data about "how bad things were," and propose solutions. Our perspective, however, reflected a somewhat different, although emerging, emphasis in the behavioral sciences. Imagine for the moment that the mental health professions primarily focused on mental *health* and wellness. Were they to do so, a substantial portion of their time and effort would be invested in defining the parameters of emotional and behavioral health, identifying characteristics of people and settings associated with healthy outcomes, and understanding the processes underlying their occurrence. In effect, their agenda would shift from focusing on defining, identifying, and removing or reducing *unwanted* developmental outcomes to defining, identifying, and enhancing *wanted* developmental outcomes. To do so applies a different set of lenses to the work of theorists such as Barker (1968), Bronfenbrenner (1979), Cicchetti (1984), Erikson (1963), Freud (1956), Lerner (1998), Piaget (1952), Rutter (2000), and Sroufe (1997). Were that to occur, the mental *health* sciences (i.e., psychiatry, clinical psychology, social work, the neurosciences, and psychopharmacology) would expand their perspective and identified partners to incorporate the theories and methods of the developmental, educational, social, and environmental sciences in their investigations.

In effect, a framework would emerge within which contributions from this broadened array of disciplines would converge toward an understanding of the emergence of behavior along the range of adaptation and adjustment across settings and over time. As the current boundaries of the various sciences flex to complement each other, the resulting science of *behavioral health* [4] would represent a whole that is substantially greater than its disciplinary parts. Whether it would be sufficient to tip the balance toward a paradigmatic shift or simply contribute to that outcome, we cannot determine. We do believe, however, that movements in this direction have import for the future of youth-oriented studies and services moving them toward positive rather than negative orientations. Inquiry into the developmental assets is an important catalyst for this movement.

Thus, a genuine integration of developmentally relevant sciences could have significant scientific and clinical ripples. As noted earlier, rather than focus on the assessment and treatment of the relatively few individuals within the population presenting *diagnostic* conditions, behavioral disorders, maladjustment, and underachievement, the emerging consortium of behavioral health disciplines would seek to find ways to sustain and increase the majority who cope, adapt, and succeed.[5] From that perspective, increasing the number and levels of assets available to youth creates an environment in which health is more likely and risky behaviors less likely. Thus, from an assets perspective, one need not choose between serving those who display positive development and those who seem to be veering toward trouble. Rather, it is assumed that increases in developmental assets, like a rising tide, raise all ships. An individual, family, neighborhood, or community with increased assets would provide an environment of care and support for those in need of treatment, of protective risk reduction for those in need of preventive interventions, and of health-promoting nurturing for the development of wellness. Rather than emphasizing risk factors

4. The term "behavioral health" reflects the authors' position that optimal development extends beyond the avoidance of disorder to the ability to recognize and respond effectively to the emotional and behavioral demands of interpersonal and noninterpersonal situations. It is also offered as a catalyst for reexamining extant knowledge bases for their potential fit in an alternative picture whereby the developmental and mental health sciences focus on positive coping and adaptation as the informational base from which maladjustment and pathology will be understood.
5. Of considerable importance to the work of this scientific consortium will be recognition of the importance of understanding how "success" is defined, who participates in that definition, and who is affected by its adoption.

that trigger vulnerability, consideration of developmental assets shifts attention to identifying and understanding those protective factors and positive experiences that contribute to the creation of healthy environments and a rising tide for all youth. The need for such a shift in perspective has long been recognized.

Nearly four decades ago, Dumont (1968) labeled as "absurd" the willingness of the mental health disciplines to wait until disorder was established before intervening. In his view, concrete evidence of that absurdity was reflected in the perspective that a "successful" practice was marked by an ever-full waiting room and an equally full "waiting list." Dumont recognized that the mental health disciplines relied for their survival on continuing need and demand for service. A related dimension of the absurdity was the assumption that professional involvement could not begin until the patient arrived. For much of the past century, mental health services overwhelmingly served those whose pathogenesis approached or met diagnostic criteria. At the same time that Dumont voiced his revelation, Caplan (1964) and others (e.g., Albee, 1982; Cowen, 1973; Kelly, 1974) recognized that delaying service delivery until need was established was driven not by avarice or choice but rather by the failure to recognize alternatives. In his seminal work, *Principles of Preventive Psychiatry,* Caplan (1964) encouraged the mental health disciplines to appreciate and adopt the long-held public health axiom that no disorder has been controlled through treatment but only through prevention. Following Caplan's lead, a few pioneers catalyzed a series of investigations that continue to the present to develop interventions which prevent the onset, continuation, and sequelae of emotional and behavioral disorder.[6] Although still early in its evolution, this movement has established the viability of early identification and reduction of risks leading to reductions in the incidence and prevalence of disorders (Albee & Gullotta, 1997; Durlak, 1997; Durlak & Wells, 1997, 1998; Mrazek & Haggerty, 1994). Evidence reported to date sustains the assertion that the mental health sciences can proactively identify and reduce factors that place individuals at risk for pathology.

It must be noted, however, that Search Institute's agenda intentionally seeks to move the mental health fields yet another step away from focusing on dysfunction and disease. As explained by Benson, Leffert, Scales, and Blyth (1998), "The framework of developmental assets establishes a set of benchmarks for positive child and adolescent development, weaving together in an a priori con-

---

6. Readers are encouraged to review Albee (1982, 1996), Cowen (1973, 1996), and Mrazek and Haggerty (1994) for descriptions of early steps in the acceptance and pursuit of preventive interventions in the mental health disciplines.

ceptual model a taxonomy of developmental targets requiring both family and community engagement to ensure their acquisition" (p. 143). Their work echoes Cowen's (2000) decade-long investigation of the seemingly simple yet clearly complex question that can be paraphrased as, "How does the majority of the population move through the life span in ways that reflect adaptation, coping, and problem-solving?" Consistent with Search Institute's position, Cowen (1994) urged the fields to move beyond risk identification and reduction to answer such questions. Calling on the idea of a rising tide, he noted that understanding the conditions under which health and wellness occur would substantially benefit not only a broad segment of the population but also those at risk for disorder. Pursuing insight into the occurrence of wellness is not, in Cowen's view, a step away from those in need. Risk reduction and prevention and health promotion and wellness are not inherently competing interests. Rather, each represents a pathway to the common goal of reducing pathology and enhancing health. In turn, health and pathology represent ongoing *processes* of interaction between the person and environment rather than fixed states.

Developmental Contributions to Health Perspectives

Understanding the processes and factors that enable most individuals to respond to daily challenges can inform the design of interventions that might introduce or increase the elements necessary for effective coping in those at risk. Furthermore, it must be explicitly recognized that those whose emotional or behavioral problems meet diagnostic criteria also display evidence of coping, adaptation, and adjustment. Health and pathology are not mutually exclusive conditions, nor do they reflect the permanent and continuous presence of one set of characteristics in the former and the total absence in the other. Bell (1986) has noted that the levels of risks vary throughout a child's lifetime; as we stated earlier, we expect the same will be true of developmental assets, thriving indexes, and risky behaviors. None of these seems to represent an invariant characteristic of either individuals or settings. Moreover, can an asset (e.g., family support or explicit boundaries) be present but not used? Can an asset be used but not effective? Work by Pike, McGuire, Hetherington, Reiss, and Plomin (1996) and Plomin and Daniels (1987) on "nonshared" environments supports these likelihoods and argues for research to identify how individuals take advantage or not of the availability of assets. Therein lies the complex defining agenda for a behavioral health science—namely, to understand most individuals across settings, circumstances, and time. In effect, a science of behavioral health must seek to promote wellness in "everyone," "every day," and "everywhere." As we discuss later, Search Institute's work on identifying the links among the presence of assets, indexes of health, and participation in risky behaviors may offer a means to test Cowen's thesis. By requiring that assets be mutable, Search Institute investigators can proactively examine the question of whether enhancing resources for health reduces vulnerability to disorder.

Developmental psychopathologists offer an important clue into understanding disorder that, we believe, applies also to health and wellness. Specifically, they have explained the difficulty of linking specific antecedents to specific disorders by demonstrating the salience of "equifinality" and "multifinality" to pathogenesis (Cicchetti & Rogosh, 1996; Sroufe, 1997). The former, equifinality, refers to evidence linking multiple antecedent conditions (e.g., familial disruption, child abuse, academic failure) to specific forms of pathology (e.g., conduct disorder); the latter, multifinality, reflects evidence linking a specific antecedent condition (e.g., familial disruption) with multiple distinct pathological outcomes (e.g., conduct disorder, substance abuse, depression). Complicating the matter is the widely recognized fact that most individuals exposed to those antecedents do not subsequently present symptoms of pathology. Lorion (2000) argued that a viable explanation for the widely varied outcomes associated with risky antecedents is that the individuals involved differ in terms of the resources (i.e., assets) they have available and the contexts in which they are required to address these risks. Adaptation and coping thus become the default condition when at least the minimal tools and situational characteristics are present to withstand and resolve the demands arising from the developmental challenges heretofore identified as risk factors. Search Institute's work is very consistent with this perspective. To exploit the opening they have provided, however, the aforementioned behavioral health consortium must combine their conceptual resources and investigatory methods.

The need for integration across multiple social, behavioral, and developmental disciplines has been recognized by those invested in the design and implementation of interventions to prevent emotional disorders and promote emotional health (e.g., Cowen, 2000; Lorion, 1999, 2000). The emergence of such interventions reflects growing scientific and lay acceptance of public health's long-standing argument for avoiding rather than treating disorder. It also reflects appreciation of the salience of contextual factors for the expression of internal states. In essence, it rests on an expanded and more complex "diathesis-stress" disease model (Lilienfeld & Lilienfeld, 1980) in which the initial reference of diathesis to individual genetic or congenital predispositions broadens to include vulnerabilities due to characteristics of settings and circumstances in which one develops, and stress refers, perhaps, to the timing, intensity, and duration of situational encounters or experiences. Seemingly, the mismatch between demands and the individual's resources to respond to those demands represents the conditions that trigger pathogenic processes whereby vulnerabilities move toward disorder and maladjustment. As Wakefield (1997) explains, disorder cannot develop without the combination of malfunctioning mechanisms that result in socially negative consequence; that is, disorder reflects "harmful dysfunction." In effect, some natural function must fail *and* that failure must result in harm to the individual as defined by her or his social context. The developmental assets approach seems consistent with that perspective. It explicitly highlights the psychosocial parameters of health and disorder and hypothesizes how external factors ally with internal strengths and weaknesses to influence developmental outcomes.

Increasingly, those involved with prevention and promotion efforts have come to recognize the importance of investigating the processes underlying individual-contextual transactions (Mrazek & Haggerty, 1994; Rutter, 2000; Sameroff, 2000; Sameroff & Chandler, 1975; Sameroff & Fiese, 1989). Of equal importance to unraveling the theoretical and methodological challenges associated with normative and pathogenic processes is solving the complications that arise as one attempts to translate theory and empirical findings into interventions that are acceptable, affordable, and, most important, demonstrably and consistently effective. If, as assumed by Search Institute, assets are, in fact, responsive to change in desired and predictable ways, significant opportunities may exist for both enhancing competencies and resources associated with the development of health and reducing risks associated with the occurrence of pathology. Within their framework, neither diathesis nor stress defines inevitability. Rather than focus on the potential for pathology in all, their perspective highlights the potential for health and positive growth in all. In their system, all soil can be enriched and all moisture and sunlight maximally used to nourish all flowers.

Presumably, therefore, the analysis and manipulation of assets open the way for the behavioral health sciences to uncover new insights into the design of human settings (e.g., homes, schools, workplaces, recreational facilities, neighborhoods, and communities) that support the development, maintenance, and application of health. The promise of Barker's concept of behavior settings may thus finally be actualized. As defined by Barker (1968; Barker & Gump, 1964; Barker & Shoggen, 1973), a behavior setting represents the organized impact of environmental characteristics on determining how individuals behave (for better or worse) within a given setting or situation. Wicker (1979) explains the underlying process as follows:

Behavior settings are self-regulating, active systems. They impose their program of activities on persons and objects within them. Essential persons and materials are drawn into settings, and disruptive components are modified or ejected. It's as if behavior settings were living systems intent on remaining alive and healthy, even at the expense of their individual components. . . .

. . . to summarize some of the essential features of behavior settings. Most of them can be presented in a single sentence: A behavior setting is a bounded, self-regulated, and ordered system composed of replaceable human and nonhuman components that interact in a synchronized fashion to carry out an ordered sequence of events called the setting program. (p. 12)

Some may read Wicker as suggesting that settings force a specific set of behaviors and only those behaviors to occur within their boundaries. Such contextual determinism was neither perceived nor intended in Barker's work. Rather, he maintains that setting characteristics contribute to the *probability* that certain behaviors will occur and that others will not. A basketball court, for example, presents strong demands for certain activities. If a ball is available, it is highly likely that someone will dribble it and attempt to shoot it through the basket. If it is not, it is likely that someone will act as if he or she is shooting a ball toward a basket. Neither behavior, however, is likely to occur if a graduation ceremony or piano recital is under way. In other cases, some individuals may simply sit in the stands and talk while others use the floor space to exercise, jog, or do nothing. Nor will all who are present in the gymnasium behave alike during an actual game. Players on the court will behave quite differently than those on the bench. Given the location and orientation of the bleachers, most in the audience will watch the game and respond positively or negatively, depending on what occurs on the floor and which player(s) or team is involved. The characteristics of the setting pull for each of these. They do not, however, preclude some in the audience from ignoring the game and socializing with those around them. They do not preclude some from reading, listening to another game on the radio, or even writing a class assignment.

Thus, the characteristics of the setting contribute to the likelihood that certain, presumably desired, behaviors will occur but cannot guarantee their occurrence. We believe that the same is true for developmental assets. External assets, in effect, represent psychosocial characteristics of settings. To the extent that assets are available to an individual, family, neighborhood, or community, the conditions are present for positive growth and development. Those outcomes thereby become more likely, though not inevitable.

The preceding discussion revisits the question of how developmental "success" is defined and measured. Reaching agreement about definitions of health and wellness represents a complex political and moral challenge for the behavioral health disciplines. For whatever agreement is reached to have salience, however, the scientists and theorists would need to involve representatives of the general public across the age span as full partners in their deliberations. The selection of participants in such deliberations would itself represent a significant political process, and, if pursued openly and patiently, could represent an unprecedented opportunity for all involved in questions of health and wellness to examine their assumptions about:

- Settings involved in the development of youth;
- Those who occupy such settings as providers of something, recipients of something, or observers of something;
- The respective roles of those occupants; and
- The value to be attached to their respective viewpoints.

We offer "deliberative conversations" as one approach that could allow for the systematic examination of Search Institute's definition of assets, risky behaviors, and thriving indicators as salient elements of human development. How much agreement is there among youth, parents, educators, and the general public about the value of each of these elements? How are disagreements across these groups to be resolved? Who decides—youth, parents, or the community—which assets to target for increase and which risky behaviors to target for reduction?

Laying a Foundation for Behavioral Health

The behavioral *health* sciences, reconceptualized as a multidisciplinary prevention and health promotive consortium of social, behavioral, and educational sciences, must, in collaboration with those they intend to study and effect, arrive at a broad-stroke blueprint of how emotional and behavioral health develops and is applied across variable and changing circumstances. Such a knowledge base would, we believe, offer an optimistic glimpse into the potential for psychological engineering whose potential to improve the human condition approaches, equals, or perhaps exceeds that promised by the Human Genome Project. Undertaking such a line of inquiry within a planned program of research would reflect, for the behavioral sciences, a paradigm shift in the fullest sense of Kuhn's (1974) articulation of that concept. Within a comprehensively ecological framework (Kelly, 1966), the emerging prevention and health promotive sciences would become conceptual and methodological partners in the systematic identification of (a) the components of effective functioning; (b) the mechanisms which trigger their emergence singly and in combination; (c) the individual and contextual conditions for their expression, inhibition, expansion, or dissipation; (d) the limits of and circumstances for determining their malleability; and (e) the conditions under which interventions for their optimization can be implemented and sustained.

Such a shift in focus from pathology to positive functioning requires the development of the capacity to assess mental *health* within an individual, family, group, neighborhood, or community. Presumably, the resulting knowledge base would inform the design of a program of research to develop psychometrically sound and culturally sensitive measures of mental *health*. Search Institute investigators offer one such approach in their assessment of thriving indicators, risky behaviors, and developmental assets. Central to any measurement approach is examination of the reactivity of the phenomenon of interest (e.g., mental *health*) to the measurement procedures themselves. How would one confirm the presence and extent of the aforementioned individual and contextual characteristics? Through interview, questionnaire, observation, or structured activity? From whom would information be gained? The individual? Those with whom he or she interacts? Those who witness such interactions? Who would gather such information? Would functioning be assessed traditionally (e.g., within a professional setting) or naturally? How would temporal characteristics within and across developmental stages be handled?

Pathology typically has been assessed by a lone professional who interacts solely with the individual being assessed. In the role of diagnostician, the professional attempts to understand how that individual child or adolescent, for example, is cognitively, emotionally, or behaviorally functioning at home, school, and in the community. The answers to those and related questions are sought in settings and under circumstances alien to the person being examined and disconnected from the circumstances for which behavioral prediction is sought. In a small proportion of assessments undertaken within a family or systems perspective, the underlying concept of pathology results in including one or more members of a family within the assessment format under controlled (or time limited) circumstances.

Based on the questions presented, the problems to be solved, and the reactions observed, the professional makes an "informed" judgment about current and future status. Presumably, insights into the nature, persistence, and precipitants of identified pathological processes allow for predictions about subsequent emotional, behavioral, and cognitive functioning. With information gained in a limited amount of time under circumstances unlike most that would be encountered by most individuals, conclusions are drawn about underlying processes that compromise an individual's capacity to adjust, adapt, and resolve demands on his or her emotional, behavioral, or cognitive capacities. Astonishingly, such assertions are generally assumed to be correct even if rarely confirmed. Once its presence has been asserted, pathology is assumed to reside within an individual, to be expressed under the "right" circumstances.

Cannot the same, therefore, be said about health and wellness? Given the relative infrequency with which pathology is reflected in epidemiological surveys and the overwhelming predominance of its absence rather than presence in the general population, should it not be assumed ever present and expressive? That such an assumption is not made, that we speak of unexpressed pathology as "in remission" rather than absent, reflects the fact that far more attention has been paid to confirming the presence of pathology than health. Thus, our assessment procedures and emphases have focused on finding weakness rather than strengths, deficits rather than talents, and failings rather than fulfillment.

What if that were not the case? How would we go about reversing this situation? At least with pathology we have available a sense of the negative and justify the narrow scope of assessment procedures by the specificity of our presumed target. By contrast, health is defined, at least in part, as the capacity to handle the familiar as well as the unfamiliar; to relate to family members and friends as well as strangers; to be at ease in known settings and to become at ease in novel circumstances. Thus, application across a broad array of settings and circumstances is a defining characteristic of that process heretofore labeled health and wellness. How such characteristics are to be represented in measurement procedures adds to the aforementioned challenges. How essential was it for Search Institute to include risky behaviors within its survey foci? Would communities and the behavioral health sciences have equal interest if assets and thriving indicators alone were being measured? To the extent that Search Institute's measures and findings lead to research and interventions focused on those elements per se, the shift from pathology to wellness can be actualized. Doing so challenges many of the field's assumptions about what is important and how its mission is defined.

As noted, the solution to this challenge is not readily found in the traditions of the mental health disciplines. Psychometric procedures have long differentiated state and trait characteristics but not the underlying mechanisms that differentiate them. Specifically, under what circumstances do the former change and the latter not? Do some characteristics have "statelike" qualities for some period before stabilizing and appearing "traitlike"? How much variability can a trait display before being considered a state? How little can a state display before being considered a trait? Those are not trivial questions, for a similar measurement perspective appears to be reflected in the procedures for measuring developmental assets. Although not asserted by Search Institute's scientists, the interpretation of reported survey findings as inventories of the number or percentage of youth from various demographic subgroups who have this asset or present that thriving indicator gives rise to the assumption that risks, thriving indicators, and even assets are somehow fixed in time. If so, how readily are any of these elements changed? If only with considerable effort, then their equation with fixed entities may be justified. If, as suggested in many of Search Institute's reports (e.g., Benson, this volume), assets are highly responsive to intervention, one must assume that they are equally responsive to secular trends, political decisions, economic shifts, and so on. If such is the case, then attempts to influence asset levels must both account for and be sufficient to overcome these other influences.

One's view of the nature and mutability of assets probably reflects one's underlying assumptions about the nature of mental health. Recently, Lorion proposed "viewing wellness or well-enough as the normative state involving the *active* pursuit of equilibrium and adaptation characteristic of most individuals under most circumstances" (2000, p. 17; emphasis added). Underscoring the qualifier "active" is intentional. Therein lies an essential distinction between conceptualizing health as a characteristic of individuals that carries across settings and situations or as a dynamic process whereby the appropriateness of emotion and behavior reflects neither deeply rooted dynamics nor historically conditioned responses but rather the results of an ongoing, immediate integration of past history, present circumstances, and future intent. From this perspective, health is a continuous reflection of ongoing developmental, emotional, and behavioral adjustment. Within this perspective, an asset is part of a system for recognizing and resolving developmental demands.

The dynamic of this system may be viewed in relation to Piaget's understanding of cognitive development and intellectual functioning:

> Piaget further proposes that organisms tend toward equilibrium with the environment. The organism—whether a human being or some other form of life—tends to organize {cognitive} structures into coherent and stable patterns. His ways of dealing with the world tend toward a certain balance. He tries to develop structures which are effective in his interactions with reality. This means that when a new event occurs he can apply

to it the lessons of the past (or assimilate the events into already existing structures), and he will easily modify his current patterns of behavior to respond to the new situation. With increasing experience he acquires more and more structures and therefore adapts more readily to an increasing number of situations. (Ginsburg & Opper, 1969, pp. 23–24)

If health represents an equally active, albeit more general, *activity* rather than a state and the *application* rather than presence of trait characteristics, then the measurement of mental *health* must necessarily be capable of representing that *process*. Resolution of that challenge appears a necessary antecedent to modeling the structure of psychological "DNA." Absent from the developmental assets framework is any way of modeling that dynamic quality. Hence, we have as yet no way of depicting how a change in an asset or a thriving indicator or a risky behavior affects the others and the functioning of each depends on the functioning of others.

As that puzzle is gradually pieced together, the mental *health* disciplines must examine explicitly whether health-related characteristics can and should be altered to optimize their level and, most important, their substantive nature (Lorion, 2000; Sarason, 1984). This question is not rhetorical, nor is its answer obvious. It is raised in appreciation of Sarason's (1984) examination of efforts to apply social and behavioral sciences to achieve "desirable" social change. His inquiry into whether "science and technology {can} continue to ignore the possibility that what they give to society is frequently a very mixed blessing, that like all other institutions they suffer from the passion of partnership and the self-serving stance" led him to assert that "because something can be studied or developed is in itself an insufficient base for doing it however wondrous it appears to be in regard to understanding and controlling our world" (p. 480). As discussed below, the question of *who* decides the defining parameters of health presents the public, policy makers, and members of the relevant scientific communities with truly difficult philosophical, ethical, and social issues. Consensus appears easier to achieve about the forms of emotional, behavioral, and social responses that are *not* desired than about those that are. Debates about the former, as yet unresolved and most troubling, appear barely to hint at the level of controversy associated with the determination of what is acceptable, from whom, under what circumstances, and for whom it is acceptable. The authors' preliminary steps toward these issues confirm that their resolution is as essential as it is challenging.

As noted earlier, antecedent to the design of interventions to achieve psychological health and wellness, we must develop reliable and valid measures of each.

Yet, as Helmstadter (1964) explained nearly four decades ago, traditional psychometric science is designed to *differentiate* individuals just as traditional statistical techniques are designed to examine levels and sources of variation within and across individuals. Were similar emphases reflected in measures of health and wellness, then:

> Whether conceptualized categorically, statistically or dynamically, wellness has the potential to become yet another parameter by which people are categorized and differentiated. If that were to occur, levels of wellness other than the idealized end-state could be interpreted as another index of relative deficiency. Inevitably, then, the "less-than-well" could be deemed in need of repair. (Lorion, 2000, p. 11)

Concern that wellness could become a proxy for yet another deficit meriting remediation applies directly to assessments of developmental assets. If conceptualized dichotomously as either present or absent, the development of assets has one meaning, namely, to increase their availability and accessibility. If, however, assets are conceptualized as relative, their development refers to efforts relative to their availability, accessibility, *and* adequacy. The last would result in interventions to increase the level of an asset and its utilization within individuals. For the authors, that in itself could become problematic.

Contrary to earlier assumptions, the prevention sciences have begun to appreciate that preventive interventions can be harmful. Years ago, Lorion (1987) urged consideration of this "other side of the coin." Gordon explicitly considers this iatrogenic potential in his alternative nosology for preventive interventions (Gordon, 1983, 1987). For both conceptual and pragmatic reasons, Gordon challenged the applicability of public health's traditional primary, secondary, and tertiary categorical triad. In its place he proposed that interventions to prevent negative emotional and behavioral conditions be differentiated into universal, selective, and indicated interventions. The titles of these categories refer to the specificity of targeting but also to the requirement that the intensity and intrusiveness of the intervention (hence, its potential for harm) must be balanced by its level of risk. Both Gordon's alternative categories and his caveat have been adopted by the Institute of Medicine's review of the prevention field. The focus on the avoidance of negative outcomes, however, has not changed. Justification for intervention has remained in the reduction of rates at which negative states occurred. The asset-building perspective offers a significant alternative whose positive focus is reflected in the fact that achievement of program goals serves all in a community whatever their level of risk.

The Development of Assets within Two Communities

Case Example 1: A Suburban Trial

One of the points of the deliberative process is to proceed through what Yankelovich (1991) calls the seven stages of moving from individual opinion to public judgment. Those seven stages move individuals and groups from unstable and varying opinions to solid and thoughtful judgment. In the first phase, "consciousness-raising," people start to recognize that there is an issue (stage 1) and develop a sense of urgency about it (stage 2). In phase two, "working through," people start to explore choices for dealing with the issue (stage 3) and then experience resistance to facing costs and trade-offs, which produces wishful thinking (stage 4) and then weighing pros and cons (stage 5). In the last phase, "resolution," people take a stand intellectually (stage 6), which ends in their making a responsible judgment morally and emotionally (stage 7). While our experience suggests that deliberative conversations are most useful in the middle stages, we have seen the contribution they can make at each of the seven stages Yankelovich discusses. We are beginning to see how the data from the *Search Institute Profiles of Student Life: Attitudes and Behaviors* survey can be used to move citizens through those stages.

Our suburban community is located west of Philadelphia near the beginning of what is known as the "Main Line." It contains mature residential communities of tree-lined streets, sylvan parks, and preserved natural areas, interspersed with dynamic commercial enclaves. The community has an approximate population of 60,000, 7% of which are minority (about two-thirds of those African American and most of the remaining, Asian). The township includes an area of 24 square miles and is one of the wealthiest communities in the state and nation. The township has many communities within its boundaries, each with its own feel and sense of identity. Many of those neighborhoods have their own smaller community shopping areas, some of which are among the region's finest upscale shopping districts. The public schools have earned the reputation as some of the best in the region as well as the country. The district offers a challenging academic program, along with a variety of extracurricular activities, including intramural and interschool athletics and instrumental and choral music at all levels. While the public schools have earned excellent reputations, the district is also home to more than 12 private schools (K–12), many of which also have excellent reputations. By most measures of social and economic capital, this setting is resource rich and, as a behavioral setting, should potentiate healthy adjustment among its youth.

The community, for example, has had a Drug and Alcohol Council for many years. In 1999, the council was expanded and renamed Community Advocates for Safe Youth (CASY), reflecting its concern following the wave of school shootings in presumably safe communities. In the process, CASY membership was expanded to include representatives from the school district, recreation department, and police departments, local hospitals, community centers, ElderNet, and Care Consortium of the Main Line, as well as teachers, counselors, parents, and students.

In 1999, CASY applied for a Healthy Communities grant offered through the county health department in order to purchase the *Search Institute Profiles of Student Life: Attitudes and Behaviors* survey. The grant was received in 1999 and again in 2000. As described earlier in this chapter, the survey was given in the spring of 2000 to the 7th–12th graders and 9th–12th graders in the public and four of the private schools in the community. A total of 3,000 students completed surveys. CASY selected the survey because it was interested in a portrait of the attitudes, behaviors, and needs of its youth, as opposed to many surveys that only ask students if they drink, take drugs, or are already engaging in a specific negative behavior. For CASY, Search Institute's tool captures information from young people about their feelings and about support systems or lack thereof, and is better able to alert CASY as to the vulnerability of some children even before the negative behaviors occur.

In the fall of 1999, the superintendent of the local school district called a meeting of some community leaders to discuss a proactive response to a series of events across the country, of which the shootings at Colorado's Columbine High School were only the most recent at the time. He thought there might be a need to create an umbrella organization that could pull together the individual initiatives in the community and become a resource in a coordinated and functional way. One goal was to make sure that resources were well known to each other so that the work of each could build on and complement the work of the others. In calling this group together, the superintendent asked one of the authors (H.S.) to facilitate the meeting. He was clear that this was to be a community activity, not one of the school district. After two meetings, a local community coalition emerged with representation from private and public schools, community government, police, health care, and state and federal government. Together, they have developed the following mission statement: "The Community Coalition is a coalition of community agencies and individuals working together to foster an atmosphere where children feel safe, secure and included. The Community Coalition will plan and conduct activities and make resources available that support the safety, security and inclusion of children in the Township and Borough. The Coalition's hope is to create a healthier community environment that will be of benefit to all residents."

Being proactive is key to the motivation behind surveying students. Residents of the township believe they have a wonderful community, which holds high academic, social, and moral expectations for its youth. Its children are high achievers, both in school and in community service. At the same time, the community realizes that neither it nor its youth are immune to the pressures that characterize contemporary life, or to the kind of exceptional behavior one saw in the shootings at Columbine and elsewhere, or to the kind of risky behaviors that show up in the press as students are seriously injured or killed in car accidents as a result of drinking or the use of inhalants.

When we received the data reports from Search Institute, a small group took on the task of working with the results, to make sense of them and figure out how best to report them back to the community. At that point the second author (R.L.) joined the working group, and together we spent about six weeks going over the data and discussing it. At the end of that period, we made several presentations, first to the heads of the schools that were involved in the survey and then to parents on the public school Inter-School Council (ISC). The response to the data at those initial meetings was disappointing but not unexpected. Administrators and community leaders were hardly surprised by the findings, whether the levels of risky behavior or the levels of thriving indicators. Nor were they surprised that students reported a weakening of boundaries as they got older. In fact, administrators, teachers, and students alike pointed to the later data as contributing to the increasing levels of risky behaviors as students moved through high school. Administrators lamented that there isn't much they can do to enforce boundaries if parents do all they can to protect their child(ren) from the consequences of breaking boundaries. Parents at the ISC meeting were less sanguine and more surprised by the data.

From those initial meetings, as well as from conversations among the working group, five themes emerged as important for the community: (1) support and communication, (2) boundaries and expectations, (3) exposure to violence, (4) the nature and extent of drug and alcohol use, and (5) sexual activity. We then used those themes as the basis for reporting the data back to the community as a whole at a community forum held at one of the local colleges. We structured the meeting to allow for both a plenary report out of the survey data, as well as small-group work with each group focusing on one of the themes. Previous experiences led us to expect around 100 people at this meeting. To our amazement and gratitude, more than 350 people came out. This unexpected turnout forced us to modify our plans for "small-group" work. For while we had sufficient rooms and facilitators to run small groups for 200 people, our space limitations forced some of the groups to encompass 30–35 people in rather cramped quarters.

The conversation in the small groups indicated that different people in the community were at different stages in their thinking about the five themes raised by Search Institute's data. Some were still at Yankelovich's "consciousness-raising" phase. For some, the data was a wake-up call, whereas for others, the data increased their sense of urgency. From the reports of those who participated in the community meeting, however, some common ground emerged.

Most who participated in the community meeting seemed beyond Yankelovich's consciousness-raising phase. The majority seemed to be at the "working through" phase (stage 3). For example, one of the small groups focusing on boundaries and expectations spent a significant amount of time and energy exploring the ways in which boundaries—primarily family boundaries—may be unclear to children and quickly acknowledged that part of the problem was the variety of boundaries different families set for children. Outlining the variety of boundaries led to a very preliminary and tentative identification of some choices for dealing with that aspect of the issue (stage 3). Almost immediately they confronted two possible barriers. The first came in their inclination to focus on "the problem." Regaining a balance between clearly identifying "the problem" and focusing on positive goals and assets will be a recurring challenge. The second barrier became clear in the question of how parents, within and across families, might come to an agreement on a common set of expectations for children and adults. Part of this is connected with the question of whose boundaries and expectations should become the community standard. In working through this issue, participants began to experience some of the resistance regarding costs and trade-offs that Yankelovich discusses. But they also began to see that they had a range of community assets that might be useful down the line.

Unlike informal conversations among friends, this meeting led neither to wishful thinking (at least not yet) nor to a sense of futility. Group members did probe each other, starting with stories and asking questions connecting actions to values, as well as questions asking people to weigh the costs they are willing to accept in order to achieve the results they want. In this way, exploring consequences and bringing together people from the same township, who were not yet neighbors or friends, seemed to generate optimism that some common ground could be reached.

We are still at the beginning of these deliberative conversations. We have much work to do if we are to get beyond the working-through phase to resolution. We know this is a slow process, and we know that only a small portion of the community is involved, but we seem to have made a good start. And we have a sense of our next steps. We have asked those involved in the community meeting to join us again, to continue those deliberative conversations in what we are calling an "intergenerational workshop to set community goals." Prior to the meeting, we continued to analyze the data and advised the media in ways that sustained community attention to the issues and continued to raise residents' consciousness about their youths' assets and risks. We continued to solicit people's input about the findings and their sense of "choices," which must be considered if they are to build community assets. The community must also begin to organize around assets, not just deficits, as it works to move through Yankelovich's stages toward the resolution of identified concerns.

Case Example 2: An Urban Trial

Two years ago, the University of Pennsylvania entered into an agreement with the School District of Philadelphia to participate financially and programmatically in the development of a K–8 neighborhood school in nearby West Philadelphia. Contiguous to the university's campus, including its schools of medicine, dentistry, and veterinary medicine and their affiliated clinical facilities, this neighborhood reflects many of the characteristics of low-income urban America. The neighborhood is economically, racially, and culturally diverse. Although its population is primarily African American, families from many cultures live within its borders. Local schools provide ESL classes for children from families speaking more than 40 different languages. A portion of that diversity reflects the families of university faculty and staff.[7] The community includes many single-parent families who are unemployed, underemployed, or have multiple jobs in order to gather adequate income. Most live in row houses (two to three floors) built in the early 1900s; many of these housing units are in need of costly maintenance. Scattered throughout the neighborhood (and increasing in frequency as one moves away from the university) are abandoned buildings that are boarded up against intruders but provide shelter to homeless individuals and families and cover for the illicit activities of drug dealers and users. Most neighborhood streets are relatively narrow, crowded with cars but improved somewhat due to a recently initiated, citywide "blight reduction" program that

---

7. Sections of the neighborhood closest to the university are disproportionately populated by students who rent apartments and the families of faculty and staff, many of whom have moved to the neighborhood in response to a university-sponsored program that subsidizes the purchase of homes in the neighborhood.

began with the removal of abandoned cars. Its next stage calls for the demolition of abandoned buildings and development of green spaces, side yards, and, hopefully, the construction of residential and business properties.

Except for the few whose parents can afford private school, most neighborhood children attend public schools that also were built in the early 1900s and designed for approximately half their current enrollment. These schools have both high turnover and high absenteeism in their staffs and students and relatively low achievement levels. Unacceptably high attrition occurs in student enrollment at significant transition points (e.g., from elementary to middle school and from middle to high school). The recent introduction of minimal achievement levels as a condition for promotion from the 4th to the 5th and from the 8th to the 9th grade and receipt of a high school diploma increases anxiety about their children's future throughout the community. Sensitive to the perception that it is seeking to "gentrify" the neighborhood, the university has made explicit its commitment to improve the quality of life for all residents. The partnership with the public schools to construct a new school, partially supported through funding, personnel, and programs, represents a central component of that commitment. As originally explained, the "PENN-assisted school" (hereafter referred to as "the school") is intended to relieve overcrowding of local schools, provide a training and continuing education resource for educators within the neighborhood and city, and serve as a laboratory for enhancing instructional strategies for urban education.

Neighborhood resistance to the school reflected concern that already understaffed and underresourced local elementary schools would be hurt as their best and brightest faculty, staff, and students transferred to the new facility. Existing collaborations between the university and neighborhood schools were deemed in jeopardy once attention focused on the school. Of critical concern was the manner in which enrollment boundaries were drawn and thus how much of the neighborhood (and which of its demographic subgroups) would benefit from the school. Many in the community assumed that the school was intended primarily for university-affiliated residents as a "gentrification engine." In response to these concerns, a team of university faculty and students (including the authors) committed themselves to the revitalization of a local elementary school with serious academic and behavioral problems. The university committed approximately $1.5 million over the next three years to support renewal of this "sister" school in parallel with the PENN-assisted school. University resources are intended to upgrade the instructional quality and materials available for improving performance in reading, literacy, and numeracy and systematically monitoring student performance. The public school system, for its part, has promised to upgrade the physical plant and enhance both its infrastructure and its appearance. A portion of the sister school is being renovated to house a new library that will be supplied with books and staffed by the university. Administrative assistance has contributed to revised class rosters, the curriculum, and student assignments to classes. The various elements are reinforced with a multiyear sequence of continuing education and professional development.

One author (R.L.) assumed primary responsibility for assisting faculty in the sister school with "behavior problems." A series of weekly meetings, increasingly involving the application of the deliberative conversation approach, clarified the ambiguity associated with this term. Initial examples ranged from rowdy behavior in the hall, to students wandering the halls to avoid classes, to an understanding that students' presence in the hall related to the absence of some teachers in the classroom, to teacher disagreements about methods for handling "difficult students," to students' fears of parental reprisal at suspension, to students' awareness of the absence of any system for tracking their whereabouts, and so forth. It soon became clear that "behavior problems" referred to far more than wandering in the hall.

A series of end-of-year conversations was held by the authors with 7th and 8th graders. Repeatedly, we heard that academic standards were low, educational materials outdated or unavailable, and the criteria for classroom management and academic assessment unpredictable. We heard about the lack of respect for students and the absence of "fairness." The latter point was most revealing, for it referred to the unfairness of students trying to learn in a building that was in serious disrepair and whose teachers did not consistently recognize academic achievement. The students expressed frustration at being unprepared for the transition into high school, ignored when they tried to raise concerns, and excluded from school management. Unfairness, for some students, also referred to their ability and that of their classmates to seemingly ignore rules with impunity.

Overall, through meetings with administrators, teachers, students, a handful of parents, and others in the system, the conversations consistently reflected perceptions of the depth of problems, the seriousness of needs, and the intransigence of the issues (one colleague reviewed the school's academic achievement, absenteeism [student and teacher], and staff turnover records for 20 years). Targeting any aspect of the problem seemed doomed to a series of "yes, but . . ." reminders of the elements remaining. The authors confronted negativism, hopelessness, pessimism, and an overall sense that anything tried would ultimately fail because it always had. Every segment of the system expressed its commitment to working for change and its conviction that other segments would undermine those efforts. Parents assumed teachers were going through the motions. Teachers assumed parents cared little about education and had few skills to support academic improvement. Administrators saw few allies and many critics, not to mention demands that they outperform their predecessors (we were working with the third principal in as many years) with limited funds and no time. Students seemed equally dulled into a series of motions that kept them within loosely drawn boundaries of academic and behavioral responsibility. Like so many in the school and the community, they seemed to move about in an implicitly choreographed dance of hopeless motion.

Six months of conversations made evident the salience of Benson et al.'s (1998) argument that the optimal development of youth was impeded by the cumulative influence of social factors (i.e., family isolation, civic disengagement, professionalization of care, inconsistent socialization, and the marginalization of youth) on this setting and population. Targeting these as the culprits seems to offer a viable alternative whereby small victories might accumulate within and across categories, gathering momentum along the way. Continuing along the path outlined in the developmental assets perspective unquestionably alters how we conceptualize the situation (as opposed to the "problem") and, most important, how we assess its alteration (as opposed to its "remediation"). Rather than conduct a needs assessment of the students that would be operationalized through such indexes as daily attendance, numbers of students in the hallway, numbers of disciplinary referrals, in-school and out-of-school suspensions, and so forth, we will undertake a comprehensive assets inventory of students and, insofar as possible, of faculty and administrators.

With the students' assistance, we plan to obtain detailed inventories of both school and community assets. We will propose that 11th and 12th graders in an adjoining high school fulfill their community service requirement by researching the history of their neighborhood, pinpointing its highs and lows, as well as identifying its most prominent residents (e.g., President Judith Rodin of the University of Pennsylvania is among them) and the high school's most prominent alumni. A similar option will be offered to 7th and 8th graders. We have proposed that parent requests for a course on parenting be answered by offering a six-week "community-school" seminar with a specific focus on the challenges of raising (pre-)adolescents. We want the course to be designed by and, at least in part, taught by (pre-)adolescents. In essence, we hope to shift attention from deficits to assets and to demonstrate concretely the knowledge, insights, and resources of youth.

Final Comments

The authors have learned much from their initial involvement with the developmental assets approach proposed by Search Institute. We have been encouraged by the positive reception of the system by the two communities with which we are working and by the sense that solutions to seemingly complex problems are possible. We continue our work with these communities. The suburban setting seems poised to open itself to sensitive and difficult conversations about its values and the demands it places on its youth. The urban community is currently struggling with an episode of a weapons offense in its school and new fears of open violence. It is not yet prepared to move ahead with the assets analysis but seems to take hope from discussions of the experience of its suburban neighbor. The developmental assets approach remains alien, mostly because so little attention has been paid in the past to positive elements of the community and its youth. At the same time, the community has now asserted itself in demanding that its university "partners" set aside their immediate agenda and respond to the school's immediate needs. With a rare explicitness, the teachers, administrators, and students seem to have coalesced around a goal, namely, to improve three major issues confronting the school's climate and capacity to educate. For the first time, the authors have witnessed assertion by this coalition of its right to a better climate and of its commitment to being active partners with the university in achieving that goal. In a sense, the soil is now tilled and ready for planting. The materials needed for a good harvest are being gathered, and the required labor is being acknowledged and commitments made to undertake it. The conditions seem ripe for pursuit of an agenda for the promotion and building of developmental assets.

References

Albee, G. W. (1982). Preventing psychopathology and promoting human potential. *American Psychologist, 37,* 1043–1050.

Albee, G. W. (1996). Evolutions and counterrevolutions in prevention. *American Psychologist, 51,* 1130–1133.

Albee, G. W., & Gullotta, T. (1997). *Primary prevention works.* Thousand Oaks, CA: Sage.

Barker, R. G. (1968). *Ecological psychology.* Stanford, CA: Stanford University Press.

Barker, R. G., & Gump, P. V. (1964). *Big school, small school: High school size and student behavior.* Stanford, CA: Stanford University Press.

Barker, R. G., & Shoggen, P. (1973). *Qualities of community life: Methods of measuring environment and behavior applied to an American and an English town.* San Francisco: Jossey-Bass.

Bell, R. Q. (1986). Age-specific manifestations in changing psychosocial risk. In D. C. Farran & J. D. McKinney (Eds.), *The concept of risk in intellectual and psychosocial development* (pp. 169–185). New York: Academic Press.

Benson, P. L., Leffert, N. , Scales, P. C., & Blyth, D. A. (1998). Beyond the "village" rhetoric: Creating healthy communities for children and adolescents. *Applied Developmental Science, 2,* 138–159.

Bronfenbrenner, U. (1977). Toward an experimental ecology of human development. *American Psychologist, 32,* 513–531.

Caplan, G. (1964). *Principles of preventive psychiatry.* New York: Basic Books.

Cicchetti, D. (1984). The emergence of developmental psychopathology. *Child Development, 55,* 1–7.

Cicchetti, D., & Rogosh, F. A. (1996). Equifinality and multifinality in developmental psychopathology. *Development and Psychopathology, 8,* 597–600.

Cowen, E. L. (1973). Social and community interventions. *Annual Review of Psychology, 24,* 423–472.

Cowen, E. L. (1994). The enhancement of psychological wellness: Challenges and opportunities. *American Journal of Community Psychology, 22,* 149–180.

Cowen, E. L. (1996). The ontogenesis of primary prevention: Lengthy strides and stubbed toes. *American Journal of Community Psychology, 24,* 235–249.

Cowen, E. L. (2000). Psychological wellness: Some hopes for the future. In D. Cicchetti, J. Rappaport, I. Sandler, & R. Weissberg (Eds.), *The promotion of wellness in children and adolescents* (pp. 477–503). Washington, DC: Child Welfare League of America, Inc.

Dumont, M. (1968). *The absurd healer: Perspectives of a community psychiatrist.* New York: Science House.

Durlak, J. A. (1997). *Successful prevention programs for children and adolescents.* New York: Plenum.

Durlak, J. A., & Wells, A. M. (1997). Primary prevention programs for children and adolescents: A meta-analytic review. *American Journal of Community Psychology, 25,* 115–152.

Durlak, J. A., & Wells, A. M. (1998). Evaluation of indicated preventive intervention (secondary prevention) mental health programs for children and adolescents. *American Journal of Community Psychology, 26,* 775–802.

Erikson, E. (1963). *Childhood and society.* New York: Norton.

Fisher, R., Ury, W., & Patton, B. (Eds.). (1992). *Getting to yes: Negotiating agreement without giving in.* Boston: Houghton Mifflin.

Freud, S. (1956). *A general introduction to psychoanalysis.* New York: Perma Books.

Ginsburg, H., & Opper, S. (1969). *Piaget's theory of intellectual development: An introduction.* Englewood Cliffs, NJ: Prentice Hall.

Gordon, R. (1983). An operational classification of disease prevention. *Public Health Reports, 98,* 107–109.

Gordon, R. (1987). An operational classification of disease prevention. In J. A. Steinberg & M. M. Silverman (Eds.), *Preventing mental disorders: A research perspective* (pp. 20–26). (DHHS Publication No. ADM 87-1492). Washington, DC: U.S. Government Printing Office.

Gutmann, A., & Thompson, D. (1996). *Democracy and disagreement.* Cambridge, MA: Belknap Press of Harvard University Press.

Heifetz, R. (1994). *Leadership without easy answers.* Cambridge, MA: Harvard University Press.

Helmstadter, G. C. (1964). *Principles of psychological measurement.* New York: Appleton-Century-Crofts.

Kelly, J. G. (1966). Ecological constraints on mental health services. *American Psychologist, 21,* 535–539.

Kelly, J. G. (1974, May). Toward a psychology of healthiness. Icabod Spencer Lecture, Union College, Schenectady, NY.

Kuhn, T. S. (1974). *The structure of scientific revolutions* (2nd ed.). Chicago: University of Chicago Press.

Leffert, N., Benson, P. L., Scales, P. C., Sharma, A., Drake, D., & Blyth, D. A. (1998). Developmental assets: Measurement and prediction of risk behaviors among adolescents. *Applied Developmental Science, 2,* 209–230.

Lerner, R. (1998). Theories of human development: Contemporary perspectives. In R. M. Lerner (Ed.), *The handbook of child psychology: Vol. 1. Theoretical models of human development* (pp. 1–24). Editor in chief: W. Damon. New York: Wiley.

Lilienfeld, A. M., & Lilienfeld, D. E. (1980). *Foundations of epidemiology*. New York: Oxford University Press.

Lorion, R. P. (1987). The other side of the coin: The potential for negative consequences of preventive interventions. In J. A. Steinberg & M. M. Silverman (Eds.), *Preventing mental disorders: A research perspective* (pp. 243–250). (DHHS Publication No. ADM 87-1492). Washington, DC: U.S. Government Printing Office.

Lorion, R. P. (1999). Community, prevention and wellness. In M. Herson and T. Ammerman (Eds.), *Advanced abnormal child psychology* (2nd ed., pp. 251–266). Hillsdale, NJ: Lawrence Erlbaum.

Lorion, R. P. (2000). Theoretical and evaluation issues in the promotion of wellness and the protection of "well enough." In D. Cicchetti, J. Rappaport, I. Sandler, & R. Weissberg (Eds.), *The promotion of wellness in children and adolescents* (pp. 1–28). Washington, DC: Child Welfare League of America, Inc.

Lorion, R. P., & Hightower, A. D. (2001). Applying psychological skills in the "real" world. In S. Walfish and A. K. Hess (Eds.), *Succeeding in graduate school: The career guide for psychology students* (pp. 369–384). Hillsdale, NJ: Lawrence Erlbaum.

Mathews, D. (1999). *Politics for people: Finding a responsible public voice*. Urbana: University of Illinois Press, 1999.

Mathews, D., & McAfee, N. (1999). *Making choices together: The power of public deliberation*. Dayton, OH: Kettering Foundation.

McCoy, M., Emigh, P., Leighninger, M., & Barrett, M. (1996). *Planning community-wide study circle programs: A step-by-step guide*. Pomfret, CT: Topsfield Foundation, Inc.

Mrazek, P. J., & Haggerty, R. J. (1994). *Reducing risks for mental disorders: Frontiers for preventive intervention research*. Washington, DC: National Academy Press.

Piaget, J. (1952). *The origins of intelligence in children*. New York: International Universities Press.

Pike, A., McGuire, S., Hetherington, E. M., Reiss, D., & Plomin, R. (1996). Family environment and adolescent depressive symptoms and antisocial behavior: A multivariate genetic analysis. *Developmental Psychology, 32*, 590–603.

Plomin, R., & Daniels, D. (1987). Why are children in the same family so different from one another? *Behavioral and Brain Sciences, 10*, 1–15.

Rutter, M. (2000). Psychosocial influences: Critiques, findings and research needs. *Development and Psychopathology, 12*, 375–406.

Rutter, M., & Sroufe, L. A. (2000). Developmental psychopathology: Concepts and challenges. *Developmental Psychopathology, 12*, 265–296.

Sameroff, A. J. (2000). Developmental systems and psychopathology. *Development and psychopathology, 12*, 297–312.

Sameroff, A. J., & Chandler, M. J. (1975). Reproductive risk and the continuum of caretaking casualty. In F. D. Horowitz, M. Hetherington, S. Scarr-Salapatek, & G. Siegel (Eds.), *Review of Child Development Research: Vol. 4* (pp. 187–244). Chicago: University of Chicago Press.

Sameroff, A. J., & Fiese, B. H. (1989). Conceptual issues in prevention. In D. Shaffer, I. Phillips, & N. B. Enzer (Eds.), *Prevention of mental disorders, alcohol and other drug use in children and adolescents* (pp. 23–54). (DHHS Publication No. ADM 89-1646). Rockville, MD: Office for Substance Abuse Prevention.

Sarason, S. B. (1984). If it can be studied or developed, should it be? *American Psychologist, 39*, 477–485.

Scales, P. C., Benson, P. L., Leffert, N., & Blyth, D. A. (2000). The contribution of developmental assets to the prediction of thriving among adolescents. *Applied Developmental Science, 4*, 27–46.

Scales, P. C., & Leffert, N. (1999). *Developmental assets: A synthesis of the scientific research on adolescent development*. Minneapolis, MN: Search Institute.

Sroufe, L. A. (1997). Psychopathology as an outcome of development. *Development and Psychopathology, 9,* 251–268.

Sullivan, M. L. (1998). Integrating qualitative and quantitative methods in the study of developmental psychopathology. *Development and Psychopathology, 10,* 377–393.

Wakefield, J. C. (1997). When is development disordered? Developmental psychopathology and the harmful dysfunction analysis of mental disorder. *Development and Psychopathology, 9,* 269–290.

Wicker, A. W. (1979). *An introduction to ecological psychology.* Monterey, CA: Brooks/Cole.

Yankelovich, D. (1991). *Coming to public judgement: Making democracy work in a complex world.* Frank W. Abrams Lectures. Syracuse, NY: Syracuse University Press.

Yankelovich, D. (1999). *The magic of dialogue: Transforming conflict into cooperation.* New York: Simon & Schuster.

7 Asset Building in Parenting Practices and Family Life

A. Rae Simpson
Massachusetts Institute of Technology
and Jolene L. Roehlkepartain
Minneapolis, Minnesota

Despite the obvious theoretical and practical connections between parenting and adolescent development, too often scholarship and practices related to parenting and family studies are disconnected from scholarship and practices in youth development. While youth development experts generally acknowledge the central, primary socializing role of parents, they tend to study and implement programs and practices that emphasize settings beyond the family—sometimes with an implicit message that these efforts are needed to compensate for the failures or limitations of parents. On the other side, parenting and family studies can so emphasize the inner dynamics of families and parent-child relationships that they ignore or downplay the vital role of community resources in contributing to young people's healthy development.

Because it recognizes and balances the multiple resources and socializing influences in young people's lives, Search Institute's framework of developmental assets offers a helpful catalyst for dialogue between the world of parenting practices and family dynamics and the world of youth development. This chapter seeks to stimulate such dialogue by summarizing the current research on parenting adolescents and correlating what is known with the framework of developmental assets. Our hope is that such dialogue will increase cooperation and collaboration among practitioners, scholars, and policy makers so that all

Adapted and expanded with permission from A. Rae Simpson (2001), *Raising Teens: A Synthesis of Research and a Foundation for Action*. Boston: Center for Health Communication, Harvard School of Public Health. Copies of the full, original report can be obtained by contacting the Center for Health Communication, Harvard School of Public Health, 677 Huntington Avenue, Suite 329, Boston, MA 02115. Telephone: 617-432-1038; fax: 617-731-8184; e-mail: chc@hsph.harvard.edu. Copies are also available for downloading on the Internet at www.hsph.harvard.edu/chc/parenting.

resources in communities—including parents, unrelated adults, and numerous organizations and institutions—can acknowledge and reinforce each other's efforts.

The Role of Parents in Asset Building

Although it is true that peers, schools, communities, and other factors take on added significance as children become teenagers, research consistently shows that parents remain a powerful influence in fostering healthy teen development and preventing negative outcomes (Borkowski, Ramey, & Bristol-Power, in press; Carnegie Council on Adolescent Development, 1995; Council of Economic Advisors, 2000; Dishion, McCord, & Poulin, 1999; Feldman & Elliott, 1990; Furstenberg, Cook, Eccles, Elder, & Sameroff, 1999; Hauser, 1991; Holden, 1997; Office of National Drug Control Policy, n.d.; Resnick et al., 1997; Small, 1990; Steinberg, 1996). Teens themselves acknowledge the influence of parents, reporting in studies that their parents remain critically important as guides, mentors, sounding boards, and advocates (Bostrom, 2000; Children Now, 1994; Families and Work Institute, 1993; Galinsky, 1999; Garbarino, 1999; Holmbeck, Paikoff, & Brooks-Gunn, 1995; Louis Harris & Associates, 1995; National Commission on Children, 1991; Osherson, 1999; Pogrebin, 1983; Smetana, 1994; Smetana & Asquith, 1994; Steinberg, 1996; Takanishi, 1993; U.S. Department of Health and Human Services, 1997).

The framework of developmental assets was constructed to recognize the important roles and responsibilities that all segments of the community and society have for contributing to young people's healthy development (Benson, 1997; Benson, Leffert, Scales, & Blyth, 1998c). The framework does not, however, overlook the role of parents and families. In fact, a recurring emphasis within the framework and the research undergirding it is the vital role of parents as asset builders (Scales & Leffert, 1999).

The unique asset-building role parents play in raising caring and responsible adolescents is highlighted within the framework itself. Five of the 40 developmental assets focus specifically on parents and families as sources of assets: #1: Family support; #2: Positive family communication; #6: Parent involvement in schooling; #11: Family boundaries; and #20: Time at home. The other 35 developmental assets have implicit roles for parents, such as having high expectations (#16), encouraging achievement motivation (#21), and instilling a sense of personal power (#37) (Benson, 1997; Leffert, Benson, & Roehlkepartain, 1997). Sixteen items on the *Search Institute Profiles of Student Life: Attitudes and Behaviors* survey, which measures the developmental assets of 6th- to 12th-grade youth, address how adolescents are parented and their home life (Benson, Scales,

Leffert, & Roehlkepartain, 1999). Researchers have found that adolescents who have a high number of assets (31 or more) are less likely to engage in risky behaviors (such as using alcohol and other drugs, being sexually active, and gambling) and are more likely to experience thriving indicators (such as overcoming adversity, exhibiting leadership, and succeeding in school) (Benson et al., 1999; Leffert et al., 1998; Scales, Benson, Leffert, & Blyth, 2000). In short, the 40 developmental assets offer a positive, protective response to the challenges and risks that adolescents face.

Engaging parents in taking a more active role in the lives of their adolescents is only one aspect of asset building. The asset-building approach emphasizes the need for broader community engagement in part to address "the isolation of families" in contemporary society (Benson et al., 1998c, p. 140). Although parents are a critical focus for asset-building efforts, parents are more effective when they are surrounded by a web of support in which individuals, organizations, and communities take an active role in bringing out the best in all young people.

The Harvard Project on the Parenting of Adolescents

In the past few years, while Search Institute was defining and refining the framework of developmental assets, the Harvard Center for Health Communication has been independently addressing the need for more and better information about the parenting of adolescents, in particular by launching a special initiative called the Harvard Project on the Parenting of Adolescents, with funding from the John D. and Catherine T. MacArthur Foundation. Particularly in the past two decades, a significant body of research, unprecedented both in quantity and in quality of methodology and analysis, has begun to accumulate on the role of parents and families in adolescence.

Indeed, in scanning more than 300 reviews of research and practice (see Simpson, 2001, for information on the research process), the Harvard Project found that there were significant areas of agreement among experts on the parenting of adolescents, in spite of the broad diversity of cultures represented in the United States, the myriad individual differences in parents and children, the usual shortcomings of social science research, and the relatively short period of time in which parenting and adolescence have been the subject of psychological research and practice (Collins, Maccoby, Steinberg, Hetherington, & Bornstein, 2000; Steinberg, 2000). This growing body of knowledge is potentially a valuable resource for parents as they consider their options. Summarizing these areas of widespread agreement resulted in a kind of job description for parents of adolescents. Like all job descriptions, however, it did not teach the skills for accomplishing the tasks within it, but rather outlined the overall task at hand, to which each individual brings different strengths, styles, interests, values, and levels of understanding.

For the purposes of this dialogue, what the Harvard Project learned about adolescence and parenting practices (with only limited contact with Search Institute) was highly consistent with the institute's asset-building approach. As we show in this chapter, virtually all the individual assets can easily be correlated with what the Harvard Project found, albeit in a slightly different framework. Thus, the developmental assets framework serves as a bridge between parent education and broader community-building strategies. Furthermore, those engaged in community-based asset building can readily apply the findings from the Harvard Project to their work.

Definitions and Assumptions

In laying out a set of principles for the parenting of adolescents, the Harvard Project has made several important assumptions about both parenting and adolescence. First, "parents" were defined broadly to encompass all those adults with responsibility for raising children, whatever their biological relationship to the child, including immediate and extended family members or kin, stepparents, guardians, foster parents, and tribe and clan members (see, for example, Carter, 1996; Stepp, 2000). Where the term *parents* appears in this chapter, it is shorthand for all these groups and for all others in parenting roles.

Second, "adolescence" was also defined broadly, in order to acknowledge that this is indeed one of the many issues on which there is no consensus. The Harvard Project has included research on adolescence that uses a broad range of biological and social definitions, such as puberty or middle school as a starting point and graduation from high school and other markers as an ending point. The Harvard Project also notes that the completion of the transition to full adult responsibilities in many ethnic groups and many areas of research involves a period that is generally regarded as occurring after adolescence (Arnett, 2000; Jessor, Donovan, & Costa, 1991; White, Speisman, & Costos, 1983).

Third, the issue of societal goals for adolescence was addressed. Implicit in most research on adolescent development and parenting are certain goals for adolescence, goals that underlie research measures of "healthy development" and "positive outcomes." The Harvard Project sought out research whose implicit or explicit goals were consistent with the goals for adolescence in the United States that hold across ethnic, socioeconomic, and religious lines. Again looking for areas of widespread agreement, the research team noted a striking similarity among broad goals for children across research areas and ethnic groups within the United States. These goals almost invariably include survival, physical and mental health, and economic self-sufficiency, and generally also include social connection and responsibility of some kind, particularly with regard to citizenship and/or family relationships (Furstenberg et al., 1999; LeVine, 1997; Small & Eastman, 1991; U.S. Department of Health and Human Services, 1997). The research team took the view, expressed by scholars previously, that some goals can be thought of as nearly universal, while other goals, as well as strategies, tend to be cultural and behaviors to be individual (Holmbeck et al., 1995; LeVine, 1988).

Finally, while this chapter focuses on providing information and support for parents, the question is often raised—appropriately—about whether efforts should be directed toward changing parents or changing the social context to allow parents to do their job more effectively (Dombro et al., 1996; Wallack et al., 1993). This chapter takes the view that the answer is not "either-or" but rather "both-and." Both approaches are important, not in the spirit of blaming parents for problems engendered by a lack of social and economic supports, but rather of partnering with parents in accomplishing their goals for their own development and their teens', both through community support and through individual and family growth.

In other words, the Harvard Project recognizes that some parents will not be able to benefit from the information in this chapter until we, as a society, first meet their basic needs for protection from the effects of poverty, violence, substance abuse, racism, untreated physical and mental illness, and the like. The research team offers its information, therefore, with the goal of reaching both parents themselves and those who are working to create a more supportive environment for parents through social services, policy, humanitarianism, community development, and other means.

The Ten Tasks of Adolescence

One of the most powerful influences on the parenting role is the set of profound developmental changes that occurs in adolescents. In a dramatic interplay of biological and social forces, over the course of adolescence, teenagers take the shape of adults in size, sexual maturity, brain characteristics, thinking capacity, knowledge, emotional sophistication, moral reasoning, peer and family relationships, and occupational readiness. Although development will continue in adulthood, critical steps in physical, social, cognitive, and emotional growth during adolescence shape teens' future life course (Carnegie Council on Adolescent Development, 1995; Fischhoff, Crowell, & Kipke, 1999). Overall, the quality and quantity of developmental change in adolescence rival that of infancy and early childhood.

Because the process of adolescent development is so closely interwoven with the parental role, the Harvard Project analyzed some of the key literature on adolescent development to identify the major developmental changes that parents could expect, and need to support, during adolescence.

The Harvard Project found that, as a reference point for thinking about the parenting role, these changes could be organized into ten tasks of adolescence. This list is not intended to suggest that teens encounter or resolve these tasks in any particular order or sequence or that they accomplish each one all at once. On the contrary, most developmental milestones evolve gradually, episodically, separately, and in combination, with pauses and regressions along the way. Also, the developmental changes during adolescence are part of a continuum of change that extends from childhood into adulthood. During adolescence, teens often rework earlier developmental tasks that they need as a foundation for current growth (Blos, 1962; Erikson, 1968; Winnicott, 1965). For these and other reasons, the tasks can be organized in a number of different ways, generating somewhat different lists. The following list is offered as a particularly short, current, and parent-oriented version, with the hope that it will generate further efforts of its kind.

The developmental tasks of adolescence confront parents with a dazzling and sometimes daunting array of changes in their teen, changes that the parenting role both responds to and supports. In a mixture of great leaps forward, reactive steps backward, and periodic pauses, teens present parents with striking evidence of these ten tasks in progress, as physical, cognitive, emotional, and social aspects of development play out gradually, unevenly, and interactively.

The ten tasks of adolescence and the 40 developmental assets complement each other well. If parents and other adults work to build the ten tasks, they'll also build the 40 developmental assets, and vice versa. (See Figure 1.) Both frameworks emphasize the basic skills and competencies that adolescents need to learn, practice, and master throughout the teen years. Each framework focuses on the positive factors that contribute to healthy development, showing the strengths young people need to overcome the challenges that can threaten their well-being so that they can grow safely and successfully into adulthood (Benson et al., 1999; Leffert et al., 1997; Simpson, 2000).

• **Task #1: Sexuality**—With regard to this first task, parents are likely to witness not only a physical "growth spurt" and maturational milestones, but also experimentation with forms of sexual behavior, romantic relationships, and the forging of a sexual identity (Brooks-Gunn & Paikoff, 1997; Brooks-Gunn, Petersen, & Eichorn, 1985; Brooks-Gunn & Reiter, 1990; Buchanan, Eccles, & Becker, 1992; Dyk, 1993; Furman, Brown, & Feiring, 1999; Furman & Wehner,

Figure 1. The Ten Tasks of Adolescence and the 40 Developmental Assets

Task #1: Adjust to sexually maturing bodies and feelings

Asset #31: Restraint and the Positive-Identity Assets (#37: Personal power, #38: Self-esteem, #39: Sense of purpose, and #40: Positive view of personal future)

Task #2: Develop and apply abstract thinking and skills

The Commitment-to-Learning assets (#21: Achievement motivation, #22: School engagement, #23: Homework, #24: Bonding to school, and #25: Reading for pleasure); also #37: Personal power and #39: Sense of purpose

Task #3: Develop and apply a more complex level of perspective taking

Assets #8: Youth as resources, #9: Service to others, #26: Caring, #27: Equality and social justice, #33: Interpersonal competence, #34: Cultural competence, and #36: Peaceful conflict resolution

Task #4: Develop and apply new coping skills in areas such as decision making, problem solving, and conflict resolution

The Social-Competencies assets (#32: Planning and decision making, #33: Interpersonal competence, #34: Cultural competence, #35: Resistance skills, and #36: Peaceful conflict resolution)

Task #5: Identify meaningful moral standards, values, and belief systems

The Positive-Values assets (#26: Caring, #27: Equality and social justice, #28: Integrity, #29: Honesty, #30: Responsibility, and #31: Restraint); also #39: Sense of purpose and #40: Positive view of personal future

Task #6: Understand and express more complex emotional experiences

Assets #2: Positive family communication, #29: Integrity, and #33: Interpersonal competence

Task #7: Form friendships that are mutually close and supportive

Assets #15: Positive peer influence and #33: Interpersonal competence

Task #8: Establish key aspects of identity

The Positive-Identity assets (#37: Personal power, #38: Self-esteem, #39: Sense of purpose, and #40: Positive view of personal future)

Task #9: Meet the demands of increasingly mature roles and responsibilities

The Empowerment assets (#7: Community values youth, #8: Youth as resources, #9: Service to others, and #10: Safety) and the Constructive-Use-of-Time assets (#17: Creative activities, #18: Youth programs, #19: Religious community, and #20: Time at home)

Task #10: Renegotiate relationships with adults in parenting roles

The Support assets (#1: Family support, #2: Positive family communication, #3: Other adult relationships, #4: Caring neighborhood, #5: Caring school climate, and #6: Parent involvement in schooling) and the Boundaries-and-Expectations assets (#11: Family boundaries, #12: School boundaries, #13: Neighborhood boundaries, #14: Adult role models, #15: Positive peer influence, and #16: High expectations)

1997; Katchadourian, 1990; Kipke, 1999; Koch, 1993; McClintock & Herdt, 1996; Miller & Benson, 1999; Rickel & Hendren, 1993; Savin-Williams & Rodriguez, 1993; Susman, 1997; Susman et al., 1987).

• **Task #2: Abstract thinking**—On a different front, parents are likely to notice surges of new sophistication in their teenager's ability to think, including a greater capacity for abstract thinking (Elkind, 1984; Fischer & Rose, 1994; Fischhoff et al., 1999; Flavell, Miller, & Miller, 1993; Kagan, 1972; Keating, 1980; Kohlberg & Gilligan, 1972; Kuhn & Angelev, 1976; Piaget, 1972). This can be a time rich in introspection and reflection, with deepened understanding of issues such as friendship, justice, identity, and religion, and with a greater capacity for relationships, academic study, and complex work.

• **Task #3: Perspective taking**—In a related development, teens typically become better at perspective taking. Although as preadolescents they probably learned how to "put themselves in another person's shoes," now they typically can do so more consistently. Also, they often begin to step outside of both their own perspective and that of another person, and to use this new ability in solving problems (Damon, 1997; Damon & Hart, 1982; Eisenberg, Murphy, and Shepard, 1997; Elkind, 1967; Selman, 1980; Selman & Schultz, 1990).

• **Task #4: Coping skills**—Thanks in part to some of these new abilities, many adolescents become more proficient at several kinds of coping skills. These new abilities can include more sophisticated decision-making, problem-solving, and conflict-resolution skills, as well as a shift toward a future orientation and greater ability to set and plan for realistic goals (Collins & Laursen, 1992; Fischhoff et al., 1999; Gordon, 1996; Hauser & Bowlds, 1990; Nurmi, 1991; Selman, 1980; Selman & Schultz, 1990; Silverberg & Gondoli, 1996; Worell & Danner, 1989).

There is significant debate among researchers about how to interpret the risk taking that many consider to be characteristic of adolescence. Many researchers and practitioners argue that, like the stubbornness of toddlers, some kinds of risk taking in adolescence are essential to healthy growth, promoting identity development, and decision-making skills (Baumrind, 1987; Garbarino, 1999; Lightfoot, 1997; Ponton, 1997). Also, although risk taking is thought to increase from childhood to adolescence, there is debate about whether adolescents in fact take greater and more frequent risks than do adults or whether it merely seems so, perhaps because they use different information in making judgment calls, and have less information about consequences, fewer options for protecting themselves from consequences, or fewer resources for recovering from failures (Beyth-Marom & Fischhoff, 1997; Carnegie Council on Adolescent Development, 1995;

Fischhoff et al., 1999; Lightfoot, 1997; Ponton, 1997; Scales & Leffert, 1999; Steinberg, 1991a; Strasburger, 1995).

• **Task #5: Morality**—Related to abstract thinking and heightened perspective taking are the major shifts teenagers typically undergo in thinking about morality, in which their understanding of right and wrong is no longer based on concrete rules but rather on principles about justice and care, as well as insights from their new skills in perspective taking and empathizing (Coles, 1997; Damon, 1997, 1999; Gilligan & Attanucci, 1988; Hoffman, 1980; Kohlberg, 1969; Kohlberg & Gilligan, 1972). There is a similar progression toward more sophisticated thinking about religion and spirituality (Fowler, Nipkow, & Schweitzer, 1991; McAdoo, 1995; McGoldrick, Giordano, & Pearce, 1996; Wallace & Williams, 1997).

• **Task #6: Emotions**—Teens also develop a more sophisticated understanding of feelings, such as the ability to think more effectively about the intentions behind actions and about hidden emotions (Brown, 1993; Fischer, Shaver, & Carnochan, 1990; Harter & Buddin, 1987; Larson & Richards, 1994; Selman, 1980; Selman & Schultz, 1990). Adults and teens alike experience adolescence temporarily as a time of more intense emotions, self-consciousness, and mood swings, although the causes, including ways they may be related to changing hormones and other aspects of development, are not clear (Brooks-Gunn & Reiter, 1990; Brown, 1993; Buchanan et al., 1992; Coleman & Hendry, 1990; Damon & Hart, 1982; Elkind, 1967; Kipke 1999; Larson & Richards, 1994).

• **Task #7: Friendships**—Peer friendships take on new importance and meaning in adolescence, and most researchers see this change as a significant milestone of social development. Friendships typically become more intimate, more stable, more time-consuming, more central to teen lives, and a cornerstone for learning about adult relationships (Berndt & Perry, 1990; Csikszentmihalyi & Larson, 1984; Furman & Wehner, 1997; Hartup & Overhauser, 1991; Maccoby, 1998; Savin-Williams & Berndt, 1990; Selman, 1980; Selman & Schultz, 1990; Way, 1998; Youniss & Smollar, 1985). Researchers also note, however, that relationships with parents remain important, and teens prefer to turn to their parents for advice on major life decisions.

• **Task #8: Identity**—At the same time, teens are struggling to establish key aspects of identity. This important, and some say central, issue in adolescence often brings times of experimentation. Teens will "try on" different temporary "identities" by exploring alternative styles of dress, jewelry, music, hair, behavior, and lifestyle, as they struggle to identify a true self amid seeming contradictions in the way they feel and act in different situations, and with different levels of thought and understanding. Included in the search are aspects of gender identity, as well as vocational identity and other issues (Baumeister & Vohs, in press; Brown & Gilligan, 1992; Erikson, 1968; Garbarino, 1999; Hamilton, 1990; Harter, 1999; Kegan, 1982, 1994; Kindlon & Thompson, 1999; Kroger, 1996; Marcia, 1980; Newberger, 1999; Pollack, 1998; Savin-Williams & Berndt, 1990; Scales, 1991; Surrey, 1991; Taylor, Gilligan, & Sullivan, 1995; Vondracek, 1994; Way, 1998; Youniss & Smollar, 1985).

A special challenge arises for teenagers in the United States with regard to forging a sense of ethnic identity. It is increasingly argued that doing so is important for European American youngsters, who must come to understand the role of ethnicity in their own identity and to develop an appreciation for the diversity of ethnicities in the United States, as well as for young people of color, who must forge their identity in the face of racism and discrimination (García Coll, Meyer, & Brillon, 1995; Hill, Soriano, Chen, & LaFromboise, 1994; McAdoo, 1999; Phinney & Kohatsu, 1997; Spencer & Markstrom-Adams, 1990; Spencer, Swanson, & Cunningham, 1991; Tatum, 1997). Additional challenges arise for teens in adoptive and immigrant families, and in other special circumstances (Brodzinsky, Smith, & Brodzinsky, 1998; Grotevant, Dunbar, Kohler, & Esau, 2000; McCubbin, Thompson, Thompson, & Fromer, 1998a; McCubbin, Thompson, Thompson, & Futrell, 1999; McGoldrick et al., 1996).

• **Task #9: Roles and responsibilities**—All these developments, in coordination with appropriate school, peer, mentoring, family, community, and work experiences, help teens learn the skills and manage the multiple demands of increasingly mature roles and responsibilities with regard to education, occupation, family, and citizenship, so that ultimately they can meet the expectations for young adulthood (Benson, Galbraith, & Espeland, 1998b; Damon, 1997; Graber, Brooks-Gunn, & Petersen, 1996; Hamilton & Lempert, 1996; Nightingale & Wolverton, 1993; Rhodes, in press; Silverberg & Gondoli, 1996; Vondracek, Lerner, & Schulenberg, 1986; Youniss & Yates, 1997; Zeldin, Camino, & Wheeler, 2000). These expectations are very similar at the general level (with regard to economic self-sufficiency, physical and mental health, family relationships, and citizenship) but they vary profoundly in details and timing, depending on a family's ethnicity, a teen's abilities, and many other factors (Arnett, 2000; Bavolek, 1997; Csikszentmihalyi & Schneider, 2000; García Coll et al., 1995; Graber et al., 1996; Harkness & Super, 1996; McAdoo, 1999; McGoldrick et al., 1996; Nightingale & Wolverton, 1993; Silverberg & Gondoli, 1996).

• **Task #10: Relationships with parents**—All these changes have an impact on teens' relationships with parents, potentially creating more conflict, criticism and self-criticism, emotional variability, self-absorption, indecisiveness, inconsistency, and distancing from family and family activities. On the other hand, they also engender more breadth and depth of discussion, new and exhilarating options for intellectual and emotional connection, and opportunities for a richer and more sophisticated range of activities in family life (Arnett, 1999; Bengtson & Kuypers, 1971; Coleman & Hendry, 1990; Collins, 1990; Collins et al., 2000; García Coll et al., 1995; Grotevant, 1998; Hauser, 1991; Holmbeck et al., 1995; Kegan, 1994; Larson, Richards, Moneta, Holmbeck, & Duckett, 1996; Noller, 1994; Shulman & Seiffge-Krenke, 1997; Silverberg & Gondoli, 1996; Youniss & Smollar, 1985). All told, they trigger ways in which parents and teens together renegotiate their relationship, separating in some ways and connecting more deeply in others, accommodating and honoring the needs and achievements of the other developmental changes and the family's values and goals.

The Five Basics of Parenting Adolescents

What does research tell us about the basic components of the parenting role in adolescence? The Harvard Project found that the ways in which parents contribute significantly to healthy adolescent development fall into five categories: (1) offering teens love and connection; (2) monitoring teen behavior and well-being; (3) offering guidance, including negotiating and setting limits; (4) providing information and consultation for understanding, interpreting, and navigating the larger world, through a process of modeling and ongoing dialogue; and (5) providing and advocating for resources, including other caring adults. The Harvard Project abbreviated these categories under these five headlines: (1) love and connect, (2) monitor and observe, (3) guide and limit, (4) model and consult, and (5) provide and advocate—the five basics of parenting adolescents.

The five categories move through issues related to providing love, safety, guidance, and environmental resources. They move from those that center mostly on the home environment to those that center mostly on influencing the supportiveness of the outside environment, reflective of the teen's movement into a larger and larger world. They acknowledge the unique skills and roles that come into play as parents both hold on to some aspects of the old relationship and let go of others, embracing and empowering their teen, by carrying out both old and new tasks in both old and new ways. All are a continuation of parenting functions from childhood, but with critical changes in emphasis and strategy to accommodate the dramatic transition that is under way from childhood to adulthood.

Although these five categories were reached independently, the Harvard Project's conclusions about the five key areas of parental influence are strikingly similar to findings from other initiatives, across children's ages and across disciplinary approaches. There are significant overlaps, for example, among these categories and those developed from analysis of research regarding the role of families in adolescence (Carnegie Council on Adolescent Development, 1995), the role of parents in earlier age periods (Bornstein, 1995; Greenspan, 1997), the role of parents during adolescence (Small & Eastman, 1991), the role of parents across the age span (Alvy, 1994; Holden, 1997; Smith, Cudaback, Goddhard, & Myers-Walls, 1994), and the role of adults more generally in adolescence (Scales & Leffert, 1999).

At the same time, however, these five categories are unusual in emphasizing the needs that are particularly important in adolescence, as opposed to earlier childhood, and the parental roles that are particularly influential, as distinguished from those of other adults and resources in teens' lives. For example, the Harvard Project has underscored the kinds of transitional parenting functions, such as monitoring and advising, that move parent-child relationships from the kinds of parental guidance that are more typical during childhood to those that are more common during adulthood. Similarly, the Harvard Project has highlighted advocacy as a separate arena because of the increasing need in the teen years for parents to seek out resources beyond the home, to supplement and enhance what they can provide in areas such as education, employment, career development, after-school activities, and community support (see also Small & Eastman, 1991).

Parenting Basic #1: Love and Connect

Teens need parents to develop and maintain a relationship with them that offers support and acceptance, while accommodating and affirming the teen's increasing maturity. Studies find that supportive relationships with both mothers and fathers are linked, for example, with lower risks of substance abuse, depression, negative peer influence, and delinquency, as well as higher levels of self-reliance, self-image, identity formation, school performance, and success in future relationships (Carnegie Council on Adolescent Development, 1995; Coleman & Hendry, 1990; Collins, 1990; Collins et al., 2000; Garbarino, 1999; Gobeli, 1999; Gray & Steinberg, 1999b; Hauser, 1991; Hauser & Bowlds, 1990; Holmbeck et al., 1995; Jessor & Jessor, 1977; Kegan, 1994; Kipke, 1999; Noller, 1994; Reiss, 2000; Resnick et al., 1997; Scales & Leffert, 1999; Smith et al., 1994; Steinberg, 1990). A baseline of nurturing, which has been variously described and studied as acceptance, warmth, affection, encouragement, connection, and support, also indirectly strengthens the ability of parents to carry out other components of their role, such as setting limits and offering guidance, and helps teens handle the stresses of their new roles (Coleman & Hendry, 1990; Garbarino, 1999; Gray & Steinberg, 1999b; Holmbeck et al., 1995; Kegan, 1994; Larson &

Richards, 1994; Maccoby & Martin, 1983; Noller, 1994; Smith, 1999; Smith et al., 1994; Steinberg, 1990; U.S. Department of Health and Human Services, 1997; Youniss & Smollar, 1985).

There is no question that teens also want increasing independence and increasing participation in decisions about themselves and family matters, but rather than disconnection, they seek a new kind of connection, one that allows for greater maturity and mastery of adult roles (Gray & Steinberg, 1999b; Hauser, 1991; Holmbeck, 1996; Shulman & Seiffge-Krenke, 1997; Silverberg & Gondoli, 1996). The change—and challenge—for many parents is that this connectedness and support must take place in the context of their teens' growing efforts to establish their own values, ideas, and identity, manifesting itself in such behaviors as increased criticism, emotional distancing, withdrawal from family activities, intensification of peer relationships, and more selective sharing of personal information (Arnett, 1999; Coleman & Hendry, 1990; Collins, 1990; Grotevant, 1998; Holmbeck et al., 1995; Kegan, 1994; Noller, 1994; Shulman & Seiffge-Krenke, 1997). Closeness must be balanced with space for individuality, connection with privacy, support with acknowledgment of differences of opinion, family time with peer time, and nurturing with accommodation of maturing bodies and minds.

Furthermore, this delicate balance must be negotiated with teens, who are typically more moody, intense, critical, and argumentative than younger children (Arnett, 1999; Coleman & Hendry, 1990; Holmbeck et al., 1995; Noller, 1994; Shulman & Seiffge-Krenke, 1997). To do so often requires parents to strengthen their skills, such as in handling criticism and anger, negotiation, problem solving, listening, conflict resolution, adapting to change, and delegating responsibility (Baumrind, 1996; Collins, 1990; Grotevant, 1998; Noller, 1994; Steinberg, 1990). Research identifies a special challenge for parents and teens arising from teens' development of sexual characteristics and behavior (Collins, 1990; Galinsky, 1987; Gray & Steinberg, 1999a; Holmbeck et al., 1995; Steinberg, 1994). All these issues may require changes in the ways in which parents express love and connection, adapting their patterns for giving physical and emotional affection to fit teens' changing needs, sensitivities, interests, and activities.

Adolescents need a variety of supports, and the developmental assets framework includes six support assets. Parents and other family members are important (Assets #1: Family support; #2: Positive family communication; and #6: Parent involvement in schooling), but so are schools (#5: Caring school climate), neighbors (#4: Caring neighborhood), and other adults, such as extended family, coaches, employers, senior citizens, health-care professionals, religious leaders, and community residents (#3: Other adult relationships) (Benson, 1997). When parents feel their adolescents pulling away, they may find it easier to deal with these times of distance and discomfort when other supports are available—for their teens as well as for themselves.

The basic parenting strategy of loving and connecting with adolescents builds a number of developmental assets. (See Figure 2.) As children become teens, "love and nurture" takes on a different quality. This includes behaviors that communicate respect, interest, warmth, and affection, so that the teen feels accepted and approved of as a person, while also allowing for increased privacy, autonomy, and differences of opinion. It means continuing both to work together and play together. It involves supporting adolescents in ways that empower

Figure 2. Strategies for Parents #1: Love and Connect

Strategies vary across culture and philosophy, and research in no way suggests that "one size fits all" with parenting strategies. These ideas offer starting points and overall guidelines from which to select and adapt, taking into account values, special needs, environmental risks, ethnic traditions, individual style, and many other factors.

- Watch for moments when you feel and can express genuine affection, respect, and appreciation for your teen—Asset #1: Family support.
- Acknowledge the good times made possible by your teen's personality and growth— Asset #2: Positive family communication.
- Expect increased criticism and debate, and strengthen your skills for discussing ideas and disagreements in ways that respect both your teen's opinions and your own—Asset #2: Positive family communication.
- Spend time just listening to your teen's thoughts and feelings about her or his fears, concerns, interests, ideas, perspectives, activities, jobs, schoolwork, and relationships—Asset #2: Positive family communication.
- Treat each teen as a unique individual distinct from siblings, stereotypes, his or her past, or your own past—The Positive-Identity assets (#37: Personal power, #38: Self-esteem, #39: Sense of purpose, and #40: Positive view of personal future).
- Appreciate and acknowledge each teen's new areas of interest, skills, strengths, and accomplishments, as well as the positive aspects of adolescence generally, such as its passion, vitality, humor, and deepening intellectual thought—the Positive-Identity assets (#37: Personal power, #38: Self-esteem, #39: Sense of purpose, and #40: Positive view of personal future).
- Provide meaningful roles for your teen in the family, ones that are genuinely useful and important to the family's well-being—Asset #8: Youth as resources.
- Spend time together one on one and as a family, continuing some familiar family routines, while also taking advantage of ways in which new activities, such as community volunteering, can offer new ways to connect—Assets #9: Service to others and #20: Time at home.

Key Message for Parents:
Most things about their world are changing. Don't let your love be one of them.

them while also building a strong sense of identity in them so that they can develop into caring, competent adults who have and want to contribute something worthwhile to society.

Parenting Basic #2: Monitor and Observe

Teens need parents to be aware of—and let teens know they are aware of—their activities, including school performance, work experiences, after-school activities, peer relationships, adult relationships, and recreation, through a process that increasingly involves less direct supervision and more communication, observation, and networking with other adults. The seemingly simple act of monitoring teens' activities—having teens report on their whereabouts and knowing where teens are—is found in studies to be linked to a lower risk of drug and alcohol use, early sexual activity, pregnancy, depression, school problems, victimization, delinquency, and negative peer influence (Chamberlain & Patterson, 1995; Garbarino, 1999; Holmbeck et al., 1995; Miller, 1998; Patterson & Forgatch, 1987; Small & Eastman, 1991; Steinberg, 1991b; U.S. Department of Health and Human Services, 1997). Monitoring also appears to communicate that parents care and are listening, to influence peer selection, help teens develop social competence, and encourage the involvement and interest of other adults, such as teachers and coaches (Brody & Flor, 1998; Chamberlain & Patterson, 1995; Elliott, Hamburg, & Williams, 1998; Garbarino, 1999; Gray & Steinberg, 1999b; Holden, 1997; Holmbeck et al., 1995; Jarrett, 1997, 1999; Miller, 1998; U.S. Department of Health and Human Services, 1997; Zill & Nord, 1994).

One of the new challenges for parents of teens is that more of the monitoring must be done indirectly, by observing changes in teen behavior, by listening to teen disclosures, and by checking in with other adults. A central theme is balance—between parents' need to supervise and teens' need for privacy.

One of the key messages of the developmental assets framework concerns keeping track of adolescents. Not only is it essential for parents (and other adults) to know where young people are, they also need to know what young people are doing, thinking, and hoping for. Adolescence is a time when young people are evaluating who they are as well as what they believe and value. Monitoring adolescents entails that parents remain involved in the lives of their teenagers while also supporting them. (See Figure 3.)

Monitoring in a few specific areas has been given particular attention:

• **School progress and environment**—Parental involvement in school activities tends to decrease dramatically in adolescence, but its impact does not (Eccles & Harold, 1996; Zill & Nord, 1994). Supervision of grades is associated with better grades, monitoring of school behavior with fewer school behavior problems, and school involvement with both higher grades and fewer problems (Brody & Flor, 1998; Carnegie Council on Adolescent Development, 1995; Dryfoos, 1998; Eccles & Harold, 1996; Entwisle, 1990; Gray & Steinberg, 1999b; Holden, 1997; Holmbeck et al., 1995; Zill & Nord, 1994). School involvement can

Figure 3. Strategies for Parents #2: Monitor and Observe

There is so much more to monitor as teens enter an ever-widening world of education, employment, activities, recreation, and friendships. With respect to monitoring teens' behavior and well-being, the following strategies emerge from the research.

- Keep track of your teen's whereabouts and activities, directly or indirectly, by listening, observing, and networking with others who come into contact with your teen—Asset #11: Family boundaries.
- Keep in touch with other adults who are willing and able to let you know of positive or negative trends in your teen's behavior, such as neighbors, family, religious and community leaders, shopkeepers, teachers, and other parents—Assets #12: School boundaries and #13: Neighborhood boundaries.
- Involve yourself in school events such as parent-teacher conferences, back-to-school nights, and special needs planning meetings—Asset #6: Parent involvement in schooling.
- Stay informed about your teen's progress in school and employment, as well as the level and nature of outside activities; get to know your teen's friends and acquaintances—Asset #6: Parent involvement in schooling.
- Learn and watch for warning signs of poor physical or mental health, as well as signs of abuse or neglect, including lack of motivation, weight loss, problems with eating or sleeping, a drop in school performance and/or skipping school, drug use, withdrawal from friends and activities, promiscuity, running away, unexplained injury, serious and persistent conflict between parent and teen, or high levels of anxiety or guilt—Assets #1: Family support and #11: Family boundaries.
- Seek guidance if you have concerns about these warning signs or any other aspect of your teen's health or behavior, consulting with teachers, counselors, religious leaders, physicians, parenting educators, family, tribal elders, and others—Assets #3: Other adult relationships, #4: Caring neighborhood, and #5: Caring school climate.
- Monitor your teen's experiences in settings and relationships inside and outside the home that hold the potential for physical, sexual, and emotional abuse, including relationships involving parental figures, siblings, extended family, caregivers, peers, partners, employers, teachers, counselors, and activity leaders—Assets #11: Family boundaries, #12: School boundaries, and #13: Neighborhood boundaries.
- Evaluate the level of challenge of proposed teen activities, such as social events, media exposure, and jobs, matching the challenges to your teen's ability to handle them—Asset #16: High expectations.

Key Message for Parents:
Monitor your teen's activities. You still can, and it still counts.

take place at a number of different levels, such as monitoring communications from school, attending parent-teacher conferences and school functions, and participating in school governance (Eccles & Harold, 1996).

• **Physical and mental health**—Although most teens navigate the physical and emotional watershed of adolescence without serious difficulty, teens are at significant risk in several ways, as their rates of suicide, mental illness, and other problems grow to be as high as those for adults. One special source of problems for adolescents centers on adjusting to sexual maturation, managing sexual feelings, and struggling to find a sexual identity. About 10%–20% of teens develop a serious emotional disorder, such as depression or an eating disorder. However, if parents respond to signs of depression and seek help, treatment can reduce depressive symptoms and increase teens' capacity to cope successfully (Compas & Hammen, 1996; Peterson, Leffert, Graham, Alwin, & Ding, 1997).

• **After-school whereabouts, friendships, and peer activities**—It has been estimated that as much as 40% of young adolescents' time is spent in unstructured, unsupervised activity (Carnegie Council on Adolescent Development, 1995; Kipke, 1999), and as many as three-quarters of teens report no organized after-school activities (Duffett, Johnson, & Farkas, 1999). Knowing a teen's whereabouts and behavior during out-of-school hours is associated with lower rates of drug and alcohol use, pregnancy, and delinquency, as well as reduced susceptibility to negative peer pressure (Carnegie Council on Adolescent Development, 1995; Chamberlain & Patterson, 1995; Gray & Steinberg, 1999b; Holmbeck et al., 1995; Miller, 1998; Steinberg, 1991b; U.S. Department of Health and Human Services, 1997). Getting to know teenagers' friends is an important part of the strategy, as is monitoring teen employment.

• **Media and other popular culture**—Virtually all American adolescents are immersed in media-related activities—television, videos, video games, movies, radio, CDs and tapes, the Internet, books, magazines, newspapers—an average of close to 7 hours a day (Children's Defense Fund, 2000; Roberts, 2000; Roberts, Foehr, Rideout, & Brodie, 1999). The use of media consumes more time than school; most use occurs out of the presence of parents (Gentile & Walsh, 1999; Roberts, 2000; Roberts et al., 1999). Although there is debate about the effects of the mass media on adolescents, the research raises concerns that certain media may influence the attitudes and behaviors of susceptible teens. There tends to be agreement, therefore, that it is appropriate for parents at least to observe and discuss, if not plan and limit, the amount and content of teens' use of electronic media (Brown & Cantor, 2000; Children's Defense Fund, 2000; Roberts, 2000).

Parenting Basic #3: Guide and Limit

Teens need parents to uphold a clear but evolving set of boundaries, maintaining important family rules and values, but also encouraging increased competence and maturity. Limit setting remains an essential dimension in parenting adolescents, correlating positively with academic performance, social competence, and prevention of problem behaviors (Baumrind, 1996; Brody & Flor, 1998; Carnegie Council on Adolescent Development, 1995; Chamberlain & Patterson, 1995; Coleman & Hendry, 1990; Holden, 1997; Holmbeck et al., 1995; Noller, 1994; Smith et al., 1994; Steinberg & Darling, 1994; U.S. Department of Health and Human Services, 1997).

The developmental assets framework includes six assets in the category of Boundaries and Expectations. These assets are about guiding and limiting adolescents as they make their way. (See Figure 4.) Limits come through setting and enforcing boundaries, such as Family boundaries (#11), School boundaries (#12), and Neighborhood boundaries (#13). Guidance occurs through Adult role models (#14), Positive peer influence (#15), and High expectations (#16). Adolescents receive clearer messages when their parents, schools, neighbor-

---

Figure 4. Strategies for Parents # 3: Guide and Limit

Parents need to engage in limit setting in ways that acknowledge and encourage their teens' own decision making and problem solving. The following strategies emerge from the research.

- Maintain family rules or "house rules," upholding some nonnegotiable rules regarding issues such as safety and central family values, while negotiating other rules regarding issues such as household tasks and schedules—Asset #11: Family boundaries.
- Communicate expectations that are high but realistic—Assets #2: Positive family communication and #16: High expectations.
- Choose battles and ignore smaller issues in favor of more important ones, such as drugs, school performance, and sexually responsible behavior—Assets #2: Positive family communication and #11: Family boundaries.
- Use discipline as a tool for teaching, not for venting or taking revenge—Asset #11: Family boundaries and the Positive-Values assets (#26: Caring, #27: Equality and social justice, #28: Integrity, #29: Honesty, #30: Responsibility, and #31: Restraint).
- Restrict punishment to forms that do not cause physical or emotional injury—Assets #11: Family boundaries, #28: Integrity, and #30: Responsibility.
- Renegotiate responsibilities and privileges in response to your teen's changing abilities, turning over some areas to the teen with appropriate monitoring—Assets #8: Youth as resources, #9: Service to others, and #30: Responsibility.

Key Message for Parents:
Loosen up, but don't let go.

hoods, and communities all have similar guidelines and expectations. Unfortunately, this type of dialogue rarely occurs, and one system (such as a family or a school) can feel unsupported by another. Adolescents benefit when all the adults in their lives team up and are intentional about setting limits (Benson, 1997).

Two principles emerge as influencing the effectiveness of limit setting, as evidenced by association with positive outcomes, including school competence, social responsibility, moral development, impulse control, self-reliance, and healthy peer choices, as well as reduction in negative outcomes, including depression and delinquent behavior.

• **Combine rules and expectations with respect and responsiveness—** "Love and limits" need to go together; neither is nearly as effective without the other. In particular, for adolescents, limits need to allow teens to develop and maintain their own opinions and beliefs, and to experience their parents as hearing and responding to these ideas in making decisions about rules. The reasoning behind rules needs to be explained. Also, emphasis needs to be placed on limit setting for protection and guidance, rather than for punishment and power (Baumrind, 1996; Brody & Flor, 1998; Coleman & Hendry, 1990; Fletcher, Steinberg, & Sellers, 1999; Holden, 1997; Holmbeck et al., 1995; Noller, 1994; Smith et al., 1994; U.S. Department of Health and Human Services, 1997).

• **Combine firmness and flexibility**—Although some rules need to be firm, allowing for the safety and security of the teen and family, others need to be flexible, allowing for the teen's increasing competence, dependability, and decision-making capacity. Teens need the experience of negotiating rules and resolving conflicts with parents in ways that are respectful to both parent and teen. The relative emphasis on firmness and flexibility varies within families, depending in part on the safety of the neighborhood and community in which the teen lives: higher-risk neighborhoods call for more emphasis on the qualities of safety and respect for authority offered by firmness, while lower-risk neighborhoods allow for more emphasis on the opportunities for learning cooperative decision making and self-expression offered by flexibility. Similarly, families' cultural traditions play a role, with more emphasis on firmness in ethnic groups that place greater value on family cohesion and respect for parental authority, and on flexibility in ethnic groups that place greater value on individuality and autonomy (Baumrind, 1996; Chao, 1994; Furstenberg et al., 1999; García Coll et al., 1995; Holden & Miller, 1999; Holmbeck et al., 1995; Steinberg, 1990; Youniss & Smollar, 1985).

As children become teens, an added challenge for many parents with regard to limit setting is that decisions about limits often take place many times a day and must be made in the context of teens' new levels of risk taking and rule testing.

Teens vigorously question rules and limits as they struggle to achieve a sense of identity, apply abstract reasoning, forge more mature peer and sexual relationships, and redefine their parental relationships (Arnett, 1999; Holmbeck et al., 1995).

Most researchers and practitioners, representing a broad range of racial and religious traditions, agree that there are better alternatives to using physical force (e.g., hitting a young person). All agree that, if used at all, physical punishment should never be delivered with intent to do physical or emotional harm (Baumrind, 1996; Brody & Flor, 1998; Dobson, 1992; Larzelere, 1996; McLoyd, 1997). The strategies identified by the Harvard Project take into account this controversy while underscoring the common themes that emerge within it and across a wide range of research literature (Brody & Flor, 1998; Chamberlain & Patterson, 1995; Collins, 1990; Eberly & Montemayor, 1999; Gray & Steinberg, 1999b; Holden, 1997; Holmbeck et al., 1995; Jarrett, 1997, 1999; Miller, 1998; Noller, 1994; Schneider & Stevenson, 1999; U.S. Department of Health and Human Services, 1997; Zill & Nord, 1994).

The disadvantages of both rigid and permissive approaches become more apparent and have higher stakes as teens acquire adult skills and rights. Lack of success with these "traditional" strategies can tempt parents to give up, in particular because learning better alternatives takes information, time, and energy, all of which are in short supply for already overstressed and overworked American parents (Holmbeck et al., 1995; Patterson & Forgatch, 1987; Phelan, 1998).

Parenting Basic #4: Model and Consult

Teens need parents to provide ongoing information and support with regard to decision making, values, skills, goals, and interpreting and navigating the larger world, teaching by example and ongoing dialogue. Although the process of setting and negotiating limits is a powerful tool for helping teens learn values and decision making, another crucial set of strategies takes this important parenting role even further by making parents available as sources of information and counsel as teens explore the widening world beyond home and family (Collins et al., 2000; Resnick et al., 1997; Riera, 1995; Steinberg, 2000; Steinberg & Levine, 1997).

There is no question that a growing circle of adults and peers influences teens' thinking and decisions during adolescence, but more surprising is the extent to which parents' values and ideas remain influential. As teens forge aspects of their sense of identity, they depend on the adults they know best to serve as steady influences, interpreters, and sounding boards. In fact, many researchers have concluded that parents are a key influence in teens' decision making in fundamental areas such as values, goals, and future directions (Bostrom, 2000b; Coleman & Hendry, 1990; Garbarino & Kostelny, 1995; Holmbeck et al., 1995; Jarrett, 1997, 1999; Noller, 1994; Resnick et al., 1997; Wallace & Williams, 1997).

A strong parental role has also been indicated regarding the formation of aspects of identity, including adoptive identity, positive racial and ethnic identity, and positive gender identity (Brodzinsky et al., 1998; Brooks, 1994; Coleman & Hendry, 1990; Grotevant et al., 2000; Harrison, Wilson, Pine, Chan, & Buriel, 1990; McAdoo, 1999; McGoldrick et al., 1996; Phinney & Kohatsu, 1997; Smith et al., 1994; Tatum, 1997; Ward, 1996). Parents exercise their influence both by what they do and by what they say. With respect to what they do, parents' modeling, or setting a good example, has been found to be linked to better skills and attitudes in the areas of academic achievement, employment, health habits, individuality, relationships, communication, coping, and conflict resolution (Coleman & Hendry, 1990; Frydenberg, 1997; Gray & Steinberg, 1999b; Hauser & Bowlds, 1990; Holden, 1997; Holmbeck et al., 1995; Noller, 1994).

With respect to what parents say, research affirms that teens are listening and talking in more ways than it may appear. Teens report that they admire their parents and turn, or wish they could turn, to them for advice and counsel regarding family problems, controversial social issues, philosophical "whys," and plans for the future (Carnegie Council on Adolescent Development, 1995; Coleman & Hendry, 1990; Hayden cited in Steinberg, 1990, p. 14; Louis Harris and Associates, 1995; Schneider & Stevenson, 1999; Youniss & Smollar, 1985).

Researchers also observe that teens tend to have values and beliefs on major issues like morality and politics that are similar to their parents. If they have strong bonds with their parents, teens even tend to choose friends with values that are consistent with those of their parents, when such peer choices are available (Collins et al., 2000; Gray & Steinberg, 1999b; Holmbeck et al., 1995; U.S. Department of Health and Human Services, 1997). Parents who have a stronger connection to their teen tend to have more influence with regard to teen decisions, as do parents who choose ways of conveying their ideas that are respectful of their teen's growing maturity of thought and action (Coleman & Hendry, 1990; Gray & Steinberg, 1999b; Holmbeck et al., 1995).

In order to strengthen their decision-making skills, teens need environments that present neither too little nor too great a level of challenge—neither an overprotective environment that presents too few opportunities for learning from mistakes and coming up against problems nor an overwhelming environment that presents too few opportunities for trying out new coping strategies and experiencing successes (Bosma & Jackson, 1990; Clarke, 1997; Eccles et al., 1993; Gibbs, 1998; Hauser & Bowlds, 1990; Kegan, 1994; McAdoo, 1999; McLoyd, 1997; Savin-Williams & Rodriguez, 1993; Taylor, 1997).

The developmental assets framework helps make sense of this balancing act. (See Figure 5.) As parents support their adolescents (assets #1–#6), they also need to set boundaries and expectations (assets #11–#16). When boundaries and expectations are set in a context of positive values (assets #26–#31), they

---

Figure 5. Strategies for Parents # 4: Model and Consult

Strategies for modeling behavior and supporting teen decision making cover a variety of areas. Central to all these strategies are communication skills, including listening, modeling, offering consultation and advice, negotiating differences, and problem solving. The research findings translate into the following strategies.

- Set a good example around risk taking, health habits, and emotional control—Assets #1: Family support and #14: Adult role models.
- Express personal positions about social, political, moral, and spiritual issues, including issues of ethnicity and gender—Assets #2: Positive family communication, #27: Equality and social justice, and #34: Cultural competence.
- Model the kind of adult relationships that you would like your teen to have—Asset #14: Adult role models.
- Answer teens' questions in ways that are truthful, while taking into account their level of maturity—Assets #2: Positive family communication and #29: Honesty.
- Maintain or establish traditions, including family, cultural, and/or religious rituals— Assets #19: Religious community, #20: Time at home, and #34: Cultural competence.
- Support teens' education and vocational training, including through participation in household tasks, outside activities, and employment that develop their skills, interests, and sense of value to the family and community—Assets #6: Parent involvement in school, #7: Community values youth, #8: Youth as resources, and the Commitment-to-Learning assets (#21: Achievement motivation, #22: School engagement, #23: Homework, #24: Bonding to School, and #25: Reading for pleasure).
- Help teens get information about future options and strategies for education, employment, and lifestyle choices—Assets #17: Creative activities, #18: Youth programs, #23: Homework, #39: Sense of purpose, and #40: Positive view of personal future.
- Give teens opportunities to practice reasoning and decision making by asking questions that encourage them to think logically and consider consequences, while providing safe opportunities to try out their own ideas and learn from their mistakes—the Social-Competencies assets (#32: Planning and decision making, #33: Interpersonal competence, #34: Cultural competence, #35: Resistance skills, and #36: Peaceful conflict resolution).

Key Message for Parents:
The teen years: Parents still matter; teens still care.

help adolescents make sense of themselves (assets #37–#40) and their world. Through modeling and consulting, parents can empower (assets #7–#10) adolescents to make healthy choices that help young people develop into caring and principled adults (Benson, 1997; Benson et al., 1998b, 1999, Scales & Leffert, 1999).

Parenting Basic #5: Provide and Advocate

Teens need parents to provide not only adequate nutrition, clothing, shelter, and health care, but also a supportive home environment and a network of caring adults. The challenge for parents is to accomplish this task in the face of barriers such as family poverty, racism, lack of child support, unemployment and underemployment, overwork, limited formal education, lack of community resources, lack of after-school options, lack of familiarity with American systems and customs, domestic violence, neighborhood poverty and violence, parental incarceration, homelessness, and parents' physical and mental illness, including disability, chronic illness, and substance abuse (Bell & Quick, 1999; Galambos & Ehrenberg, 1997; Garbarino, 1999; Gray & Steinberg, 1999b; Laub & Lauritsen, 1998; McLoyd, 1997, 1998; Scales & Leffert, 1999). The challenges are increased by a tendency at adolescence for specialized services to be less common and for some problems, such as mental illness and substance abuse, to become more common (Carnegie Council on Adolescent Development, 1995; Furstenberg et al., 1999; Schulenberg, Maggs, & Hurrelmann, 1997).

Less widely recognized is the concept that teens also need parents to help provide "social capital," that is, to seek out relationships within the community that supplement what the immediate family can or even should provide in the way of resources, guidance, training, and support. This parental function, sometimes called family management, advocacy, sponsorship, or community bridging, is observed in parenting across ethnic and socioeconomic groups, particularly in adolescence, as the child prepares for and enters a widening world and spends more and more time in unstructured and unsupervised settings (see Furstenberg et al., 1999, on family management; Myers-Walls, 1999; Small & Eastman, 1991; and Smith et al., 1994, on advocacy; Jarrett, 1999, on community bridging; and Laub & Lauritsen, 1998, on social capital).

It's also important for teens to develop meaningful competencies through jobs, after-school activities, community activism, and volunteer work, especially when needed to combat inadequate, mismatched, and discriminatory distribution of resources in schools, neighborhoods, workplaces, and other settings (Côté & Allahar, 1996; Damon, 1997; Hamilton, 1990; Jarrett, 1999; Larson, 2000; Newman, 1999; Youniss & Yates, 1997; Youth Development Directions

Project, 2000). Parents can assist adolescents in finding these opportunities at school and in the community, but they'll be more successful when systems are in place that are easy to find and access (Benson, 1997; Scales & Leffert, 1999). Mentoring has also received significant attention lately as a means of providing additional adult support, guidance, and training (Rhodes, in press). Mentoring is one way to provide adult role models (asset #14) and other adult relationships (asset #3) while giving teenagers the opportunities to build their social competencies (assets #32–#36). Numerous activities (from athletics to the arts to volunteering to participating in a religious community) also can provide opportunities for young people to connect with caring adults, even though they're not set up to be mentoring activities (Benson, 1997).

A key part of this concept involves collaborating with teens themselves, working together as allies, in addressing the problems they face. Youth empowerment is a key aspect of the developmental assets framework, with four assets specifically addressing this issue: #7: Community values youth; #8: Youth as resources; #9: Service to others; and #10: Safety. When adolescents are given useful, meaningful roles at home and in the community, they learn basic competencies (assets #32–#36) while developing a stronger positive sense of their own identity (assets #37–#40). When parents provide and advocate for their adolescents, they can help their teenagers find programs, people, and opportunities that allow adolescents to grow and develop into well-rounded people. (See Figure 6.)

Implications for Research, Policy, and Practice

One of the most important kinds of wealth that we must share as a nation is information. In the past few decades, a significant body of knowledge has accumulated about the parenting of adolescents. Although consolidating and disseminating that knowledge is no panacea, it is one powerful strategy, in combination with other strategies, for strengthening families and improving outcomes for America's children and teens.

We must build much more effective bridges among all those who are addressing the raising of teenagers. We must promote an exchange of information among researchers, parents, practitioners, and policy makers, so that each group benefits from the others' feedback. We must discover or strengthen systems for sharing knowledge among parenting education and other fields—and increase a sense of collegiality and shared goals. We must create more effective means of consolidating information, making it available, and conveying it back and forth; and we must support the senders, the synthesizers, and the seekers within each group. Together, we can make this work.

Parents need a "dictionary" that translates adolescent behaviors—from their strange clothes to their hostile outbursts to their risk taking—into developmental terms. They need to understand that some of these behaviors are not permanent and that most reflect and contribute to healthy development. Parents need to know approximately when they are likely to occur—often earlier than most parents expect.

Like parents of younger children, they also need "ages and stages" information to help them understand what the developmental milestones look like and roughly when to expect them. Although they can see physical growth and sexual maturing, what about the "growth spurts" in cognitive, social, and emotional

---

Figure 6. Strategies for Parents # 5: Provide and Advocate

A subset of these strategies addresses the need for parents to advocate for their teens by involving themselves in various aspects of their teens' lives, such as at school, at activities, and by advocating for better or more appropriate services. These strategies also help combat the reduction in opportunities for lasting adult-teen relationships that characterize American culture more broadly.

Specific strategies for which there is broad research support include the following:

- Network within the community as well as within schools, family, religious organizations, and social services to identify resources that can provide positive adult and peer relationships, guidance, training, and activities for your teen—Assets #3: Other adult relationships, #4: Caring neighborhood, #5: Caring school climate, #6: Parent involvement in schooling, #17: Creative activities, #18: Youth programs, and #19: Religious community.
- Make informed decisions among available options for schools and educational programs, taking into account such issues as safety, social climate, approach to diversity, community cohesion, opportunities for peer relationships and mentoring, and the match between school practices and your teen's learning style and needs—Assets #5: Caring school climate, #7: Community values youth, #10: Safety, #14: Adult role models, #15: Positive peer influence, and #32: Planning and decision making.
- Make similarly informed decisions among available options for neighborhoods, community involvement, and youth programs—Assets #4: Caring neighborhood, #7: Community values youth, #10: Safety, #14: Adult role models, #15: Positive peer influence, #18: Youth programs, and #32: Planning and decision making.
- Arrange or advocate for preventive health care and treatment, including care for mental illness—Assets #3: Other adult relationships, #31: Restraint, and #37: Personal power.
- Identify people and programs to support and inform you in handling parental responsibilities and in understanding the societal and personal challenges in raising teens—Assets #3: Other adult relationships, #4: Caring neighborhood, and #5: Caring school climate.

Key Message for Parents:
You can't control their world, but you can add to or subtract from it.

development? What do major leaps in abstract thinking look like at home, in school, and in relationships? Is it "normal" for teens to become self-conscious, self-centered, and self-absorbed, and will it pass? What are the developmental steps that follow adolescence, and how can parents support these steps during and after adolescence?

Available more extensively for parents of young children, this kind of developmental information is essential for helping parents adjust their expectations appropriately and plan how best to support their teen's growth. While there may be more variability within the phases of adolescence than of childhood, nonetheless some characteristic changes distinguish preadolescence, early adolescence, middle adolescence, late adolescence, and young adulthood. Therefore, it would be a powerful asset for parents to have this information more readily available in usable formats.

This developmental information also needs to be linked to strategies for parents. Parents need to know which characteristics of each phase they can influence directly, and which ones they can influence indirectly, within schools and communities, through decision making, monitoring, and advocacy. They need information that allows them to sort out image from reality, unfounded fears from real risks, and typical teen behaviors from the uncommon ones that tend to attract media and community attention.

A single, major, national clearinghouse is urgently needed to link these efforts and catalyze the creation of new ones to fill in the gaps, across states, ages of children, classes, and ethnicities, including an emphasis on quality information for parents of teens as well as younger children. These resources should include referrals to print and electronic information, and to people and programs from whom parents can seek personal contact, exchange, and support. Also needed is an increase in the quality and quantity of parenting and family support programs for those raising teenagers, designed for their needs, with effective outreach, staff training, curriculum development, evaluation, and coordination with other local services.

Especially important are initiatives that strengthen community involvement, mobilizing parents, other adults, and teens, formally and informally, on behalf of positive youth development. Also important is the need to make information more accessible to the professional groups with whom parents come into contact and to whom they often turn for advice and information, such as teachers, physicians, religious leaders, mental health counselors, community groups, and the media. These professional groups have a unique opportunity and responsibility to support and encourage the efforts of parents. Communicating with parents and involving parents must be viewed as an integral part of working effectively with teens, including within school systems and community programs.

At the same time, all these groups, including parents, need assistance in evaluating the parenting resources that do exist. Given the confusing array of experts and options available in the media and the community, professionals and parents alike need information about how to assess the credibility of experts and ideas, as well as how to determine which ones are appropriate for specific families and circumstances. Linking the efforts of youth development and parent education may also help parents of adolescents find information and resources.

These efforts should be coordinated with those of advocacy organizations and community initiatives in which parents join with community leaders, policy makers, practitioners, religious leaders, researchers, and others in collaborative efforts to create safe and healthy schools, neighborhoods, and other support systems for teens and families. In some ways, teens and their parents are reflecting back to us the problems in American families and the larger society. More mechanisms are needed that allow us to listen, join together, and respond. We have an opportunity to revolutionize the way in which we, as a society, think about parenting, in particular the parenting of adolescents.

The framework of the 40 developmental assets offers one way to assist parents in raising competent, caring adolescents. While the framework has been measured among close to 100,000 6th to 12th graders in 213 communities and towns across the nation (Benson et al., 1999), it also has been translated so that parents have guidance in how to build these developmental assets in their children from birth through age 18 (see Benson et al., 1998a, 1998b; Roehlkepartain & Leffert, 2000). Recognizing that parents cannot do the work of raising adolescents alone, Search Institute launched a national Healthy Communities • Healthy Youth (HC • HY) initiative in 1996 to support communities. These initiatives build assets in young people while also providing networking and support for individuals, families, and organizations within a community (Benson, 1997). Currently, 600 communities in 41 states and three Canadian provinces have started an HC • HY initiative along with 24 states that have created statewide initiatives (www.search-institute.org). These community initiatives can be an important resource for building bridges in the world of practice between fields of youth development and parenting education.

We can raise awareness about the importance of parenting during adolescence, we can shift negative perceptions about parenting and adolescence, and we can provide tools for raising healthy teenagers. The power to do so is well within our grasp, and the effects will reverberate throughout our schools, our courts, our workplaces, our neighborhoods, and our lives.

References

Alvy, K. T. (1994). *Parent training today: A social necessity.* Studio City, CA: Center for the Improvement of Child Caring.

Arnett, J. J. (1999). Adolescent storm and stress, reconsidered. *American Psychologist, 54,* 317–326.

Arnett, J. J. (2000). Emerging adulthood: A theory of development from the late teens through the twenties. *American Psychologist, 55,* 469–480.

Baumeister, R. F., & Vohs, K. (in press). The pursuit of meaningfulness in life. In C. R. Snyder (Ed.), *Handbook of positive psychology.* New York: Oxford University Press.

Baumrind, D. (1987). A developmental perspective on adolescent risk-taking behavior in contemporary America. *New Directions for Child Development, 37,* 93–126.

Baumrind, D. (1996). The discipline controversy revisited. *Family Relations, 45,* 405–414.

Bavolek, S. J. (Ed.). (1997). *Multicultural parenting educational guide: Understanding cultural parenting values, traditions and practices* (Vol. 1). Park City, UT: Family Development Resources.

Bell, M. M., & Quick, S. (1999). Parents in prison. In C. A. Smith (Ed.), *The encyclopedia of parenting theory and research* (pp. 338–340). Westport, CT: Greenwood.

Bengtson, V. L., & Kuypers, J. A. (1971). Generational difference and the developmental stake. *Aging and Human Development, 2,* 249–260.

Benson, P. L. (1997). *All kids are our kids: What communities must do to raise caring and responsible children and adolescents.* San Francisco: Jossey-Bass.

Benson, P. L., Galbraith, J., & Espeland, P. (1998a). *What kids need to succeed: Proven, practical ways to raise good kids.* Minneapolis: Free Spirit Publishing.

Benson, P. L., Galbraith, J., & Espeland, P. (1998b). *What teens need to succeed: Proven, practical ways to shape your own future.* Minneapolis: Free Spirit Publishing.

Benson, P. L., Leffert, N., Scales, P. C., & Blyth, D. A. (1998c). Beyond the "village" rhetoric: Creating healthy communities for children and adolescents. *Applied Developmental Science, 2,* 138–159.

Benson, P. L., Scales, P. C., Leffert, N., & Roehlkepartain, E. C. (1999). *A fragile foundation: The state of developmental assets among American youth.* Minneapolis: Search Institute.

Berndt, T. J., & Perry, T. B. (1990). Distinctive features and effects of early adolescent friendships. In R. Montemayor, G. R. Adams, & T. P. Gullotta (Eds.), *From childhood to adolescence: A transitional period?* (pp. 269–287). Newbury Park, CA: Sage.

Beyth-Marom, R., & Fischhoff, B. (1997). Adolescents' decisions about risks: A cognitive perspective. In J. Schulenberg, J. L. Maggs, & K. Hurrelmann (Eds.), *Health risks and developmental transitions during adolescence* (pp. 110–135). Cambridge: Cambridge University Press.

Blos, P. (1962). *On adolescence: A psychoanalytic interpretation.* New York: Free Press.

Borkowski, J. G., Ramey, S. L., & Bristol-Power, M. (Eds.). (2001). *Parenting and the child's world: Influences on academic, intellectual, and social-emotional development.* Mahwah, NJ: Lawrence Erlbaum.

Bornstein, M. H. (1995). Parenting infants. In M. H. Bornstein (Ed.), *Handbook of parenting: Vol. 1. Children and parenting* (pp. 3–39). Mahwah, NJ: Lawrence Erlbaum.

Bosma, H., & Jackson, S. (Eds.). (1990). *Coping and self-concept in adolescence.* New York: Springer-Verlag.

Bostrom, M. (2000). The 21st century teen: Public perception and teen reality. In *Reframing youth issues: Working papers of the FrameWorks Institute and the Center for Communications and Community, UCLA.* Washington, DC: FrameWorks Institute.

Brody, G. H., & Flor, D. L. (1998). Maternal resources, parenting practices, and child competence in rural, single-parent African American families. *Child Development, 69,* 803–816,

Brodzinsky, D. M., Smith, D. W., & Brodzinsky, A. B. (1998). *Children's adjustment to adoption: Developmental and clinical issues* (Vol. 38). Thousand Oaks, CA: Sage.

Brooks, J. B. (1994). *Parenting in the 90s.* Mountain View, CA: Mayfield.

Brooks-Gunn, J., & Paikoff, R. (1997). Sexuality and developmental transitions during adolescence. In J. Schulenberg, J. L. Maggs, & K. Hurrelmann (Eds.), *Health risks and developmental transitions during adolescence* (pp. 190–219). Cambridge: Cambridge University Press.

Brooks-Gunn, J., Petersen, A. C., & Eichorn, D. (1985). The study of maturational timing effects in adolescence. *Journal of Youth and Adolescence, 14,* 149–161.

Brooks-Gunn, J., & Reiter, E. O. (1990). The role of pubertal processes. In S. S. Feldman and G. R. Elliott (Eds.), *At the threshold: The developing adolescent* (pp. 16–53). Cambridge, MA: Harvard University Press.

Brown, D. (1993). Affect development, psychopathology, and adaptation. In S. L. Ablon, D. Brown, E. J. Khantzian, & J. Mack (Eds.), *Human feelings: Explorations in affect development and meaning* (pp. 5–66). Hillsdale, NJ: Analytic Press.

Brown, J. D., & Cantor, J. (2000). An agenda for research on youth and the media. *Journal of Adolescent Health, 27* (2, supplement 1), 2–7.

Brown, L. M., & Gilligan, C. (1992). *Meeting at the crossroads: Women's psychology and girls' development.* Cambridge, MA: Harvard University Press.

Buchanan, C. M., Eccles, J. S., & Becker, J. B. (1992). Are adolescents the victims of raging hormones: Evidence for activational effects of hormones on moods and behavior at adolescence. *Psychological Bulletin, 111,* 62–107.

Carnegie Council on Adolescent Development. (1995). *Great transitions: Preparing adolescents for a new century.* New York: Carnegie Corporation of New York.

Carter, N. (1996). *See how we grow: A report on the status of parenting education in the US.* Philadelphia: Pew Charitable Trusts.

Chamberlain, P., & Patterson, G. R. (1995). Discipline and child compliance in parenting. In M. H. Bornstein (Ed.), *Handbook of parenting: Applied and practical parenting* (Vol. 4, pp. 205–225). Mahwah, NJ: Lawrence Erlbaum.

Chao, R. K. (1994). Beyond parental control and authoritarian parenting style: Understanding Chinese parenting through the cultural notion of training. *Child Development, 65,* 1111–1119.

Children Now. (1994). *Tune in or tuned out? America's children speak out on the news media.* Los Angeles: Children Now.

Children's Defense Fund. (2000). *The state of America's children yearbook.* Washington, DC: Children's Defense Fund.

Clarke, A. S. (1997). The American Indian child: Victims of the culture of poverty or cultural discontinuity? In R. D. Taylor & M. C. Wang (Eds.), *Social and emotional adjustment and family relations in ethnic minority families* (pp. 63–81). Mahwah, NJ: Lawrence Erlbaum.

Coleman, J. C., & Hendry, L. (1990). *The nature of adolescence.* (2nd ed.). New York: Routledge.

Coles, R. (1997). *The moral intelligence of children: How to raise a moral child.* New York: Plume.

Collins, W. A. (1990). Parent-child relationships in the transition to adolescence: Continuity and change in interaction, affect and cognition. In R. Montemayor, G. R. Adams, & T. P. Gullotta (Eds.), *From childhood to adolescence: A transitional period?* (Vol. 2, pp. 85–106). Newbury Park, CA: Sage.

Collins, W. A., & Laursen, B. (1992). Conflict and relationships during adolescence. In C. U. Shantz & W. W. Hartup (Eds.), *Conflict in child and adolescent development* (pp. 216–241). Cambridge: Cambridge University Press.

Collins, W. A., Maccoby, E. E., Steinberg, L., Hetherington, E. M., & Bornstein, M. H. (2000). Contemporary research on parenting: The case for nature and nurture. *American Psychologist, 55,* 218–232.

Compas, B. E., & Hammen, C. L. (1996). Child and adolescent depression: Covariation and comorbidity in development. In R. J. Haggerty, L. R. Sherrod, N. Garmezy, & M. Rutter (Eds.), *Stress, risk, and resilience in children and adolescents: Processes, mechanisms, and interventions* (pp. 225–267). Cambridge: Cambridge University Press.

Côté, J. E., & Allahar, A. L. (1996). *Generation on hold: Coming of age in the late twentieth century.* New York: New York University Press.

Council of Economic Advisors. (2000). *Teens and their parents in the 21st century: An examination of trends in teen behavior and the role of parental involvement.* Paper prepared for the White House Conference on Teenagers, Washington, DC, May 2.

Csikszentmihalyi, M., & Larson, R. (1984). *Being adolescent: Conflict and growth in the teenage years.* New York: Basic Books.

Csikszentmihalyi, M., & Schneider, B. (2000). *Becoming adult: How teenagers prepare for the world of work.* New York: Basic Books.

Damon, W. (1997). *The youth charter: How communities can work together to raise standards for all our children.* New York: Free Press.

Damon, W. (1999, August). The moral development of children. *Scientific American* 72–78.

Damon, W., & Hart, D. (1982). The development of self-understanding from infancy through adolescence. *Child Development, 53,* 841–864.

Dishion, T. J., McCord, J., & Poulin, F. (1999). When interventions harm: Peer groups and problem behavior. *American Psychologist, 54,* 755–764.

Dobson, J. (1992). *The new dare to discipline.* Wheaton, IL: Tyndale House.

Dombro, A. L., O'Donnell, N. S., Galinsky, E., Melcher, S. G., & Farber, A. (1996). Engaging the public, *Community mobilization: Strategies to support young children and their families* (Chap. 9). New York: Families and Work Institute.

Dryfoos, J. G. (1998). *Safe passage: Making it through adolescence in a risky society.* New York: Oxford University Press.

Duffett, A., Johnson, J., & Farkas, S. (1999). *Kids these days '99: What Americans really think about the next generation.* New York: Public Agenda.

Dyk, P. H. (1993). Anatomy, physiology, and gender issues in adolescence. In T. P. Gullotta, G. R. Adams, & R. Montemayor (Eds.), *Adolescent sexuality* (pp. 35–56). Newbury Park, CA: Sage.

Eberly, M. B., & Montemayor, R. (1999). Chores. In C. A. Smith (Ed.), *The encyclopedia of parenting theory and research* (pp. 68–70). Westport, CT: Greenwood.

Eccles, J. S., & Harold, R. D. (1996). Family involvement in children's and adolescents' schooling. In A. Booth & J. Dunn (Eds.), *Family-school links: How do they affect educational outcomes?* (pp. 3–34). Hillsdale, NJ: Lawrence Erlbaum.

Eccles, J. S., Midgley, C., Wigfield, A., Buchanan, C. M., Reuman, D., Flanagan, C., & Iver, D. M. (1993). Development during adolescence: The impact of stage-environment fit on young adolescents' experiences in schools and in families. *American Psychologist, 48,* 90–101.

Eisenberg, N., Murphy, B. C., & Shepard, S. (1997). The development of empathic accuracy. In W. Ickes (Ed.), *Empathic accuracy* (pp. 73–116). New York: Guilford.

Elkind, D. (1967). Egocentrism in adolescence. *Child development, 38,* 1025–1034.

Elkind, D. (1984). *All grown up and no place to go: Teenagers in crisis.* Reading, MA: Addison-Wesley.

Elliott, D. S., Hamburg, B. A., & Williams, K. R. (Eds.). (1998). *Violence in American schools: A new perspective.* Cambridge: Cambridge University Press.

Entwisle, D. R. (1990). Schools and the adolescent. In S. S. Feldman & G. R. Elliott (Eds.), *At the threshold: The developing adolescent* (pp. 197–224). Cambridge, MA: Harvard University Press.

Erikson, E. H. (1968). *Identity, youth, and crisis.* New York: Norton.

Families and Work Institute. (1993). Unpublished data from the National Study of the Changing Workforce, provided courtesy of the Families and Work Institute, New York.

Feldman, S. S., & Elliott, G. R. (Eds.). (1990). *At the threshold: The developing adolescent.* Cambridge, MA: Harvard University Press.

Fischer, K. W., & Rose, S. P. (1994). Dynamic development of coordination of components in brain and behavior: A framework for theory and research. In G. Dawson & K. W. Fischer (Eds.), *Human behavior and the developing brain.* New York: Guilford.

Fischer, K. W., Shaver, P. R., & Carnochan, P. (1990). How emotions develop and how they organize development. *Cognition and Emotion, 4,* 81–127.

Fischhoff, B., Crowell, N. A., & Kipke, M. (1999). *Adolescent decision making: Implications for prevention programs.* Washington, DC: National Academy Press.

Flavell, J. H., Miller, P. H., & Miller, S. A. (1993). *Cognitive development.* Englewood Cliffs, NJ: Prentice-Hall.

Fletcher, A. C., Steinberg, L., & Sellers, E. B. (1999). Adolescents' well-being as a function of perceived interparental consistency. *Journal of Marriage and the Family, 61,* 599–610.

Fowler, J. W., Nipkow, K. E., & Schweitzer, F. (Eds.). (1991). *Stages of faith and religious development: Implications for church, education, and society.* New York: Crossroad.

Frydenberg, E. (1997). *Adolescent coping: Theoretical and research perspectives.* New York: Routledge.

Furman, W., Brown, B., & Feiring, C. (Eds.). (1999). *The development of romantic relationships in adolescence.* Cambridge: Cambridge University Press.

Furman, W., & Wehner, E. (1997). Adolescent romantic relationships: A developmental perspective. In S. Shulman & W. A. Collins (Eds.), *Romantic relationships in adolescence: Developmental perspectives* (pp. 21–36). San Francisco: Jossey-Bass.

Furstenberg, F. F., Cook, T. D., Eccles, J., Elder, G. H., & Sameroff, A. (1999). *Managing to make it: Urban families and adolescent success.* Chicago: University of Chicago Press.

Galambos, N. L., & Ehrenberg, M. F. (1997). The family as health risk and opportunity: A focus on divorce and working families. In J. Schulenberg, J. L. Maggs, & K. Hurrelmann (Eds.), *Health risks and developmental transitions during adolescence* (pp. 139–160). Cambridge: Cambridge University Press.

Galinsky, E. (1987). *The six stages of parenthood.* Reading, MA: Addison-Wesley.

Galinsky, E. (1999). *Ask the children.* New York: William Morrow.

Garbarino, J. (1999). *Lost boys: Why our sons turn violent and how we can save them.* New York: Free Press.

Garbarino, J., & Kostelny, K. (1995). Parenting and public policy. In M. H. Bornstein (Ed.), *Handbook of parenting: Vol. 3. Status and social conditions of parenting* (pp. 419–436). Mahwah, NJ: Lawrence Erlbaum.

García Coll, C. T., Meyer, E. C., & Brillon, L. (1995). Ethnic and minority parenting. In M. H. Bornstein (Ed.), *Handbook of parenting: Vol. 2. Biology and ecology of parenting* (pp. 189–209). Mahwah, NJ: Lawrence Erlbaum.

Gentile, D. A., & Walsh, D. A. (1999). *MediaQuotient: National survey of family media habits, knowledge, and attitudes.* Minneapolis: National Institute on Media and the Family.

Gibbs, J. T. (1998). Conclusions and recommendations. In J. T. Gibbs, A. F. Brunswick, M. E. Connor, R. Dembro, T. E. Larson, R. J. Reed, & B. Solomon (Eds.), *Young, black, and male in America: An endangered species* (pp. 317–363). Dover, MA: Auburn House.

Gilligan, C., & Attanucci, J. (1988). Two moral orientations. In C. Gilligan, J. Ward, J. Taylor, & B. Bardige (Eds.), *Mapping the moral domain: A contribution of women's thinking to psychological theory and education* (pp. 73–86). Cambridge, MA: Harvard University Press.

Gobeli, V. (1999). Recognition/encouragement. In C. A. Smith (Ed.), *The encyclopedia of parenting: Theory and research* (pp. 351–352). Westport, CT: Greenwood.

Gordon, C. P. (1996). Adolescent decision making: A broadly based theory and its application to the prevention of early pregnancy. *Adolescence, 31,* 561–584.

Graber, J. A., Brooks-Gunn, J., & Petersen, A. C. (1996). Adolescent transitions in context. In J. A. Graber, J. Brooks-Gunn, & A. C. Petersen (Eds.), *Transitions through adolescence: Interpersonal domains and context* (pp. 369–383). Mahwah, NJ: Lawrence Erlbaum.

Gray, M. R., & Steinberg, L. (1999a). Adolescent romance and the parent-child relationship: A contextual perspective. In W. Furman, B. B. Brown, & C. Feiring (Eds.), *The development of romantic relationships in adolescence* (pp. 235–265). Cambridge: Cambridge University Press.

Gray, M. R., & Steinberg, L. (1999b). Unpacking authoritative parenting: Reassessing a multidimensional construct. *Journal of Marriage and the Family, 61*, 574–587.

Greenspan, S. I., with Benderly, B. L. (1997). *The growth of the mind*. Reading, MA: Perseus.

Grotevant, H. D. (1998). Adolescent development in family contexts. In W. Damon & N. Eisenberg (Eds.), *Handbook of child psychology: Vol. 3. Social, emotional and personality development* (5th ed., pp. 1097–1149). New York: John Wiley.

Grotevant, H. D., Dunbar, N., Kohler, J. K., & Esau, A. M. L. (2000). Adoptive identity: How contexts within and beyond the family shape developmental pathways. *Family Relations, 49*, 379–387.

Hamilton, S., (1990). *Apprenticeship for adulthood: Preparing youth for the future*. New York: Free Press.

Hamilton, S. F., & Lempert, W. (1996). The impact of apprenticeship on youth: A prospective analysis. *Journal of Research on Adolescence, 6*, 427–455.

Harkness, S., & Super, C. M. (Eds.). (1996). *Parents' cultural belief systems: Their origins, expressions, and consequences*. New York: Guilford.

Harrison, A. O., Wilson, M. N., Pine, C. J., Chan, S. Q., & Buriel, R. (1990). Family ecologies of ethnic minority children. *Child Development, 61*, 347–362.

Harter, S. (1999). *The construction of the self: A developmental perspective*. New York: Guilford.

Harter, S., & Buddin, B. (1987). Children's understanding of the simultaneity of two emotions: A five-stage developmental acquisition sequence. *Developmental Psychology, 23*, 388–399.

Hartup, W. W., & Overhauser, S. (1991). Friendships. In R. M. Lerner, A. C. Petersen, & J. Brooks-Gunn (Eds.), *Encyclopedia of adolescence* (Vol. 1, pp. 378–384). New York: Garland.

Hauser, S. T., & Bowlds, M. K. (1990). Stress, coping, and adaptation. In S. S. Feldman & G. R. Elliott (Eds.), *At the threshold: The developing adolescent* (pp. 388–413). Cambridge, MA: Harvard University Press.

Hauser, S. T., with Powers, S. I., & Noam, G. G. (1991). *Adolescents and their families: Paths of ego development*. New York: Free Press.

Hoffman, M. L., (1980). Moral development in adolescence. In J. Adelson (Ed.), *Handbook of adolescent psychology*. New York: John Wiley.

Holden, G. W. (1997). *Parents and the dynamics of child rearing*. Boulder, CO: Westview.

Holden, G. W., & Miller, P. C. (1999). Enduring and different: A meta-analysis of the similarity in parents' child rearing. *Psychological Bulletin, 125*, 223–254.

Holmbeck, G. N. (1996). A model of family relational transformations during the transition to adolescence: Parent-adolescent conflict and adaptation. In J. A. Graber, J. Brooks-Gunn, & A. C. Petersen (Eds.), *Transitions through adolescence: Interpersonal domains and context*. Mahwah, NJ: Lawrence Erlbaum.

Holmbeck, G. N., Paikoff, R. L., & Brooks-Gunn, J. (1995). Parenting adolescents. In M. H. Bornstein (Ed.), *Handbook of parenting: Vol. 1. Children and parenting* (pp. 91–118). Mahwah, NJ: Lawrence Erlbaum.

Jarrett, R. L. (1997). African American family and parenting strategies in impoverished neighborhoods. *Qualitative Sociology, 20*, 275–288.

Jarrett, R. L. (1999). Successful parenting in high-risk neighborhoods. *The Future of Children: When School Is Out, 9*, 45–50.

Jessor, R., Donovan, J. E., & Costa, F. M. (1991). *Beyond adolescence: Problem behavior and young adult development*. Cambridge: Cambridge University Press.

Jessor, R., & Jessor, S. L. (1977). *Problem behavior and psychosocial development: A longitudinal study of youth*. New York: Academic Press.

Kagan, J. (1972). A conception of early adolescence. In J. Kagan & R. Coles (Eds.), *Twelve to sixteen: Early adolescence* (pp. 90–105). New York: Norton.

Katchadourian, H. (1990). Sexuality. In S. S. Feldman & G. R. Elliott (Eds.), *At the threshold: The developing adolescent* (pp. 330–351). Cambridge, MA: Harvard University Press.

Keating, D. P. (1980). Thinking processes in adolescence. In J. Adelson (Ed.), *Handbook of adolescent psychology* (pp. 211–246). New York: John Wiley.

Kegan, R. (1982). *The evolving self: Problems and process in human development.* Cambridge, MA: Harvard University Press.

Kegan, R. (1994). *In over our heads: The mental demands of modern life.* Cambridge, MA: Harvard University Press.

Kindlon, D., & Thompson, M. (1999). *Raising Cain: Protecting the emotional life of boys.* New York: Ballantine.

Kipke, M. D. (1999). *Adolescent development and the biology of puberty: Summary of a workshop on new research.* Washington, DC: National Academy Press.

Koch, P. B. (1993). Promoting healthy sexual development during early adolescence. In R. Lerner (Ed.), *Early adolescence: Perspectives on research, policy, and intervention* (pp. 293–307). Hillsdale, NJ: Lawrence Erlbaum.

Kohlberg, L. (1969). Stage and sequence: The cognitive-developmental approach to socialization. In D. A. Goslin (Ed.), *Handbook of socialization theory and research* (pp. 347–480). Chicago: Rand McNally.

Kohlberg, L., & Gilligan, C. (1972). The adolescent as philosopher: The discovery of the self in a post-conventional world. In J. Kagan & R. Coles (Eds.), *Twelve to sixteen: Early adolescence* (pp. 144–179). New York: Norton.

Kroger, J. (1996). *Identity in adolescence: The balance between self and other* (2nd ed.). New York: Routledge.

Kuhn, D., & Angelev, J. (1976). An experimental study of the development of formal operational thought. *Child Development, 47,* 697–706.

Larson, R. W. (2000). Toward a psychology of positive youth development. *American Psychologist, 55,* 170–183.

Larson, R., & Richards, M. H. (1994). *Divergent realities: The emotional lives of mothers, fathers, and adolescents.* New York: Basic Books.

Larson, R. W., Richards, M. H., Moneta, G., Holmbeck, G., & Duckett, E. (1996). Changes in adolescents' daily interactions with their families from ages 10 to 18: Disengagement and transformation. *Developmental Psychology, 32,* 744–754.

Larzelere, R. E. (1996). A review of the outcomes of parental use of nonabusive or customary physical punishment. *Pediatrics, 98,* 824–828.

Laub, J. H., & Lauritsen, J. L. (1998). The interdependence of school violence with neighborhood and family conditions. In D. S. Elliott, B. A. Hamburg, & K. R. Williams (Eds.), *Violence in American schools: A new perspective* (pp. 127–155). Cambridge: Cambridge University Press.

Leffert, N., Benson, P. L., & Roehlkepartain, J. L. (1997). *Starting out right: Developmental assets for children.* Minneapolis: Search Institute.

Leffert, N., Benson, P. L., Scales, P. C., Sharma, A., Drake, D., & Blyth, D. A. (1998). Developmental assets: Measurement and prediction of risk behaviors among adolescents. *Applied Developmental Science, 2,* 209–230.

LeVine, R. A. (1988). Human parental care: Universal goals, cultural strategies, individual behavior. In R. A. LeVine, P. M. Miller, & M. M. West (Eds.), *Parental behavior in diverse societies* (pp. 3–12). San Francisco: Jossey-Bass.

LeVine, R. A. (1997, April 7). Personal communication.

Lightfoot, C. (1997). *The culture of adolescent risk-taking.* New York: Guilford.

Louis Harris & Associates (1995). *Between hope and fear: Teens speak out on crime and the community.* Washington, DC: National Teens, Crime, and the Community Program.

Maccoby, E. E. (1998). *The two sexes: Growing up apart, coming together.* Cambridge, MA: Harvard University Press.

Maccoby, E. E., & Martin, J. A. (1983). Socialization in the context of the family: Parent-child inter-action. In P. H. Mussen (Ed.), *Handbook of child psychology* (4th ed., Vol. 4, pp. 1–101). New York: John Wiley.

Marcia, J. E. (1980). Identity in adolescence. In J. Adelson (Ed.), *Handbook of adolescent psychology* (pp. 159–187). New York: John Wiley.

McAdoo, H. P. (1995). Stress levels, family help patterns, and religiosity in middle- and working-class African American single mothers. *Journal of Black Psychology, 21,* 424–449.

McAdoo, H. P. (Ed.). (1999). *Family ethnicity: Strength in diversity* (2nd ed.). Thousand Oaks, CA: Sage.

McClintock, M. K., & Herdt, G. (1996). Rethinking puberty: The development of sexual attraction. *Current Directions in Psychological Science, 5,* 178–183.

McCubbin, H. I., Thompson, E. A., Thompson, A. I., & Fromer, J. E. (Eds.). (1998). *Resiliency in Native American and immigrant families.* Thousand Oaks, CA: Sage.

McCubbin, H. I., Thompson, E. A., Thompson, A. I., & Futrell, J. A. (Eds.). (1999). *The dynamics of re-silient families.* Thousand Oaks, CA: Sage.

McGoldrick, M., Giordano, J., & Pearce, J. K. (Eds.). (1996). *Ethnicity and family therapy* (2nd ed.). New York: Guilford.

McLoyd, V. C. (1997). The impact of poverty and low socioeconomic status on the socioemotional functioning of African American children and adolescents: Mediating effects. In R. D. Taylor & M. C. Wang (Eds.), *Social and emotional adjustment and family relations in ethnic minority families* (pp. 7–34). Mahwah, NJ: Lawrence Erlbaum.

McLoyd, V. C. (1998). Socioeconomic disadvantage and child development. *American Psychologist, 53,* 185–204.

Miller, B. C. (1998). *Families matter: A research synthesis of family influences on adolescent pregnancy.* Washington, DC: National Campaign to Prevent Teen Pregnancy.

Miller, B. C., & Benson B. (1999). Romantic and sexual relationship development during adolescence. In W. Furman, B. B. Brown, & C. Feiring (Eds.), *The development of romantic relationships in adoles-cence* (pp. 99–121). Cambridge: Cambridge University Press.

Myers-Walls, J. A. (1999). Advocacy. In C. A. Smith (Ed.), *The encyclopedia of parenting theory and re-search* (pp. 23–24). Westport, CT: Greenwood Press.

National Commission on Children. (1991). *Speaking of kids: A national survey of children and parents.* Washington, DC: National Commission on Children.

Newberger, E. H. (1999). *The men they will become: The nature and nurture of male character.* Cambridge, MA: Perseus.

Newman, K. S. (1999). *No shame in my game: The working poor in the inner city.* New York: Alfred A. Knopf and Russell Sage Foundation.

Nightingale, E., & Wolverton, L. (1993). Adolescent rolelessness in modern society. In R. Takanishi (Ed.), *Adolescence in the 1990s: Risk and opportunity* (pp. 14–28). New York: Teachers College Press.

Noller, P. (1994). Relationships with parents in adolescence: Process and outcome. In R. Montemayor, G. R. Adams, & T. P. Gullotta (Eds.), *Personal relationships during adolescence* (Vol. 6, pp. 37–77). Thousand Oaks, CA: Sage.

Nurmi, J. E. (1991). How do adolescents see their future? A review of the development of future ori-entation and planning. *Developmental Review, 11,* 1–59.

Office of National Drug Control Policy. (n.d.). National youth anti-drug campaign: Communication strategy statement. Washington, DC: Office of National Drug Control Policy.

Osherson, S. (1999). *The hidden wisdom of parents.* Holbrook, MA: Adams Media.

Patterson, G., & Forgatch, M. (1987). *Parents and adolescents living together: Part 1. The basics.* Eugene, OR: Castalia.

Peterson, A. C., Leffert, N., Graham, B., Alwin, J., & Ding, S. (1997). Promoting mental health during the transition into adolescence. In J. Schulenberg, J. L. Maggs, & K. Hurrelmann (Eds.), *Health risks and developmental transitions during adolescence* (pp. 471–497). Cambridge: Cambridge University Press.

Phelan, T. W. (1998). *Surviving your adolescents: How to manage and let go of your 13–18 year olds* (2nd ed.). Glen Ellyn, IL: Child Management.

Phinney, J. S., & Kohatsu, E. L. (1997). Ethnic and racial identity development and mental health. In J. Schulenberg, J. L. Maggs, & K. Hurrelmann (Eds.), *Health risks and developmental transitions during adolescence* (pp. 420–443). Cambridge: Cambridge University Press.

Piaget, J. (1972). Intellectual evolution from adolescence to adulthood. *Human Development, 15,* 1–12.

Pogrebin, L. C. (1983). *Family politics: Love and power on an intimate frontier.* New York: McGraw-Hill.

Pollack, W. (1998). *Real boys: Rescuing our sons from the myths of boyhood.* New York: Random House.

Ponton, L. E. (1997). *The romance of risk: Why teenagers do the things they do.* New York: Basic Books.

Reiss, D., with Neiderhiser, J. M., Hetherington, E. M., & Plomin, R. (2000). *The relationship code: Deciphering genetic and social influences on adolescent development.* Cambridge, MA: Harvard University Press.

Resnick, M. D., Bearman, P. S., Blum, R. W., Bauman, K. E., Harris, K. M., Jones, J., Tabor, J., Beuhring, T., Sieving, R. E., Shew, M., Ireland, M., Bearinger, L. H., & Udry, J. R. (1997). Protecting adolescents from harm: Findings from the national longitudinal study on adolescent health. *Journal of the American Medical Association, 278,* 823–232.

Rhodes, J. (in press). *Older and wiser: Risks and rewards in youth mentoring.* Cambridge, MA: Harvard University Press.

Rickel, A. U., & Hendren, M. C. (1993). Aberrant sexual experiences in adolescence. In T. P. Gullotta, G. R. Adams, & R. Montemayor (Eds.), *Adolescent sexuality* (Vol. 5, pp. 141–160). Newbury Park, CA: Sage.

Riera, M. (1995). *Uncommon sense for parents with teenagers.* Berkeley, CA: Celestial Arts.

Roberts, D. F. (2000). Media and youth: Access, exposure, and privatization. *Journal of Adolescent Health, 27* (2, supplement 2), 8–14.

Roberts, D. F., Foehr, U. G., Rideout, V. J., & Brodie, M. (1999). *Kids & media @ the new millennium.* Menlo Park, CA: Henry J. Kaiser Family Foundation.

Roehlkepartain, J. L., & Leffert, N. (2000). *What young children need to succeed: Working together to build assets from birth to age 11.* Minneapolis: Free Spirit Publishing.

Savin-Williams, R. C., & Berndt, T. J., (1990). Friendship and peer relations. In S. S. Feldman & G. R. Elliott (Eds.), *At the threshold: The developing adolescent* (pp. 277–307). Cambridge, MA: Harvard University Press.

Savin-Williams, R. C., & Rodriguez, R. G. (1993). A developmental, clinical perspective on lesbian, gay, male, and bisexual youths. In T. P. Gullotta, G. R. Adams, & R. Montemayor (Eds.), *Adolescent sexuality* (pp. 77–101). Newbury, Park, CA: Sage.

Scales, P. C. (1991). *A portrait of young adolescents in the 1990s.* Minneapolis: Search Institute.

Scales, P. C., Benson, P. L., Leffert, N., & Blyth, D. A. (2000). The contribution of developmental assets to the prediction of thriving outcomes among adolescents. *Applied Developmental Science, 4,* 27–46.

Scales, P. C., & Leffert, N. (1999). *Developmental assets: A synthesis of the scientific research on adolescent development.* Minneapolis: Search Institute.

Schneider, B., & Stevenson, D. (1999). *The ambitious generation: America's teenagers, motivated but directionless.* New Haven, CT: Yale University Press.

Schulenberg, J., Maggs, J. L., & Hurrelmann, K. (Eds.). (1997). *Health risks and developmental transitions during adolescence.* Cambridge: Cambridge University Press.

Selman, R. L. (1980). *The growth of interpersonal understanding: Developmental and clinical analyses.* New York: Academic Press.

Selman, R. L., & Schultz, L. H. (1990). *Making a friend in youth: Developmental theory and pair therapy.* New York: Aldine de Gruyter.

Shulman, S., & Seiffge-Krenke, I. (1997). *Fathers and adolescents: Developmental and clinical perspectives.* New York: Routledge.

Silverberg, S. B., & Gondoli, D. M. (1996). Autonomy in adolescence: A contextualized perspective. In G. R. Adams, R. Montemayor, & T. J. Gullotta (Eds.), *Psychosocial development during adolescence: Progress in developmental contextualism* (pp. 12–15). Thousand Oaks, CA: Sage.

Small, S. A. (1990). *Preventive programs that support families with adolescents.* Washington, DC: Carnegie Council on Adolescent Development.

Small, S. A., & Eastman, G. (1991). Rearing adolescents in contemporary society: A conceptual framework for understanding the responsibilities and needs of parents. *Family Relations, 40,* 455–462.

Smetana, J. G. (1994). Parental styles and beliefs about parental authority. In J. G. Smetana (Ed.), *Beliefs about parenting: Origins and developmental implications* (pp. 21–36). San Francisco: Jossey-Bass.

Smetana, J. G., & Asquith, P. (1994). Adolescents' and parents' conceptions of parental authority and personal autonomy. *Child Development, 65,* 1147–1162.

Smith, C. A. (Ed.). (1999). *Encyclopedia of parenting theory and research.* Westport, CT: Greenwood.

Smith, C. A., Cudaback, D., Goddhard, H. W., & Myers-Walls, J. A. (1994). *National extension parent education model of critical parenting practices.* Manhattan: Kansas Cooperative Extension Service.

Spencer, M. B., & Markstrom-Adams, C. (1990). Identity processes among racial and ethnic minority children in America. *Child Development, 61,* 290–310.

Spencer, M. B., Swanson, D. P., & Cunningham, M. (1991). Ethnicity, ethnic identity, and competence formation: Adolescent transition and cultural transformation. *Journal of Negro Education, 60,* 366–387.

Steinberg, L. (1990). Autonomy, conflict, and harmony in the family relationship. In S. S. Feldman & G. R. Elliott (Eds.), *At the threshold: The developing adolescent* (pp. 255–276). Cambridge, MA: Harvard University Press.

Steinberg, L. (1991a). Adolescent transitions and alcohol and other drug use prevention. In E. N. Goplerud (Ed.), *Preventing adolescent drug use: From theory to practice* (pp. 13–51). Rockville, MD: Office for Substance Abuse Prevention.

Steinberg, L. (1991b). The logic of adolescence. In P. B. Edelman & J. Ladner (Eds.), *Adolescence and poverty: Challenge for the 1990s* (pp. 19–36). Washington, DC: Center for National Policy Press.

Steinberg, L. (1996). *Beyond the classroom: Why school reform has failed and what parents need to do.* New York: Simon & Schuster.

Steinberg, L. (2000, April). *We know some things: Parent-adolescent relations in retrospect and prospect, presidential address.* Paper presented at the Conference of Society for Research on Adolescence, Chicago.

Steinberg, L., & Darling, N. (1994). The broader context of social influence in adolescence. In R. K. Silbereisen & E. Todt (Eds.), *Adolescence in context: The interplay of family, school, peers, and work in adjustment* (pp. 25–45). New York: Springer-Verlag.

Steinberg, L., & Levine, A. (1997). *You and your adolescent: A parent's guide for ages 10–20* (Rev. ed.). New York: HarperPerennial.

Steinberg, L., with Steinburg, W. (1994). *Crossing paths: How your child's adolescence triggers your own crisis.* New York: Simon & Schuster.

Stepp, L. S. (2000). *Our last best shot: Guiding our children through early adolescence.* New York: Riverhead.

Strasburger, V. C. (1995). *Adolescents and the media: Medical and psychological impact.* Thousand Oaks, CA: Sage.

Surrey, J. L. (1991). The self-in-relation: A theory of women's development. In J. V. Jordan, A. G. Kaplan, J. B. Miller, I. P. Stiver, & J. L. Surrey (Eds.), *Women's growth in connection: Writings from the Stone Center* (pp. 51–66). New York: Guilford.

Susman, E. J. (1997). Modeling developmental complexity in adolescence: Hormones and behavior in context. *Journal of Research on Adolescence, 7,* 286–306.

Susman, E. J., Inoff-Germain, G., Nottelmann, E. D., Loriaux, D. L., Cutler, G. B. J., & Chrousos, G. P. (1987). Hormones, emotional dispositions, and aggressive attributes in young adolescents. *Child Development, 58,* 1114–1134.

Takanishi, R. (1993). Changing views of adolescence in contemporary society. In R. Takanishi (Ed.), *Adolescence in the 1990s: Risk and opportunity* (pp. 1–7). New York: Teachers College Press.

Tatum, B. D. (1997). *"Why are all the black kids sitting together in the cafeteria?" and other conversations about race.* New York: Basic Books.

Taylor, J. M., Gilligan, C., & Sullivan, A. M. (1995). *Between voice and silence: Women and girls, race and relationships.* Cambridge, MA: Harvard University Press.

Taylor, R. D. (1997). The effects of economic and social stressors on parenting and adolescent adjustment in African American families. In R. D. Taylor & M. C. Wang (Eds.), *Social and emotional adjustment and family relations in ethnic minority families* (pp. 35–52). Mahwah, NJ: Lawrence Erlbaum.

U.S. Department of Health and Human Services. (1997). *Understanding youth development: Promoting positive pathways of growth.* Washington, DC: Family and Youth Services Bureau.

Vondracek, F. W. (1994). Vocational identity development in adolescence. In R. K. Silbereisen & E. Todt (Eds.), *Adolescence in context: The interplay of family, school, peers, and work in adjustment.* New York: Springer-Verlag.

Vondracek, F. W., Lerner, R. M., & Schulenberg, J. E. (1986). *Career development: A life-span developmental approach.* Hillsdale, NJ: Lawrence Erlbaum.

Wallace, J. M., Jr., & Williams, D. R. (1997). Religion and adolescent health-compromising behavior. In J. Schulenberg, J. L. Maggs, & K. Hurrelmann (Eds.), *Health risks and developmental transitions during adolescence* (pp. 444–468). Cambridge: Cambridge University Press.

Wallack, L., Darfman, L., Jernigen, D., & Themba, M. (1993). *Media advocacy and public health: Power for prevention.* Newbury Park, CA: Sage.

Ward, J. V. (1996). Raising resisters: The role of truth telling in the psychological development of African American girls. In B. J. R. Leadbeater & N. Way (Eds.), *Urban girls: Resisting stereotypes and creating identities* (pp. 85–99). New York: New York University Press.

Way, N. (1998). *Everyday courage: The lives and stories of urban teenagers.* New York: New York University Press.

White, K. M., Speisman, J. C., & Costos, D. (1983). Young adults and their parents: Individuation to mutuality. In H. D. Grotevant & C. R. Cooper (Eds.), *Adolescent development in the family* (Vol. 22, pp. 61–76). San Francisco: Jossey-Bass.

Winnicott, D. W. (1965). *The family and individual development.* London: Tavistock.

Worell, J., & Danner, F. (Eds.). (1989). *The adolescent as decision-maker.* San Diego: Academic Press.

Youniss, J., & Smollar, J. (1985). *Adolescent relations with mothers, fathers, and friends.* Chicago: University of Chicago Press.

Youniss, J., & Yates, M. (1997). *Community service and social responsibility in youth.* Chicago: University of Chicago Press.

Youth Development Directions Project. (2000). *Youth development: Issues, challenges, and directions.* Philadelphia: Public/Private Ventures.

Zeldin, S., Camino, L., & Wheeler, W. (2000). *Applied developmental science: Special issue: Promoting adolescent development in community context: Challenges to scholars, nonprofit managers, and higher education, 4* (supplement 1).

Zill, N., & Nord, C. W. (1994). *Running in place: How American families are faring in a changing economy and individualistic society.* Washington, DC: Child Trends.

8 Nonparental Adults as Asset Builders in the Lives of Youth

Jean E. Rhodes and Jennifer G. Roffman
University of Massachusetts, Boston

Supportive relationships with nonparent adults are considered to be among the key developmental assets predicting positive youth outcomes. Indeed, researchers at Search Institute have identified "supportive relationship with three or more other adults," "adult role models," and "adults in community value youth" as essential to youths' healthy development and well-being (Benson, Leffert, Scales, & Blythe, 1998; Scales & Leffert, 1999). Similarly, researchers working from within a risk-and-resilience framework have repeatedly called attention to the protective influence of supportive relationships with adults (Garmezy, 1985; Masten & Coatsworth, 1998; Werner & Smith, 1982). In this chapter, we will describe the ways in which nonparental adults function as resources in the lives of adolescents. Within this context, we will review mentoring relationships and the settings in which they are most likely to emerge. We will also discuss strategies for maximizing the benefits of mentoring and look at the underlying processes that might affect developmental outcomes. As we will describe, mentoring can occur naturally or through formal assignments, and the characteristics of mentoring relationships are as varied as the youth and mentors who enter into them.

Natural Mentors

Perhaps the most basic form of supportive bond between adolescents and mentors occurs within the extended family. Particularly among youth growing up in low-income communities, ties to grandparents, aunts and uncles, and adult cousins and siblings often develop into enormously influential bonds. Similarly, in many ethnic minority and immigrant communities, ties to extended family adults and close friends are important resources to youth (Chase-Lansdale, Brooks-Gunn, & Zamsky, 1994; Taylor, Casten, & Flickinger, 1993). Collins (1987), for example, has described the protective influence of African American women who provide guidance to younger members of the community, often acting as surrogate parents. Similarly, many Latino families are embedded in extended kinship systems that include not only blood relatives but other important adults as well.

Researchers have documented the benefits of such ties, particularly in the face of adversity. For example, Beier, Rosenfeld, Spitalny, Zanksy, and Bontemmpo (2000) found that adolescents with natural mentors were significantly less likely to participate in risky behaviors, including carrying a weapon, illicit drug use, smoking, and unsafe sex. Similarly, Zimmerman, Bingenheimer, and Notaro (in press) surveyed low-income, urban adolescents, noting that those with natural mentors had more positive attitudes toward school and were less likely to use alcohol, smoke marijuana, and be involved in delinquency. Additionally, Rhodes and colleagues have found a consistently positive pattern of mentor influence in the lives of pregnant and parenting adolescents. In addition to improved psychological functioning, adolescents with natural mentors exhibit better vocational and educational outcomes and lower levels of alcohol consumption during pregnancy than those without such supports (Klaw & Rhodes, 1995; Rhodes, Contreras, & Mangelsdorf, 1994; Rhodes & Davis, 1996; Rhodes, Ebert, & Fischer, 1992; Rhodes, Gingiss, & Smith, 1994).

Unfortunately, nonparent adults are far less available to youth than they were just a few decades ago (McLoyd, 1990; Putnam, 2000; Wilson, 1987). Women's entry into the workforce has created greater needs for supervision outside the home, and shifting marital, economic, and residential patterns have undermined extended-family networks. Additionally, declining neighborhood safety has led to social isolation and restricted opportunities for informal contact between adults and youth. Particularly in urban neighborhoods, where a growing number of adolescents live, there is decreasing coherence in the social fabric.

These changes have placed additional burdens on school systems to provide youth with supervision and meaningful adult contact. For many adolescents, teachers signify a stable source of nonparental support. Indeed, a national survey revealed that, after parents, teachers and coaches were the single most important adults in adolescents' lives (see also Beam, Chen, & Greenberger, in press). Although support from teachers has been associated with emotional, behavioral, and scholastic adjustment (Roeser & Eccles, 1998), students' access to teachers and other school adults often diminishes as students move through school. In contrast to students in elementary school, middle and high school students typically interact with multiple teachers, moving from classroom to classroom, in crowded settings that are characterized by increasing demands on both teachers and students. These changes occur at a time when students often feel increasing needs for nonparent guidance and support (Eccles et al., 1993). For youth attending underresourced schools in low-income communities, large class sizes and low teacher-to-student ratios present additional barriers to relationships. A paucity of clubs, sports, and other extracurricular activities in these settings further reduces the availability of caring adults in these environments (Katz, 1999; McLaughlin, Irby, & Langman, 1994).

Thus, despite the apparent benefits of natural mentoring relationships, many of the institutions that have historically been sources of intergenerational contact—extended families, neighborhoods, and schools—have changed in ways that have dramatically reduced the availability of caring adults. To address the needs of adolescents who lack close attention from prosocial adults, volunteer mentoring programs have been increasingly advocated.

Volunteer Mentors

Mentoring programs have become enormously popular in recent years, and this trend shows no signs of decline. An estimated five million American youth are involved in school- and community-based volunteer mentoring programs, nearly half of which were established between 1994 and 1999 (Sipe & Roder, 1999). Although the structure and specific practices of these programs vary widely, the vast majority of such efforts involve the pairing of an adult mentor with one youth. Adults and children typically meet on a regular basis during which adults provide ongoing guidance, instruction, and encouragement aimed at developing the competence and character of their protégés (Rhodes, 2002).

Despite the current popularity of mentoring, only a handful of evaluations have been published on the topic, and few studies have included comparison groups, statistical controls for initial differences, or follow-up evaluations. Additionally, mentoring programs are often encompassed by larger interventions, making it difficult to isolate their influence. Despite these difficulties, a growing number of well-designed evaluations suggest that volunteer mentoring relationships can positively influence a range of outcomes, including improvements in peer and parental relationships, academic achievement, and self-concept, as well as lower recidivism rates among juvenile offenders and reductions in substance abuse (Davidson & Redner, 1998; Grossman & Tierney, 1998; LoSciuto, Rajala, Townsend, & Taylor, 1996; McPartland & Nettles, 1991).

The largest, most influential evaluation of mentoring to date is the impact study of Big Brothers Big Sisters of America (Grossman & Tierney, 1998). This study is particularly important because of its scope (a sample of more than one thousand youth), its longitudinal status (extending over 18 months), and its experimental nature (youth were either on a waiting list or paired with a volunteer). The sample was diverse in terms of gender, race, and age, and the data collected included baseline and follow-up information on youth antisocial activities, academic outcomes, family and peer relationships, and self-concept, in addition to data on the duration, content, and nature of youths' relationships with their mentors. Although all youth exhibited gradual increases in problem behaviors over time, program participants increased at a slower rate than control group youth. At follow-up, youth who were matched with mentors reported lower levels of substance use and initiation, less physical aggression, more positive parent and peer relationships, and higher scholastic competence, attendance, and grades than control youth (Grossman & Tierney, 1998).

Since mentoring programs vary considerably, however, it is difficult to draw definitive conclusions regarding the overall effectiveness of this intervention strategy. Big Brothers Big Sisters is a large, prominent program with a long history and a standardized, intensive set of guidelines by which mentors are recruited, screened, and assigned to protégés. These guidelines encourage and facilitate the formation of long-term relationships between mentors and protégés, and typically provide the dyads with ongoing support and supervision. Other mentoring programs emphasize different elements of the intervention, and most offer far less guidance to their volunteers. In a meta-analysis of evaluations of mentoring programs, the study by DuBois, Holloway, Valentine, and Cooper (in press) found the overall effects of mentoring as an intervention to be relatively modest, especially when compared to other interpersonal interventions designed to improve youth outcomes. They attributed these attenuated effects to wide variation in quality across programs. Their study revealed a range of program practices that were associated with stronger effects, including training for mentors, structured activities for mentors and youth, and careful monitoring of matches.

Taken together, these practices converge with those identified by other researchers and are associated with more sustained relationships (Sipe, 1998). Relationship longevity is a particularly important consideration, especially since youth who are referred to mentoring programs often come from single-parent homes, and many have experienced multiple failed or disappointing relationships with adults. For these youth, the failure of yet another bond with an adult can undermine their sense of well-being. Grossman and Rhodes (in press) recently explored the predictors and effects of relationship duration, testing the hypothesis that the effects of mentoring would grow stronger over time, and that relatively short matches would lead to negative outcomes. Youth who were in relationships that lasted a year or longer reported improvements in academic, psychosocial, and behavioral outcomes; and progressively fewer effects emerged among youth who were in relationships that terminated between six months and a year or between three and six months. Additionally, adolescents who were in relationships that terminated within a very short period of time reported decrements in several indicators of functioning. Premature terminations occurred for a variety of reasons, ranging from competing time demands on the part of the volunteer to the presence of preexisting emotional problems on the part of the youth. The findings underscore the need for sufficient program resources to ensure reasonable levels of mentor screening, training, and post-match support.

Unfortunately, only a minority of mentoring programs provide adequate levels of training to volunteers, or make an effort to contact and regularly supervise volunteers (Sipe & Roder, 1999). For example, only about 40% of mentoring programs require that mentors make a commitment to participate for at least a full year, and as many as half of all relationships terminate within the first few months (Sipe & Roder, 1999). Those programs that do provide more intensive training and support often have long waiting lists of youth who qualify for the intervention but are not paired with mentors for months or even years. The time spent languishing on waiting lists can be even longer for youth with special requirements for the match, such as minority youth desiring a same-race mentor or immigrant youth experiencing language barriers (Rhodes, Reddy, Grossman, & Lee, in press; Roffman, Suárez-Orozco, & Rhodes, in press).

Given the need for adequate infrastructure, and the costs and delays involved in providing it, alternative solutions to the problem of the dwindling availability of nonparent adults should also be considered. Moreover, the intensive one-on-one emotional connection that lies at the heart of a mentoring relationship may not be necessary, appropriate, or even desirable for all youth. The needs of lower-risk youth might be satisfied through their contact with adult staff members in organized sports, activities, clubs, and other community settings.

Mentoring within the Community

Community-based settings may represent an appropriate, less-intensive alternative context for youth to forge ties with caring adults. Adolescents and adults often come into informal contact with each other in such settings and form close relationships as a by-product of their mutual involvement in recreational or educational activities. For example, youth often encounter community youth workers through their involvement in such organizations as the YM-YWCA or the Boys and Girls Clubs of America. Some of these programs are funded by municipal grants designed to provide after-school or summer activities for youth in parks, schools, or other public spaces. Still others are smaller, localized programs designed to meet the needs of a particular segment of the population by providing tutoring, career guidance, or other targeted services.

Regardless of size or scope, many of the programs that provide youth with adult guidance, supervision, and support are oriented toward a "youth development" philosophy (Larson, 2000; Lerner, Fisher, & Weinberg, 2000; Roth, Brooks-Gunn, Murray, & Foster, 1998). In contrast with the "deficit" philosophy of many programs designed to prevent negative outcomes among youth, a youth development program emphasizes the positive attributes and strengths that children and adolescents possess, and attempts to provide the support and encouragement needed for vulnerable youth to achieve their goals and reach their potential. In community agencies oriented toward a youth development approach, adult volunteers and staff members typically demonstrate many of the qualities of successful volunteer mentors. These include an understanding of youths' family dynamics and an ability to work with both youth and parents; the ability to create safe, collaborative spaces for learning and exploration in which youth take ownership and responsibility for their activities; a belief in youth potential; and an enthusiasm for and commitment to youth work (Baker, Pollack, & Kohn, 1995; Camino, 1994; Heath, 1994; McLaughlin et al., 1994; Morrow & Styles, 1995).

At the most basic level, youth who participate in community programs are enjoying out-of-school time that is not spent in isolation, unsupervised, or on the streets with their peers. Participants in such programs often describe them as safe havens from the pressures of the streets or as "second homes"—places where adolescents feel comfortable expressing themselves and letting down their guard (Hirsch et al., 2000; Villaruel & Lerner, 1994). Settings in which youth can congregate, socialize, and participate in recreational activities during their out-of-school hours represent an important option for those youth who may lack supervision while parents are at work or otherwise unavailable. This option provides youth with supervision from caring adults, while at the same time allowing them the independence needed to choose activities and interact freely with peers, an autonomy that becomes increasingly important as youth grow older (Beck, 1999; Bryant, 1989). Parents know that their children are in a safe setting and are unlikely to feel threatened by the intensity of a one-on-one relationship between their children and a volunteer mentor.

As is true of many volunteer mentors, the adults who work in community programs are often prepared to provide tutoring, educational guidance, advice about the college application process, and job search assistance. Staff members at community youth-serving agencies often report that they believe an important part of their role to be the reversal of inner city schools' and teachers' negative impact on the scholastic competence of low-income and minority youth (Heath, 1994; McLaughlin et al., 1994). In this way, community youth workers seek to provide some of the support that teachers who are constrained by shortages of resources and time are not able to provide.

Some researchers have characterized community youth centers in disadvantaged communities as performing a "bridging" function, discussing the link these programs provide between two disparate cultures—that of the inner city and that of the mainstream population. In addition, Heath (1994) characterized youth programs as a "border zone" between the streets and the mainstream culture. McLaughlin et al. (1994) described the adults working in the "urban sanctuaries" they evaluated as providing bridges between the inner city and the outside world of mainstream employment. This "bridge" role appears to be performed somewhat uniquely by community youth workers. In research comparing the types of support provided by extended-family adults, school adults, and staff members at Boys and Girls Clubs in several disadvantaged urban communities, Hirsch, Roffman, Pagano, and Deutsch (2000) found that club staff members were more likely than the other two types of adults to be described as having diffuse, complex relationships that were characteristic of mentoring. In addition, while school adults tended to provide instruction only in academic skills, relationships with club staff members tended to involve mentoring in a combination of skills and life lessons. The skills they taught included academics—they were the only one of the three groups of nonparental adults to provide help with homework—but also extended to sports and the arts. The life lessons they provided included ways to mediate conflicts, the avoidance of drugs and pregnancy, and the need to maintain lofty career goals and aspirations for the future.

These findings are complemented by other research on community-based youth programs. For example, Gamboni and Arbreton (1997) found that social support from adult staff was a major force motivating youth participation in after-school programs. The provision of this support was facilitated by structural features of the programs and specific staff practices, several of which are similar to the program practices that have been associated with more successful volunteer mentoring programs. Structural program elements included a high staff-youth ratio, a high level of staff stability, and time in the schedule for informal staff-youth interactions. Staff practices included growing familiarity with youth's outside lives (at home and at school) and making time to talk with youth about their progress and concerns. By focusing on the potential of youth, and operating in a respectful and informal manner, community-based programs provide an opportunity for youth who might not have access to adults through social networks or mentoring programs.

In summary, the literature suggests that, across many contexts, caring non-parental adults can be important developmental resources in the lives of adolescents. A continuing challenge will be to identify and enhance the settings in which positive interactions between nonparental adult mentors and youth can be formed and sustained. It will also be important for researchers to develop and test conceptual models that help to explain the underlying processes by which nonparent adult relationships influence developmental outcomes. A deeper understanding of the processes that govern mentoring relationships, and the conditions under which they occur, is likely to bring needed theoretical grounding to researchers and additional clarity to practitioners who are overseeing matches. In light of the diverse backgrounds of both youth and mentors, as well as the many forms that mentoring takes, there are likely to be a number of interacting processes by which mentoring affects youth outcomes. For example, whereas socioemotional processes may account for the improvements that are sometimes observed in adolescents' close relationships, cognitive processes may best explain the more advanced thinking skills that sometimes emerge from the bonds. Similarly, role modeling, shaping, and other behavioral processes may account for some of the positive changes in adolescents' behavior and life goals (Darling, Hamilton, & Niego, 1994; Rhodes, 2002). In the following section, each of these processes will be described.

A Conceptual Understanding of Mentoring

Mentors sometimes influence adolescents' approaches to other relationships and, in doing so, bring about positive change. For example, Rhodes, Grossman, and Resch (2001) have presented evidence to suggest that the effects of mentoring may be mediated through improvements in adolescents' relationships with their parents. Support for this potential can be found in attachment theory. In particular, children are thought to construct cognitive representations of relationships through their early experiences with primary caregivers. These beliefs and expectations, or working models, are then incorporated into the personality structure, where they are triggered and played out in new relationships throughout and beyond childhood. Although relatively stable, working models are thought to be flexible to revision in response to changing life circumstances, such as engagement in consistently supportive relationships with teachers or other adults. In fact, with the increase in perspective taking and interpersonal understanding that accompanies this stage of development, adolescence may lend itself uniquely to the revision and reconceptualization of working models (Main, Kaplan, & Cassidy, 1985). For example, adolescents can begin to compare relationships and, in doing so, recognize that some relationships may be better than others in meeting their attachment needs (Allen & Land, 1999). Similarly, adolescents' differentiation from and decreased reliance on parents as attachment figures create openings for the transfer of attachment needs to others.

A related pathway by which mentors may bring about change is through their influence on adolescents' cognitive development. Adolescence is characterized by heightened logical and abstract reasoning abilities, which are often shaped through social interactions. Since adolescents frequently are reluctant to discuss sensitive issues with their parents, mentors can provide a safe context for disclosures, transmitting adult values, advice, and perspectives. Given this privileged position, and the openings provided by adolescents' growing capacity for understanding and reflecting, mentors are uniquely situated to help youth stay in touch with their sense of self and advance their understanding of relationships. Adolescents' capacity for critical thinking and self-awareness may be advanced through their ongoing conversations on meaningful topics with mentors (Darling, Hamilton, & Hames, in press). In doing so, mentors can help adolescents test their ideas and engage in cognitive skills beyond those they are capable of handling on their own. The cognitive processes that emerge from such conversations can then be appropriated by adolescents, extending their existing base of knowledge and skills (Rogoff, 1990).

A final pathway by which positive bonds with mentors might influence adolescent developmental outcomes is through role modeling and shaping. Mentors can serve as concrete models of success, exemplifying qualities that adolescents might wish to emulate. By observing and comparing their own and their mentors' performance, adolescents can incorporate new behavioral repertoires. This modeling process, which sometimes occurs through formalized apprenticeships, is thought to be reinforced through mentors' support, feedback, and encouragement, and is intimately tied with the cognitive developmental processes described above (Darling et al., in press). Even when mentors do not serve as direct models or apprentices, they can be influential in shaping outcomes. For example, mentors can provide a safe and encouraging context for adolescents to explore different identities and experiment with new behavioral repertoires. Mentors can also hold adolescents to higher standards or introduce new visions of what adolescents can achieve. Along these lines, they can help their protégés establish connections and make use of resources in the community.

Of course, it is likely that these processes are interwoven and activated in conjunction with one another over time. For example, adolescents' shifting perspectives on relationships are mobilized by their emerging cognitive skills and operate according to social-cognitive rules (Erikson, 1993). Similarly, adolescents' capacity to engage in relationships and selectively attend to qualities of importance governs the extent to which their behavior can be effectively shaped by adults. It is also likely that different processes are amplified in different relationships. For example, adolescents who have had good relationships with their parents may be drawn to adults as role models and confidants, whereas those who have experienced unsatisfactory parental ties may develop compensatory bonds with mentors that address their social and emotional needs. An important role of mentors in this capacity may be to provide an emotionally secure base from which adolescents can explore and regulate their emotions. To the extent that mentors can provide scaffolding in this process, adolescents may be able to develop an independent, potentially healthier approach to emotional regulation than the approach that was developed in relation to their parents.

The benefits that adolescents derive from mentoring relationships may also vary as a function of their age, gender, or other preferences. For example, as older adolescents become increasingly drawn to peer relationships and activities, they tend to place greater emphasis on the vocational skill-building and role-modeling aspects of the relationships (Darling et al., in press). Gender may also affect the nature of the emotional connection that is formed with a mentor. Several researchers have concluded that girls form bonds with adults more readily than do boys (Blyth, Hill, & Thiel, 1982; Darling et al., 1994), although other research suggests that, especially among ethnic minorities, gender differences may be masking more complex patterns. For example, in her investigation of African American adolescents' support networks, Coates (1987) found that although girls reported more frequent contact with support figures and estimated larger networks than boys, there were no gender differences in the actual numbers of supportive adults that were listed and described. Other researchers have indicated that girls may be more linked to extended family adults, whereas boys may more readily cultivate ties outside the family (Feiring & Coates, 1987; Feiring & Lewis, 1989).

These gender issues may translate into differences in the processes at work in mentoring relationships. Liang, Tracy, Taylor, and Williams (in press) explored a relational model of mentoring and concluded that young women's successful ties with mentors may be more likely than those of boys or men to involve empathy, engagement, authenticity, and empowerment, as opposed to more instrumental, goal-based activities. Finally, Rhodes, Reddy, and Osborne (2001) found that adolescent girls who were referred to volunteer mentoring programs had lower initial levels of communication, trust, and intimacy with their mothers than did adolescent boys in mentoring relationships.

The personal preferences of both the mentor and the protégé undoubtedly influence the nature of the emotional connection that forms. For some, a relationship characterized by conversation and the sharing of confidences will fulfill a need, whereas others will prefer to spend time engaging in activities such as sports or skill-based exercises (Hamilton & Hamilton, 1992). Regardless of differences in the actual ways in which mentors and protégés spend their time together, it appears that successful mentor-youth bonds are characterized by a basic level of trust and emotional connection that, in turn, enables other pathways to be pursued (Rhodes, 2002).

Conclusions

Adolescence marks a time of multiple transitions, setting the stage for stress and uncertainty. Mentoring relationships can facilitate the successful navigation of these challenges. Such relationships can develop naturally or through programs, and their influence occurs through multiple, interacting pathways of influence. To the extent that these pathways become better understood, researchers will be better equipped to target and maximize the influence of the relationships. Irrespective of context or the underlying processes that are activated, successful relationships all share an emphasis on intensity and duration. Strong, long-term bonds require adequate resources and a careful consideration of factors that facilitate longevity. In volunteer mentoring programs, adequate training and supervision can make the difference between the premature termination of a relationship and the formation of a long-term bond. For youth workers and teachers, training and supervision can provide insights and skills that may not be part of the regular job of teaching or leading activities. Adults who feel confident in their abilities and skills are likely to be more effective in providing support and encouragement that matches the needs of the youth in their care.

It is also important to consider ways to bridge the gaps that may exist among adolescents' homes, schools, communities, and peer groups. Youth who lack adult support in any one of these settings may fall into risky behaviors and dangerous choices. To the extent that families, schools, and communities can marshal and coordinate their resources and strengths to foster the formation of enduring intergenerational bonds, one of the most critical developmental needs of adolescents can be effectively met.

References

Allen, J. P., & Land, D. (1999). Attachment in adolescence. In J. Cassidy, P. R. Shaver, et al. (Eds.), *Handbook of attachment: Theory, research, and clinical applications* (pp. 319–335). New York: Guilford Press.

Baker, K., Pollack, M., & Kohn, I. (1995). Violence prevention through informal socialization: An evaluation of the South Baltimore Youth Center. *Studies on Crime and Crime Prevention, 4,* 61–85.

Beam, M. R., Chen, C., & Greenberger, E. (in press). The nature of adolescents' relationships with their "very important" nonparental adults. *American Journal of Community Psychology.*

Beck, E. L. (1999). Prevention and intervention programming: Lessons from an after-school program. *Urban Review, 31,* 107–124.

Beier, S. R., Rosenfeld, W. D., Spitalny, K. C., Zanksy, S. M., & Bontemmpo, A. N. (2000). The potential role of an adult mentor in influencing high-risk behaviors in adolescents. *Archives of Pediatric Medicine, 154,* 327–331.

Benson, P. L., Leffert, N., Scales, P. C., & Blyth, D. (1998). Beyond the "village" rhetoric: Creating healthy communities for children and adolescents. *Applied Developmental Science, 2,* 138–159.

Blyth, D., Hill, J., & Thiel, K. (1982). Early adolescents' significant others: Grade and gender differences in perceived relationships with familial and nonfamilial adults and young people. *Journal of Youth and Adolescence, 11,* 425–450.

Bryant, B. K. (1989). The need for support in relation to the need for autonomy. In D. Belle (Ed.), *Children's social networks and social supports* (pp. 332–351). New York: John Wiley & Sons.

Camino, L. A. (1994). Refugee adolescents and their changing identities. In L. A. Camino & R. M. Krulfeld (Eds.). *Reconstructing lives, recapturing meaning: Refugee identity, gender, and culture change* (pp. 29–56). Amsterdam: Gordon & Breach.

Chase-Lansdale, L., Brooks-Gunn, J., & Zamsky, E. Y. (1994). *African-American intergenerational families in poverty: Quality of mothering and grandmothering.* Chicago: Irving B. Harris Graduate School of Public Policy.

Coates, D. (1987). Gender differences in the structure and support characteristics of Black adolescents' social networks. *Sex Roles, 17,* 667–687.

Collins, P. H. (1987). The meaning of motherhood in black culture and black mother/daughter relationships. *Sage: A Scholarly Journal of Black Women, 4,* 3–10.

Darling, N., Hamilton, S. F., & Hames, K. (in press). Relationships outside the family: Unrelated adults. *American Journal of Community Psychology.*

Darling, N., Hamilton, S., & Niego, S. (1994). Adolescents' relations with adults outside the family. In P. Montemayor, G. Adams, & T. Gullotta (Eds.), *Personal relationships during adolescence. Advances in adolescent development: An annual book series,* Thousand Oaks, CA: Sage.

Davidson, W. S., & Redner, R. (1988). The prevention of juvenile delinquency: Diversion from the juvenile justice system. In R. H. Price, E. L. Cowen, R. P. Lorion, & J. Ramos-McKay (Eds.), *Fourteen ounces of prevention: Theory, research, and prevention* (pp. 123–137). New York: Pergamon.

DuBois, D. L., Holloway, B. E., Valentine, J. C., & Cooper, H. (in press). Effectiveness of mentoring programs for youth: A meta-analytic review. *American Journal of Community Psychology.*

Eccles, J. S., Midgley, C., Wigfield, A., Buchanan, C. M., Reuman, D., Flanagan, C., & MacIver, D. (1993). Development during adolescence: The impact of stage-environment fit on young adolescents' experiences in schools and in families. *American Psychologist, 48,* 90–101.

Erikson, E. (1993). *Childhood and society.* New York: W. W. Norton.

Feiring, C., & Coates, D. (1987). Social networks and gender differences in the life space of opportunity: Introduction. *Sex Roles, 17,* 611–620.

Feiring, C., & Lewis, M. (1989). The social networks of girls and boys from early through middle childhood. In D. Belle (Ed.), *Children's social networks and social supports* (pp. 119–150). New York: John Wiley & Sons.

Gamboni, M., & Arbreton, A. (1997). *Safe havens: The contributions of youth organizations to healthy adolescent development.* Philadelphia: Public/Private Ventures.

Garmezy, N. (1985). Stress resistant children: The search for protective factors. In J. E. Stevenson (Ed.), *Recent research in developmental psychopathology* (pp. 220–227). Oxford: Pergamon.

Grossman, J. B., & Rhodes, J. E. (in press). The test of time: Predictors and effects of duration in youth mentoring relationships. *American Journal of Community Psychology.*

Grossman, J. B., & Tierney, J. P. (1998). Does mentoring work? An impact study of the Big Brothers/ Big Sisters program. *Evaluation Review, 22,* 403–426.

Hamilton, S., & Darling, N. (1989). Mentors in adolescents' lives. In K. Hurrelmann (Ed.), *The social world of adolescents: International perspectives* (pp. 121–140). Berlin: Walter de Gruyter.

Hamilton, S. F., & Hamilton, M. A. (1992). Mentoring programs: Promise and paradox. *Phi Delta Kappan, 73,* 546–550.

Heath, S. B. (1994). The project of learning from the inner-city youth perspective. *New Directions for Child Development, 63,* 25–34.

Hirsch, B. J., Roffman, J. G., Pagano, M. E., & Deutsch, N. L. (2000, March–April). *The role of youth-staff relationships in Boys & Girls Clubs.* Paper presented as part of a symposium, *Natural and volunteer mentoring relationships of adolescents,* at the Society for Research in Adolescence meetings, Chicago.

Hirsch, B. J., Roffman, J. G., Deutsch, N. L., Flynn, C. A., Loder, T. L., & Pagano, M. E. (2000). Inner-city youth development programs: Strengthening programs for adolescent girls. *Journal of Early Adolescence, 20,* 210–230.

Katz, S. R. (1999). Teaching in tensions: Latino immigrant youth, their teachers and the structures of schooling. *Teachers College Record, 100,* 809–840.

Klaw, E., & Rhodes, J. (1995). Mentor relationships and the career development of pregnant and parenting African-American teenagers. *Psychology of Women Quarterly, 19,* 551–562.

Larson, R. W. (2000). Toward a psychology of positive youth development. *American Psychologist, 55,* 170–183.

Lerner, R. M., Fisher, C. B., & Weinberg, R. A. (2000). Toward a science for and of the people: Promoting civil society through the application of developmental science. *Child Development, 71,* 11–20.

Liang, B., Tracy, A. J., Taylor, C. A., & Williams, L. M. (in press). Mentoring college-age women: A relational approach. *American Journal of Community Psychology.*

LoSciuto, L., Fox, M., Hilbert, S. M., & Sonkowsky, M. (1999). The mentoring factor: Evaluation of the Across Ages' intergenerational approach to drug abuse prevention. *Child and Youth Services, 20,* 77–99.

LoSciuto, L., Rajala, A. K., Townsend, T. N., & Taylor, A. S. (1996). An outcome evaluation of Across Ages: An intergenerational mentoring approach to drug prevention. *Journal of Adolescent Research, 11,* 116–129.

Luthar, S. S. (1991). Vulnerability and resilience: A study of high-risk adolescents. *Child Development, 62,* 600–616.

Main, M., Kaplan, N., & Cassidy, J. (1985). Security in infancy, childhood, and adulthood: A move to the level of representation. In I. Bretherton & E. Waters (Eds.), *Growing points of attachment theory and research. Monographs of the Society for Research in Child Development, 50,* 11–15.

Masten, A. S. & Coatsworth, J. D. (1998). The development of competence in favorable and unfavorable environments: Lessons from research on successful children. *American Psychologist, 53,* 205–220.

McLaughlin, M., Irby, M., & Langman, J. (1994). *Urban sanctuaries: Neighborhood organizations in the lives and futures of inner-city youth.* San Francisco: Jossey-Bass.

McLoyd, V. (1990). The impact of economic hardship on black families and children: Psychological distress, parenting, and socioemotional development. *Child Development, 61,* 311–346.

McPartland, J. M. & Nettles, S. M. (1991). Using community adults as advocates or mentors for at-risk middle school students: A two-year evaluation of Project RAISE. *American Journal of Education, 99,* 568–586.

Morrow, K. V., & Styles, M. B. (1995). *Building relationships with youth in program settings: A study of Big Brothers/Big Sisters*. Philadelphia: Public/Private Ventures.

Putnam, R. D. (2000). *Bowling alone: The collapse and revival of American community*. New York: Simon & Schuster.

Rhodes, J. E. (2002). *Older and wiser: Risks and rewards in youth mentoring*. Cambridge, MA: Harvard University Press.

Rhodes, J. E. (in press). Mentoring programs. In A. E. Kazdin (Ed.), *Encyclopedia of psychology*. Washington, DC: American Psychological Association.

Rhodes, J. E., Contreras, J., & Manglesdorf, S. (1994). Natural mentor relationships among Latina adolescent mothers. *American Journal of Community Psychology, 22*, 211–228.

Rhodes, J. E., & Davis, A. A. (1996). Supportive ties between nonparent adults and urban adolescent girls. In B. J. Leadbeater & N. Way (Eds.), *Urban girls: Resisting stereotypes, creating identities* (pp. 213–249). New York: New York University Press.

Rhodes, J. E., Ebert, L., & Fischer, K. (1992). Natural mentors: An overlooked resource in the social networks of young, African American mothers. *American Journal of Community Psychology, 20*, 445–461.

Rhodes, J. E., Gingiss, P. L., & Smith, P. B. (1994). Risk and protective factors for alcohol use among pregnant African American, Hispanic, and White adolescents: The influence of peers, sexual partners, family members, and mentors. *Addictive Behaviors, 19*, 555–564.

Rhodes, J. E., Grossman, J. B., & Resch, N. L. (2001). Agents of change: Pathways through which mentoring relationships influence adolescents' academic adjustment. *Child Development, 71*, 1662–1671.

Rhodes, J. E., Haight, W. L., & Briggs, E. C. (1999). The influence of mentoring on the peer relationships of foster youth in relative and nonrelative care. *Journal of Research on Adolescence, 9*, 185–201.

Rhodes, J. E., Reddy, R., Grossman, J. B., & Lee, J. M. (2001). *Volunteer mentoring relationships with minority youth: An analysis of same- versus cross-race matches*. Manuscript under review.

Rhodes, J. E., Reddy, R., & Osborne, L. N. (2001). *Protégé baseline characteristics as predictors of youth outcomes in mentoring programs*. Manuscript in preparation.

Roeser, R., & Eccles, J. S. (1998). Adolescents' perceptions of middle school: Relation to longitudinal changes in academic and psychological adjustment. *Journal of Research on Adolescence, 8*, 123–158.

Roffman, J. G., Suárez-Orozco, C., & Rhodes, J. E. (in press). Facilitating positive development in immigrant youth: The role of mentors and community organizations. In D. F. Perkins, L. M. Borden, J. G. Keith, & F. A. Villaruel (Eds.), *Positive youth development: Creating a positive tomorrow*. Norwell, MA: Kluwer Academic Press.

Rogoff, B. (1990). *Apprenticeship in thinking: Cognitive development in social context*. New York: Oxford University Press.

Roth, J., Brooks-Gunn, J., Murray, L., & Foster, W. (1998). Promoting healthy adolescents: Synthesis of youth development program evaluations. *Journal of Research on Adolescence, 8*, 423–459.

Scales, P. C., & Leffert, N. (1999). *Developmental assets: A synthesis of the scientific research on adolescent development*. Minneapolis, MN: Search Institute.

Sipe, C. L. (1998). Mentoring adolescents: What have we learned? In J. B. Grossman (Ed.), *Contemporary issues in mentoring* (pp. 11–23). Philadelphia: Public/Private Ventures.

Sipe, C. L., & Roder, A. E. (1999). *Mentoring school-age children: A classification of programs*. Philadelphia: Public/Private Ventures.

Taylor, R., Casten, R., & Flickinger, S. (1993). Influence of kinship social support on the parenting experiences and psychosocial adjustment of African-American adolescents. *Developmental Psychology, 29*, 382–388.

Villaruel, F. A., & Lerner, R. M. (1994). *Promoting community-based programs for socialization and learning.* San Francisco: Jossey-Bass.

Werner, E. E., & Smith, R. S. (1982). *Vulnerable but invincible: A study of resilient children.* New York: McGraw-Hill.

Wilson, W. J. *The truly disadvantaged: The inner city, the underclass, and public policy.* Chicago: University of Chicago Press, 1987.

Zimmerman, M. A., Bingenheimer, J. B., & Notaro, P. C. (in press). Natural mentors and adolescent resiliency: A study with urban youth. *American Journal of Community Psychology.*

Part IV

A Vision for the Future

9 Toward Asset-Building Communities: How Does Change Occur?

Peter L. Benson
Search Institute

The concept of developmental assets was premiered in 1990 (Benson, 1990) and quickly became linked with other theories and models of developmental strengths, including resiliency (Garmezy, 1991), protective factors (Hawkins, Catalano, & Miller, 1992), and positive youth development (Benson & Pittman, 2001). In 1997, the Presidents' Summit for America's Future convened in Philadelphia with the participation of then president Bill Clinton and former presidents George Bush, Jimmy Carter, and Gerald Ford. The summit gave birth to America's Promise under the leadership of General Colin Powell. This effort has provided an additional language of developmental strengths as it rallies communities to promote five fundamental resources: ongoing relationships with caring adults, access to and engagement in safe places with structured activities, a healthy start, the development of marketable skills, and opportunities for community service and civic engagement.

It could be said, then, that the 1990s triggered an unprecedented proliferation of models and research dedicated to naming developmental nutrients and, as a corollary, introduced a new organizing principle into policy debates about how to advance child and adolescent well-being. Since the 1960s, deficit reduction has been the dominant organizing framework (Benson, 1997). It gave impetus for the aggressive growth of prevention programs and funding initiatives as well as a series of national social indicator studies that track youth engagement in health-compromising behaviors (e.g., violence, adolescent pregnancy, alcohol and tobacco use, illicit drug use). The organizing principle suggested by models of developmental nutrients, on the other hand, emphasizes promotion rather than prevention and requires an alternative indicator system—not yet institutionalized at the federal level—that tracks youth access to and utilization of the kinds of supports and opportunities suggested by emerging developmental nutrient models.

Why this second organizing principle is emerging now would be a useful line of historical and sociological inquiry. However, the most compelling questions emerging from the evolving study of developmental strengths/nutrients have to do with the processes and procedures of increasing access and utilization on a rather massive scale. And truth be told, though all architects of developmental nutrient models are deeply interested in application, the science of how change occurs is in its infancy. We have invested much more intellectual and research energy in naming the positive building blocks of development and demonstrating their predictive utility for enhancing health and academic outcomes than in studying the complex array of strategies and procedures for moving the developmental needle forward.

In this concluding chapter, my intent is to look at the chapters in this volume for clues about sector, community, and social change. My interest here is both in advancing how to think about change and in discovering initial hypotheses about how change is triggered and sustained.

Promoting Positive Human Development: Six Essential Questions

An applied science devoted to increasing access to supports and opportunities must address several interrelated questions. Here are six crucial ones:

A. What are the necessary and essential building blocks of positive development during the second decade of life? How must these be calibrated to gender, age, and other aspects of individual-level diversity?

B. How do these building blocks (i.e., developmental assets, nutrients) inform youth outcomes (e.g., health behaviors, academic achievement, thriving)? Are assets additive? Do effects hold across demographic categories?

C. What are the sources, both direct and indirect, of the building blocks? Who and what have capacity? How efficacious are relationships with adults, positive peer influence, developmental ecologies such as families, neighborhoods and schools, programs, and policy? Is community a viable "delivery system"?

D. What do these "delivery systems"—whether ecologies, programs, or relationships—look like when they function at optimal levels? In asset language, what does an asset champion look like? What do asset-building places, programs, and sectors look like? And, on a bigger canvas, what do asset-building communities and society look like?

E. In moving delivery systems from the status quo to these optimal levels, what theories and models of change and transformation should guide us?

F. What are the actual techniques and practices that effectively create desirable change?

In (E) theories of change and (F) the practice of change, the range of issues that need to be explored is extensive and compelling. A few include building effective, cross-sector collaborations; leadership development; building shared vision; activating collective and personal efficacy; building social trust; building receptivity to change; transforming the cultures of schools, neighborhoods, and congregations; mobilizing adults and youth; connecting the dots and sustaining energy.

Several points are made clearer when these six questions are placed in a flow chart (see Figure 1).

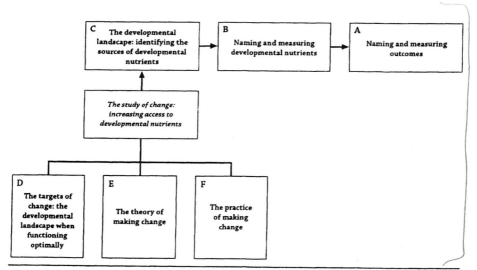

Figure 1. *Framing an Applied Science for Positive Human Development*

Figure 1 is certainly an oversimplified, minimalist picture of the arenas of inquiry within an "applied science for positive human development." But it helps to make three major points:

1. For cells A, B, and C, individuals may be the focal units of analysis; for cells D, E, and F, social entities are the focal analysis units. Examples include schools, neighborhoods, families, communities, and society. D, E, and F, then, are about the scientific inquiry needed to optimize and mobilize the sources found in C. By viewing it in this way, it becomes obvious that in understanding how to move the developmental needle forward for America's young, we need more than good developmental

science. We also need to draw on a series of disciplines—sociology, history, anthropology, political science, economics, and community development among them—to create the knowledge and wisdom for bringing about change at the citizen, sector, community, and societal levels.

2. A disproportionate amount of scientific energy is devoted to cells B and A and their intersection. Less energy is directed to conceptualizing the developmental landscape (C). Bronfenbrenner's (1979) pioneering conceptualization of the interlocking layers of environmental influence remains one of the major theoretical efforts seeking to articulate the richness and complexity of this domain.

3. The theoretical and empirical void becomes most pronounced at points D, E, and F in the diagram. These are three interlocking areas of inquiry necessary to advance knowledge and practice in making change (that is, in mobilizing the nutrient-delivering capacity of settings and relationships). This stream of scientific work requires, at a minimum, conceptualizations of "what it looks like when we get there" (D), theories of change (E), and knowledge about effective strategies and practices (F).

For now let us call the combination of D, E, and F the scientific study of pathways to change. In both the more basic research tradition in developmental psychology and the more applied tradition of youth development, research rarely makes it beyond the C, B, A cells in Figure 1 (Benson & Pittman, 2001). Among the exceptions are efforts to build logic models for expanding access to developmental nutrients (e.g., Connell & Kubisch, 2001)—cell E in Figure 1—and to identify characteristics and features of developmentally rich ecologies (e.g., Elder & Conger, 2000). This line of inquiry emerges from the John D. and Catherine T. MacArthur Foundation's Network on Successful Adolescence in High Risk Settings and is among the few conceptual projects we could include in framing cell D.

In building a science around pathways to change, we would be well served to look at and learn from scholarship devoted to promoting change in other arenas. We would suspect that one could map out fairly comprehensive understandings of D, E, and F in the arenas of organizational development, economic policy, economic development, marketing, and nation building.

The intriguing issue is how to build a line of inquiry that integrates all of the cells in Figure 1. It is rare, of course, for any of us to be trained (or rewarded) to think on the big canvas that this multidisciplinary line of inquiry requires. But it certainly would be both socially important and intellectually enticing to create those new alliances, dissemination vehicles, conversations, and funding streams to further this critical area of inquiry.

Pathways to Change

A science of change and change making in the service of advancing access to multiple developmental nutrients would explore five pathways and the interactions among them:

- Pathways to adult engagement (how to mobilize adults, both within communities and as a national force engaging in asset-building actions);
- Pathways to adolescent engagement (how to mobilize adolescents to become proactive in their own developmental journey and to activate their asset-building capacity with peers and younger children);
- Pathways to sector transformation (how to increase the delivery of developmental nutrients by means of extant socializing systems, including families, neighborhoods, congregations, schools, youth organizations, and places of work);
- Pathways to community change (how to orchestrate and sustain transformation and engagement within and across multiple actors, settings, and ecologies); and
- Pathways to social change (how to promote developmentally attentive and asset-enhancing social norms, national policy, local policy, and media influence).

Each of these five pathways can, of course, be examined through the D, E, and F lenses in Figure 1 to identify "what it looks like when we get there" (D), the theory of change (E), and the strategy and practice of change (F).

Each of the chapters in this volume provides perspective and insight on one or more of these pathways. It is fitting, then, to examine them through this pathways lens and to conclude this chapter with a series of 10 initial principles germane to increasing access to developmental nutrients. In so doing, I take considerable liberty in weaving themes across multiple authors. I think of these principles as a shared work, inspired by our collective pursuit of social change, and as a preliminary attempt to frame some of the mandates, possibilities, and strategies for advancing the science, the practice, and the civic engagement needed to transform American communities.

1. Change the language used to describe children and adolescents. Recasting youth as resources to be developed rather than "problems to be fixed" is a reframing necessary for reengaging and reenergizing citizens and social institutions in creating asset-building relationships

with youth. Two particular strategies are needed here: creating and disseminating an alternative set of social indicators (which track how well communities—and the nation as a whole—are providing developmental nutrients); and providing training, technical assistance, and incentives for the print and broadcast news media to draw citizens toward youth rather than away from them.

2. Transform public perceptions of youth and personal capacity. Part of this process will emerge as principle 1 above is achieved. However, reigniting adult engagement in the lives of children and adolescents requires more than changing the valence of adult sentiments. Also needed is attention to providing the public with skill, practice, and social norms that demand and expect constructive engagement. Recent research on social norms suggests a variety of strategies for norm change (Scales et al., 2001).

3. Mobilize local communities to identify common ground. A critical developmental process is to embed children and adolescents in networks of citizens and social institutions who speak with harmony of voice about locally prized and locally developed expectations and values. Multiple chapters speak to the power of this dynamic, its relative absence in contemporary community life, and the feasibility of orchestrating community-wide dialogues to bring forth a common vision. Innovations like Damon's youth charter (see Chapter 3) deserve broad support and implementation.

4. Position children and adolescents as necessary and essential change agents in the transformation of community life. The wisdom found in these chapters provides a multilevel understanding of youth engagement. Three strategies are highlighted: the active inclusion of youth in naming and documenting developmental nutrients; the engagement of youth in community-based public dialogues designed to establish common ground and local change-making strategies; and the positioning of youth as critical actors in creating and providing asset-building supports and opportunities. We might go so far as to say that changing the developmental landscape in American communities cannot occur, on a significant scale, without deep attention to youth as agents of change. And, if we are to create a science that is useful for articulating and triggering new frames, new strategies, and new practices, that inquiry must engage youth as experts and co-learners.

The connection between the developmental landscape (cell C in Figure 1) and the developing adolescent (cell B) is not unidirectional.

Indeed, a developmental system approach suggests that the influence is bidirectional (Lerner, 1996, 2002). Accordingly, strategies for increasing the asset-building capacity of developmental ecologies should include the positioning of youth as prime actors in effecting ecological transformation.

5. Activate sustained relationships. Two lines of scientific work discussed in these chapters are important here: one demonstrates that quality relationships are *a* if not *the* primary delivery system for many developmental nutrients. The other is the importance of sustained relationships (or what Jean Rhodes [2001] calls relationship longevity) in maximizing the asset-building capacity of adult-youth connectedness. There is mounting evidence that local communities are organized around providing short-term, transitory relationships. For spreading access to supports and opportunities, there may be no more critical need than to build a science, a practice, and a public will to discover (or perhaps rediscover) the nature and dynamics of intergenerational community.

6. Position the family as an essential partner in strengthening the developmental landscape. Al Gore's foreword to this volume clearly signals this issue and the ways communities can and should use their family-strength-building capacities. Rae Simpson's testimony regarding families' asset-building capacities pushes us to contemplate with her how to organize and orchestrate a nationwide process to disseminate practical tools and ideas designed to nudge families forward. It is worth noting at this point that youth development conversations in the United States tend to view the family as a secondary player. Indeed, there may even be a nonpartisan political process emerging here. Mr. Gore's ideas could be seen as groundbreaking and bridge building in his attempt to bring family, community, and youth into a single, nonpartisan framework.

7. Treat community as a pivotal entry point for making change. It is clear across many chapters in this volume that advancing the developmental needle requires forms of synergy, shared purpose, and public engagement that no single social institution can hope to achieve. Watch out, several authors suggest, for the ease and dispatch with which initiatives become owned (either in reality of perception) by a school district, an agency, or a governmental entity. Much work is needed to discover how to successfully position and sustain a change-making effort as a public idea, as an enterprise that belongs to "all of us."

8. In disseminating new ideas and new strategies for the local production of developmental nutrients, pay attention to process and individual differences. There may be stages in both individual and community readiness.

9. Trust the people. Much expertise and wisdom about human development are grounded in community memory and tradition. An applied
   science of positive human development—to be helpful rather than ir-
   relevant to making change—learns how to learn what the people
   know.

10. In evolving this applied science of positive human development, at-
    tend to contemporary developmental system theory and several key
    constructs. "Relative plasticity" in development suggests there are
    considerable possibilities during the second decade of life to orches-
    trate interactions among developmental ecologies that can inform de-
    velopmental trajectories. These ecologies and contexts involve multi-
    ple levels, including proximal social relationships, macroinstitutions
    from public policy to economics, and the natural and designed physi-
    cal ecologies of human development.

In crafting this synthesis of core ideas, I am struck by what the chapters do
not discuss. With rare exception, public policy is a quiet, in-the-background
theme. And as such, this silent theme suggests a major idea, one that deserves
considerable conversation and debate: when it comes to spreading access to developmental nutrients, the *lead* actors are the people, and the traditional stuff
of policy—regulation, resources, funding—is best positioned as a *supporting*
actor in assisting people to imagine and create developmentally attentive
communities.

References

Benson, P. L. (1990). *The troubled journey: A portrait of 6th–12th grade youth.* Minneapolis: Search
   Institute.
Benson, P. L. (1997). *All kids are our kids: What communities must do to raise caring and responsible children
   and adolescents.* San Francisco: Jossey-Bass.
Benson, P. L., & Pittman, K. J. (Eds.). (2001). *Trends in youth development: Visions, realities and challenges.*
   Norwell, MA: Kluwer Academic Publishers.
Bronfenbrenner, U. (1979). *The ecology of human development: Experiments by nature and design.*
   Cambridge, MA: Harvard University Press.
Connell, J. P., & Kubisch, A. C. (2001). Community approaches to improving outcomes for urban chil-
   dren, youth, and families: Current trends and future directions. In A. Booth & A. C. Crouter (Eds.),
   Does it take a village? Community effects on children, adolescents, and families (pp. 177–201).
   Mahwah, NJ: Lawrence Erlbaum.

Elder, G. H., & Conger, R. D. (2000). *Children of the land: Adversity and success in rural America.* Chicago: University of Chicago Press.

Garmezy, N. (1991). Resiliency and vulnerability to adverse outcomes associated with poverty. *American Behavioral Scientist, 34,* 416–430.

Hawkins, J. D., Catalano, R. F., & Miller, J. Y. (1992). Risk and protective factors for alcohol and other drug problems in adolescence and early adulthood: Implications for substance abuse prevention. *Psychological Bulletin, 112,* 64–105.

Lerner, R. M. (1996). Relative plasticity, integration, temporality, and diversity in human development: A developmental contextual perspective about theory, process, and method. *Developmental Psychology, 32,* 781–786.

Lerner, R. M. (2002). *Concepts and theories of human development (3rd ed.).* Mahwah, NJ: Lawrence Erlbaum.

Rhodes, J. E. (2001). *Older and wiser: Risks and rewards in youth mentoring.* Cambridge, MA: Harvard University Press.

Scales, P. C., Benson, P. L., Roehlkepartain, E. C., Hintz, N. R., Sullivan, T. K., & Mannes, M. (2001). The role of neighborhood and community in building developmental assets for children and youth: A national study of social norms among American adults. *Journal of Community Psychology, 29,* 703–727.

10 Afterword: Toward an Asset-Based Policy Agenda for Children, Families, and Communities

Neal Halfon
University of California at Los Angeles

This volume has presented a practical and pathbreaking approach to linking youth and community development strategies pioneered by Search Institute. The volume also offers critical reflections by researchers and practitioners on the importance and applicability of this approach to youth and community development. In addition to the enormous potential value that this approach has for communities seeking to fashion new strategies for creating and promoting the resources for youth development, the assumptions, ideas, and evidence presented also have broader implications for national, state, and local public policy focused on work, family, health, and education.

As the title, *Developmental Assets and Asset-Building Communities: Implications for Research, Policy, and Practice*, suggests, this volume links theoretical and practical traditions in a new and more integrative approach to human and community development. Developmental assets (DA) are an important bridging concept that encompasses and organizes rich empirical and theoretical traditions in developmental psychology and human development in a way that makes these traditions available for community practice. Asset-building communities (ABCs) are also a bridging concept that reflects and integrates the research and practice traditions in community organizing, community development, and community building. ABCs also provide a bridge to the public health field, where community-based practice has moved well beyond notions of community health to broad integrative initiatives using similar asset-based frameworks focused on building healthy communities. This unified DA-ABCs approach incorporates into the logic of individual and community transformation the understanding that strategies that foster individual development must be nested within and integrated into broad-based strategies for family-centered community building. The powerful new practice and intervention framework created by Search Institute does just that: it integrates individual and family change processes focused on positive health and human development, with a complementary set of community-building activities. In years to come, development assets and asset-building communities are likely to become important icons of a powerful policy agenda, and like the icons on a desktop computer, clicking on the DA icon will unpack a powerful set of tools and applications that not only can be used to construct ABCs but also help create the conditions for the development of asset-building cultures.

By focusing public policy making on creating ABCs, it is possible to redirect large social institutions (e.g., health and educational systems) and community-based organizations (e.g., schools, clubs, and religious organizations) to support the relationships that bind communities together and promote the building of developmental assets. Such relationships are conducive to reciprocal altruism and support the social values of generosity, gratitude, and trust (Wright, 2000). Implicit in this work is that asset-building cultures can help transmit these values—to individuals, families, and entire communities.

In the same way that the contributors to this volume have demonstrated how applied developmental science can be used to align human development with a changing social context, so also can appropriate public policy be used to align social programs and resource allocation with the building of developmental assets for individuals, families, and communities. The DA-ABCs approach constitutes a powerful framework for developing a vision for U.S. domestic policy and can inform strategic initiatives to fulfill a new vision for communities. The organization of developmental assets into arrays of easily understandable categories provides multiple entry points for community-based change. The DA-ABCs approach also supports the development of positive relationships within families, new relationships between families, and a different set of relationships between families and community institutions, organizations, and agencies. This rich web of asset-building relationships facilitates learning, development, and fulfillment, as well as the greater realization of human potential.

A communication strategy that frames asset-based community building and positive youth development can be targeted not just at changing how children, youth, and parents view their roles and relationships in a community, but also at reframing how community-based institutions, stakeholders, and policy makers understand their own roles and goals. In this way, asset-based principles and values become an organizing framework for developing policy and communicating the mechanisms a community can use and devise to ensure that its youth develop intellectually, morally, socially, emotionally, and physically.

Broader Policy Implications

A wide range of policies can be implemented to support community builders and to align political and economic resources in order to further asset building at the neighborhood, family, and individual levels. A general principle is that beneficial policy would align community goals, resources, and assets with the human development priorities of that community. In addition, policies should contribute to the development of social capital by supporting positive relationships between individuals, within and between families, and between families and community-based institutions such as schools, congregations, law enforcement, recreational centers, and other organizations and agencies.

Three major areas in which policy development could advance the goals of asset building and asset-based community building are:

- Health policy;
- Education policy; and
- Family and work policy.

Each of these public policy domains is accountable for enormous expenditures at the federal, state, and local level each year. They are also responsible for supporting and sustaining a significant proportion of the human services infrastructure in many communities. While it is impossible to provide a comprehensive breakdown of how the framework of developmental assets can be used to transform all the policies in any domain, I will attempt to make some illustrative suggestions. A more complete list of potential policies could be developed, but I offer the following as a way of stimulating this next round of discussions.

Health Policy

Health policy encompasses those policies that affect both the delivery of services to individuals by physicians, hospitals, and health-care organizations (e.g., HMOs) and policies that affect the delivery of public health services. Both the personal and public health-care systems continue to focus on traditional modes of diagnosis, treatment, and prevention of disease, but both also are increasingly focusing on new morbidities (e.g., mental health problems) and what can be done to promote the health of individuals, populations, and communities. As the personal health-care system wrestles with runaway costs, it must consider how to redirect more of its resources into long-term prevention strategies, including preventing the onset and minimizing the impact of chronic diseases that affect so many Americans and clearly have their origins in many of the behaviors that are adopted early in life. National public health policy is also increasingly directed toward strategies intended to promote health, such as the Department of Health and Human Services' Healthy People program, whose goal is to build protective factors and health-promoting behaviors (read "developmental assets").

One of the burgeoning areas of health policy focus is mental health. The recent Surgeon General's report on mental health has documented the toll of mental health problems on individuals, families, and society (including skyrocketing health-care and work-related costs). (The report can be found at www.surgeongeneral.gov/library/mentalhealth/home.html.) The Surgeon General's report also makes it clear that many mental health problems have their origins early in life, have long, definable predisease pathways, and are often preventable through a combination of effective early interventions and mental health promotion strategies (read "developmental assets").

As the Institute of Medicine's report on the future of public health suggests, the core functions of public health are assessment, assurance, and policy development (Institute of Public Medicine, 1988). Many public health departments in states and communities throughout the United States are aligning their assessment functions with their assurance of appropriate health-promoting interventions and resources. As a result, the potential for public health departments to get more into the business of measuring developmental assets, and allocating their formidable data collection and analysis capacities to this cause, is increasingly feasible. Moreover, aligning strategies for creating ABCs with community health initiatives coming out of public health departments also seems like a natural alliance.

Therefore, to begin to determine how health policy could be informed by and support the developmental assets and asset-building communities, the appropriate agencies and institutions should consider:

- Redirecting and further aligning the $1.3 trillion in personal medical care expenditures and services with health-promoting services that build developmental assets with and for individuals and families. A greater focus on financing and investing in healthy development could provide a new set of strategic resources to promote asset building (Halfon & Hochstein, 2002).
- Aligning existing pubic health system functions of assessment assurance and policy development with the goals of asset building. Rather than the measurement of developmental assets being something that is "done" only as a part of a "special project," the routine monitoring and promotion of developmental assets in neighborhoods and communities should become an essen-

tial component of what public health systems do for the communities they serve.

- Incorporating into popular and ever increasing health service integration initiatives an asset-building approach that can foster collaboration across different public systems through a broad network of resources that cross traditional boundaries and challenge traditional assumptions.

Education Policy

Another major focus of U.S. domestic policy is education. The same is true at the state level, where nearly half of state budgets are allocated to education. The importance of education in American politics and policy development has also been demonstrated in several recent mayoral elections in which education was among the dominant issues, even in cities where the mayor has no legal or statutory authority over this domain of public life. Across the nation many communities are considering how to reconfigure their school systems, updating and modernizing buildings, introducing more accountability for outcomes, but also redefining their social compact so that schools can assume a more active role as community centers and institutions of lifelong learning.

The recent brain science revolution that has accentuated the importance of the early years and the need for more public investment in early care and education is driving state and local reform efforts to create early childhood educational systems. The National Association for the Education of Young Children (NAEYC) has promulgated principles of school readiness that are quite consistent with the developmental asset approach. NAEYC's readiness principles emphasize how parents, schools, and communities must support the developmental assets of young children. Therefore the design for these early childhood systems is also clearly conducive to promoting development assets for young children and asset-building communities focused on the early years (Halfon, McLearn, & Schuster, 2002).

A community-based educational model that is increasingly embraced by early childhood educators has its origins in the educational system in the town of Reggio, Italy (Gardner, 1999). The Reggio model is a northern Italian version of an asset-building community that is focused on promoting developmental assets for young children (Edwards, Gandini, & Forman, 1998). The Reggio model of education supports the enhancement of learning and critical thinking capacities by mobilizing community resources in service to young children's burgeoning abilities to explore and actively learn in a community-supported environment.

The coming years are likely to see a greater integration of research and policy development focused on the early years and school readiness with similar efforts focused on enhancing developmental assets for older children and youth. In order to determine how education policy can be further informed by and support developmental assets and the creation of asset-building communities, the appropriate agencies and institutions should consider:

- Supporting the movement for schools to become community learning centers and essential partners in building developmental assets in communities.
- Providing resources for schools to develop family resource centers on school campuses and provide other services that are essential in overcoming barriers to learning. Beacon Schools, 21st Century Schools, and Comer Schools are all examples of models that are heading in this direction.
- Creating greater developmental integrity and continuity in schools by considering K–12 school sites, to provide greater developmental support and continuity of relationships. Also worthy of consideration are new school models that integrate early and primary education in one continuum (birth to 8-year-old learning systems) and 8- to 18-year-olds into another linked system.
- Introducing a community-building component into middle and high school curriculums that allows for students to take part in family-centered community-building activities.
- Expanding service-learning opportunities beginning in elementary school in order to embed a service ethos into educational practice, and to link education with community-building efforts.

Family and Work Policy

Families in the United States are being stretched in many directions. The demands of care giving coupled with the demands of earning a livelihood are stretching many families to the max. In a recent survey of 5,000 parents in California, nearly 85% of parents reported that they go to bed exhausted each night, with nearly that proportion also reporting that they have no time for themselves. For parents to have the ability to invest their time and energy in the relationships within their family and their community that are going to promote the development of essential assets that their children require, changes in work and family leave policy are essential. To pave the way for greater family involvement in asset-building community activities, changes in public policy that mediate the role of work in families' lives are essential. The appropriate agencies and institutions should consider:

- Expanding family leave provisions to permit greater involvement in essential family and youth development activities.

- Expanding workplace-focused parental support programs to facilitate communication and relationship building skills by parents with their children and youth.
- Increasing the availability of affordable housing to reduce the necessity for parents to work extended hours to meet their families' financial needs.
- Increasing the minimum wage to a living wage reflective of the regional cost of living. Fairer wages can further the ability for parents to sufficiently provide for their families within reasonable work hours and increase their involvement with family members.
- Providing good-quality child care for low-wage earners. The provision of affordable care can reduce unsupervised time for children, and enable parents to work full time, attend school, or receive job training.

This preliminary list of policy initiatives is meant to begin a dialogue about how developmental assets and asset-building communities can be more widely supported. It is also meant to show the potential synergies between the initiatives and practice strategies of Search Institute and larger policy agendas that are emerging, and to support broader collaborative efforts that can stimulate and sustain community-building initiatives. Creating the programmatic and policy agenda that supports the powerful vision embodied in this approach will facilitate the further development of asset building within communities throughout the United States.

References

Edwards, C., Gandini, L., & Forman, G. (1998). *The hundred languages of children: The Reggio Emilia approach.* Westport, CT: Ablex Publishing.

Gardner, H. (1999). *The disciplined mind: What all students should understand.* New York: Simon and Schuster.

Halfon, N., & Hochstein, M. (2002). Life course health development: An integrated framework for developing health, policy, and research. *Milbank Review, 80,* 433–479.

Halfon, N., McLearn, K. T., & Schuster, M. A. (Eds.). (2002). *Child rearing in America: Challenges facing parents with young children.* Cambridge: Cambridge University Press.

Institute of Medicine. (1988). *The future of public health.* Washington, DC: National Academy Press.

Wright, R. (2000). *Non-zero: The logic of human destiny.* New York: Pantheon.

Contributors

Peter L. Benson has served since 1985 as president of Search Institute in Minneapolis, a national nonprofit research organization dedicated to promoting the well-being of children and adolescents. Benson also is adjunct professor in the Department of Educational Policy and Administration at the University of Minnesota and the first Visiting Scholar at the William T. Grant Foundation in New York City. Among his books on children, adolescents, and the community forces that shape their lives are *All Kids Are Our Kids: What Communities Must Do to Raise Caring and Responsible Children and Adolescents; The Fragile Foundation: The State of Developmental Assets among American Youth*; and *Religion on Capitol Hill: Myths and Realities*. His work has been reported in *Time, Newsweek, U.S. News and World Report*, the *New York Times*, and the *Washington Post*.

Mary Carlson is associate professor of psychiatry at Harvard Medical School. With a background in neuroscience, she currently conducts research within a framework of child rights.

Brian Chan is a student at Harvard Medical School. He plans to pursue his interests in children's health and well-being in a career at the junction of medicine and public health.

William Damon is the director of the Stanford Center on Adolescence, which provides guidance for parenting, improved educational practice, and youth development in a wide variety of community settings by offering cross-departmental collaboration on critical problems in youth development. In addition to his work on the development of youth charters for schools and communities nationwide, Damon writes on intellectual and moral development through the life span; among his books are *Greater Expectations: Overcoming the Culture of Indulgence in Our Homes and Schools* and *The Moral Child: Nurturing Children's Natural Moral Growth*. He also serves as editor in chief of *New Directions for Child and Adolescent Development* and *The Handbook of Child Psychology*.

Felton Earls is professor of social medicine at Harvard Medical School. He is a child psychiatrist and epidemiologist with long-standing interests in international child health.

Al Gore is currently a visiting professor teaching a course on family-centered community building at Middle Tennessee State University in Murfreesboro and at Fisk University in Nashville. He and Tipper Gore are also writing a book on the family's role in American life. Recently, Al Gore became vice chair of MetWest, a financial services firm, where he assists the firm in global strategy and in exploring new business opportunities. As a former vice president, senator, and member of Congress, Mr. Gore frequently speaks out on public issues.

Anne Gregory is a doctoral candidate in the clinical science program at the University of California, Berkeley. Her intervention interests include addressing youth problems from an ecological perspective. Her research interests focus on socialization in schooling, with an emphasis on the quality and significance of teacher-student relationships. Currently, Gregory is examining the role of culture and ethnicity during disciplinary interactions in classrooms. Her publications include "The Youth Charter: Towards the Formation of Adolescent Moral Identity."

Neal Halfon is professor of pediatrics in the School of Medicine and professor of Community Health Sciences in the School of Public Health at the University of California, Los Angeles, where he directs the UCLA Center for Healthier Children, Families and Communities, as well as the National Center for Infancy and Early Childhood Health Policy Research. Halfon also chairs the National Community and Academic Consortium on Family-Centered Community Building. He is coeditor (with Kathryn T. McLearn and Mark A. Schuster) of *Child Rearing in America: Challenges Facing Parents with Young Children.*

Karen Hein, M.D., became president of the William T. Grant Foundation in 1998. Hein is also clinical professor of pediatrics, epidemiology, and social medicine at Albert Einstein College of Medicine in New York. She has worked on health-care reform as a member of the U.S. Senate Finance Committee staff, drafting legislation related to health benefits, workforce, and financing medical education and academic health centers. In 1987, Hein founded the nation's first adolescent HIV/AIDS program and worked closely with the Board of Education to expand AIDS education to the more than one million students in the New York City public school system. She has written more than 150 articles, chapters, and abstracts related to adolescent health, particularly focusing on high-risk youth. Her book *AIDS: Trading Fears for Facts,* has sold over 100,000 copies.

Richard M. Lerner is the Bergstrom Chair in Applied Developmental Science at Tufts University. He is the author or editor of 45 books and more than 300 scholarly articles and chapters. Lerner is known for his theory of, and research into, relations between life-span human development and contextual or ecological change. He is also a leader in the study of public policies and community-based programs aimed at the promotion of positive youth development.

Raymond P. Lorion is professor and director of clinical training for the doctoral program in school, community and clinical-child psychology in the University of Pennsylvania's Penn Graduate School of Education. His research has examined epidemiological factors related to learning disorders, alcohol, tobacco, and other drug use, and community violence. Lorion has written extensively on conceptual, methodological, and policy issues related to prevention science and practice in the mental health disciplines. His current work focuses on understanding the nature and consequences of pervasive community violence and developing comprehensive intervention strategies for responding to this threat to children and their families.

Jean E. Rhodes is professor of psychology at the University of Massachusetts in Boston. For more than a decade, she has conducted research on the mentoring of children and adolescents, including an extensive analysis of the Big Brothers Big Sisters national impact study. In addition, she has explored the influence of natural and assigned mentors on adolescent mothers. Rhodes is a Fellow in the American Psychological Association and the Society for Research and Community Action, a member of the MacArthur Foundation Research Network on the Transition to Adulthood, and a research consultant to the National Mentoring Partnership. She has published three books and more than 30 articles and chapters on the topic of youth mentoring.

Jolene L. Roehlkepartain is a parent educator, author, and speaker on family and children's issues. Involved in Search Institute's early efforts regarding children's assets, she was a coauthor of the 1997 report titled *Starting Out Right: Developmental Assets for Children*. Previously, she was the editor of *Parents of Teenagers* magazine and the founding editor of *Adoptive Families* magazine. She is the author or coauthor of 20 books, including *Raising Healthy Children Day by Day, An Asset Builder's Guide to Youth and Money, What Young Children Need to Succeed, A Leader's Guide to What Young Children Need to Succeed,* and *Building Assets Together.*

Jennifer G. Roffman is a postdoctoral researcher in the Department of Psychology at the University of Massachusetts in Boston. She received a Ph.D. in 2000 from Northwestern University in human development and social policy. Roffman's work focuses on the impact on youth well-being of mentors and other significant nonparent adults.

A. Rae Simpson is administrator of parenting programs at the Massachusetts Institute of Technology and consultant to the Center for Health Communication at the Harvard School of Public Health. Having initiated the center's efforts in the area of parenting and media, she prepared a report in 2001 titled *Raising Teens: A Synthesis of Research and a Foundation for Action* and a report in 1997 titled *The Role of the Mass Media in Parenting Education*. Simpson has written and lectured extensively for both professional and popular audiences on the role of the mass media in communicating science and health information to the public. She consults nationally and locally on issues in parenting education and mass communication with corporations, advertising firms, media, government, and foundations. Simpson is founding chair of the National Parenting Education Network and founding president of the Parenting Education Network of Massachusetts.

Harris Sokoloff is director of the Center for School Study Councils at the University of Pennsylvania's Penn Graduate School of Education, where he also serves as adjunct associate professor and certification officer. His main professional development work is with school superintendents, school boards, and district staff to help them keep pace with state-of-the-art educational and management theory, research, and practice. Sokoloff's applied research is with school districts and community organizations to build stronger, more productive relationships between schools and their communities, particularly the (re)building of a public for public education through the use of deliberative public forums on different public policy issues.

Barbara Trickett is a project coordinator at Harvard Medical School. She has a background as a science teacher and currently applies her skills to research in international child development.

Author Index

Subject Index

CPSIA information can be obtained at www.ICGtesting.com
Printed in the USA
LVOW072335051112

306010LV00008B/77/A